INDIA'S DANCES

INDIA'S DANCES

Their History, Technique and Repertoire

Reginald Massey

abhinav publicaTions

NEW DELHI

First published in India 2004

© Reginald Massey

Publishers
Shakti Malik
Abhinav Publications
E-37, Hauz Khas
New Delhi-110016 (INDIA)
Phones: 26566387, 26562784, 26524658
Fax: 91-11-26857009
e-mail: shakti@nde.vsnl.net.in
Website: http//www.abhinavexports.com

ISBN 81-7017-434-1

Lasertypeset by
S.R. Enterprises
Lajpat Nagar-IV
New Delhi-110024
Phone: 26236663

Printed at
D.K. Fine Art Press Pvt. Ltd.
Ashok Vihar, Delhi

CONTENTS

ACKNOWLEDGEMENTS

T.R. Aggarwal; Bharatiya Vidya Bhavan, London; Sheel Chandra; Mary Clarke; Indian Council for Cultural Relations, New Delhi; Dr Sunil Kothari; Jamila Massey; Marcus Massey; Dr M.N. Nandakumara; Asavari Pawar; Sangeet Natak Akademi, New Delhi; Anjana Sharma; Shanta Serbjeet Singh; *The Dancing Times*, London; *The Guardian*, London; *The Times*, London; Muthusamy Varadarajan; Dr Kapila Vatsyayan.

BHARATA NATYAM	- Tanjore, Madurai, Madras, Belur
KATHAKALI	- Kerala
KATHAK	- Lucknow, Jaipur, Delhi
MANIPURI	- Manipur
ODISSI	- Orissa

The main centres of classical dancing in the India-Pakistan subcontinent

INTRODUCTION

$\mathcal{I}$ndian dance is now a widely recognised and respected art form throughout the world. Many young, and some not so young, people from non-Indian backgrounds are learning Indian dance with great interest and enthusiasm. This has not happened overnight and must not be taken for granted by those who practise Indian dance in India or abroad. It has been a difficult, uphill struggle covering a period of several decades and many have dedicated their lives to the cause of propagating Indian dance.

Just over a century ago Tagore founded Santiniketan with, it is germane to mention, assistance from the English educationist Leonard Elmhirst. In 1930, the Kerala poet Vallathol estabished the Kerala Kala Mandalam to fulfil his dream of reinstating Kathakali to its former glory. In Tamil Nadu the stigma of temple prostitution continued for a long time and it took years for crusaders like E. Krishna Iyer and Rukmini Devi to make Dasi Attam acceptable.

There were, however, a few western dancers who were captivated by Indian dance. The American Ruth St Denis toured the world with her 'Oriental' *Radha Dance* and when she and her husband Ted Shawn started their dance centre at Jacob's Pillow they welcomed Indian dancers there.

Martha Graham, who trained at Jacob's Pillow, had the highest regard for India's dance culture, and the exotic Mata Hari toured far and wide with her 'Oriental' temple dances. Inspired by the Krishna legend, Fokine and Cocteau created *Le Dieu Bleu* in which the god was danced by Nijinsky and Karsavina was Radha.

In the 1920s the great Pavlova toured India and the Far East. In Chennai her Indian hosts informed her that Indian dance had all but died out and what was left was not worth watching. But, ever a searcher, she persevered and visited temples where the devadasis still danced. It was Pavlova who advised Rukmini Devi to give up studying Russian ballet and to rediscover the dance heritage of her own country. Pavlova also inspired Menaka who became the first famous Kathak dancer who was not a *bai* or *tavaif* (courtesan). In 1924, Uday Shankar met Pavlova in London and danced with her for a year and a half. He then formed his own company and became an extraordinary Indian dance missionary.

The other genius who took Indian dance to the West was Ram Gopal who was trained and honed by gurus such as Kathakali's Kunju Kurup and Dasi Attam's Meenakshi Sundaram Pillai. He first toured abroad with the American *danseuse* La Meri and later, on his own, took America by storm. In 1939, his London debut heralded a meteoric career; he was invited to meet Queen Mary and leading figures in the ballet world became his friends. Nijinsky himself came to see him dance. Later, Markova danced Radha to Ram Gopal's Krishna.

In the 1960s I worked with Ram Gopal for a short time and had the opportunity of studying him at close quarters. He believed that dancers transcend race, style and technique.

To use his words, theirs is a "universal language of the body in any rhythm of the dance, be it Eastern or Western".

Indian dance is today taught in many cities, both in India and abroad, but it has to be accepted that Delhi has now attracted a very large number of practitioners representing a variety of styles from all over India. Hence it is appropriate and indeed necessary for me to make a few observations on India's chief city.

Delhi (also pronounced Dilli or even Dehli) on the banks of the Yamuna has been identified with Indraprastha which is mentioned in the *Mahabharata*. Raja Dillu gave his name to the city and it became the capital of the Rajput kings. In 1192, however, the valiant Prithviraj Chauhan was vanquished by the Afghan invader Shahab-ud-Din Ghuri and the city passed into Muslim hands. Sultans of various dynasties, Persians, Turks, Afghans and others, made Delhi their political and military headquarters before the Mughal adventurer Babur shattered in 1526, at Panipat just north of Delhi, the army of the then ruling Afghan sultan Ibrahim Lodi. Babur, it must be remembered, wrested the sultanate of Delhi from his Muslim co-religionists rather than from the Hindus. Later, for good measure, Babur dealt with the turbulent Hindu Rajputs in similar fashion. One of his distasteful legacies is, of course, the bleeding wound of the Ram temple-Babri mosque controversy.

It was, however, Babur's grandson Akbar who expanded and consolidated the Mughal empire and made the very word "Mughal" synonymous with magnificence, opulence, grandeur and greatness.

There was, in spite of the political and dynastic upheavals, much give and take between the Hindus of Hindustan and the Muslims from Central Asia and Persia. The adjustments found expression in many ways. The Bhagti movement, for instance, stressed the brotherhood of man irrespective of religion or social and caste background. It combined the most attractive features of both Hinduism and Islam and produced saints like Kabir (1440–1518) who, though born a Muslim, renounced formal Islam and became the generative source of great poetry and music. Bhagti encouraged mysticism as did Sufism, which was a pantheistic type of Islam, and both relied heavily on the use of music. It was the tremendous influence of Sufi thought throughout the Islamic world that led the later Muslim monarchs in India to encourage and even foster the Hindu arts. Many Muslims became great *ustads*, masters, of Hindustani music, that is, the classical music of north India. However, classical dance in every part of India was, and still is, taught and practised largely by Hindus.

It is significant that the classical Kathak dance of north India, a masterful blend of the best in Hindu and Islamic aesthetics, arrived at a recognisable point of excellence during Akbar's benign rule. The same happened with music. The emperor's favourite musician Miyan Tansen was made one of the Nine Gems of the empire. By virtue of his high status Tansen had immense influence in political, diplomatic, religious and financial matters. Before Tansen, however, there was Amir Khusro who served successive sultans in Delhi. He was born in 1234 and lived till the age of ninety. Although born in the Etah district in north India, his forbears were Turks and he thus called himself a Hindu Turk. He studied Indian music for many years and wrote: "Indian music, the fire that burns heart and soul, is superior to the music of any other country."

Khusro, however, enriched Hindustani music by introducing Arabic and Persian elements and thus endowed it with greater grace and elegance. He encouraged the *qawwali*, a form of Muslim religious singing still heard at the shrines of the Sufi saints. He was also the originator of the *tarana* style of music.

Akbar's reign was marked by tolerance and understanding and the promulgation of just laws. The *jizya*, poll tax on non-Muslims, was abolished and Hindus were appointed to the highest posts in the government as well as in the army. Philosophers and divines of every faith were invited to court. There was complete religious freedom in the emperor's domains at a time when, for instance, in England Roman Catholics and Protestants were burning each other at the stake.

The reigns of Akbar's son Jehangir (1605–1627) and grandson Shahjehan (1628–1658) were, in many ways, even more artistically productive. Music, dance, painting, poetry and architecture flourished. It is not without significance that the mothers of both these emperors were Hindu Rajput princesses.

Unfortunately a family feud commenced when Shahjehan fell seriously ill in 1657. The emperor's third son, Aurangzeb, came out on top after he had had his three brothers put to death and his father imprisoned in the Agra fort. It is a tragedy for India that the saintly scholar-prince Dara Shikoh, Shahjehan's eldest son, could not become emperor. He strove to build bridges between Hindu and Muslim thought and would most probably have surpassed the great Akbar. Aurangzeb however undid his ancestor's achievements. During the fifty years of his reign he was particularly harsh towards his Hindu subjects and succeeded in destroying much of the goodwill that had been carefully nurtured between Hindus and Muslims. A puritan in his personal life, Aurangzeb was imperious and headstrong and a Sunni fanatic. Apart from the Hindus, he also persecuted Shias, Sufis and Sikhs. He has also been accused of being anti-Art. Aurangzeb was, in fact, fond of music but had convinced himself that rulers ought to suppress their natural inclinations and devote themselves to duties of state. He did, however, maintain musicians and dancers for the entertainment of his wives and daughters.

Niccolao Manucci, an Italian adventurer who was in India during Aurangzeb's reign, has written about the many performing artists at the Mughal court and notes that they were given names like "Ruby" and "Gazelle-eyed". But since the emperor had withdrawn his personal patronage the best artists left the imperial court to seek employment in provincial centres under local rajahs and nawabs.

Many weak and incompetent emperors succeeded Aurangzeb. Of these particular mention must be made of Jehandar Shah and Mohammad Shah since both were notorious for their profligacy, a vice which Aurangzeb disapproved of most strongly. The former spent most of his time with his low born mistress Lal Kunwar, a dancer and singer. The emperor, infatuated by her, handed out the highest positions to her friends and relatives. The latter's reign lasted till the middle of the 18th century and was politically disastrous. However, the musicians at his court were Sadarang and Adarang who brought the *khayal* style to its fullest perfection. This style, fluid and fired with imagination and improvisation, soon became the dominant genre of classical music. Sadarang wrote thousands of compositions that gained for *khayal* a level of respectability. Also at this time the *tappa* style of music was refined and introduced into the classical repertoire by Miyan Shori. *Tappas* were songs composed and sung by Punjabi camel drivers and Miyan Shori, seeing that they had strength and feeling, made them acceptable to sophisticated audiences.

In general parlance Mohammad Shah is always referred to as Mohammad Shah *Rangila*; the word *rangila* (colourful) meaning a man given to worldly and artistic pleasures. When Nadir Shah, the Persian conqueror, was advancing on Delhi in 1739 the emperor was watching a musical drama and no one dared interrupt his enjoyment of it. The producer did some quick thinking. He forced one of the performers, who was doing a comic part, to sing the news on the stage as part of the play. Still the emperor refused to get the dire message. Very soon Mohammad Shah paid heavily for his dereliction of duty. Nadir Shah entered Delhi and put thousands to the sword and as part of the fabulous loot he carried away were the Koh-é-Noor diamond and Shahjehan's magnificent Peacock Throne.

The Mughal empire, as an effective political entity, could be said to have lasted for about three centuries: from the mid-16th to almost the mid-19th century. Certainly there was an emperor in Delhi right up to 1857 but he was an emperor in name only. He became, in effect, a puppet of both the Marathas and the British and they, for their own reasons of convenience, recognised him as Emperor of Hindustan. In these circumstances the Mughals fought shy of asserting their authority lest it be proved, not least to themselves, that they had little or no means of exercising that authority. They retreated from political affairs and responsibilities and spent much time in artistic endeavour, quite clearly as a form of spiritual and emotional compensation for the loss of empire.

After the miserable collapse of the Great Rebellion of 1857, the last Mughal emperor, Bahadur Shah II, was held prisoner by the British in Delhi's Red Fort which was built by his ancestor Shahjehan the creator of the Taj Mahal. The emperor was a poet (his pen name was Zafar) who wrote numerous *ghazals,* poems set to music, and *thumris,* romantic lyrics, which became immensely popular and remain so today. Zafar is also remembered as the patron and friend of the poets Naseer, Zouq and Ghalib.

Zafar was put on trial, humiliated, deposed and sent into exile. He died in Rangoon in 1862. This was the official end of the Mughal empire with Zafar lamenting his fate in memorable verse.

The historian Percival Spear dwells at length on the level of cultural activity in Delhi even while the Mughal empire was in its final death throes. There was communal harmony in Delhi with Hindus and Muslims celebrating each other's festivals with enthusiasm. Zafar himself set an example in this respect, as the *Delhi Urdu Akhbar* reported in its issue of March 1, 1840:

"The king met Raja Sohan Lal in private. Nawab Hamid Ali Khan requested that he would like to attend the *mela* (festival) of Gul Chathar. His Majesty allowed him to do so. On the 22nd of the previous month the courtiers and princes had celebrated the festival of Basant. His Majesty ordered that everyone should come to court dressed in yellow. It was a great occasion. Nearly four thousand people gathered. It looked as if it were a field of *zaffran* (saffron) because everyone present was wearing *basanti* colour turbans and shawls. There was plenty of music and dance. The dancers were given a large amount of *inam* (presents)."

Spear quotes the following entries from Zafar's palace diary:

"At night His Majesty witnessed a *naach* (dance performance) and fireworks in the courtyard of the Diwané-Khas on the occasion of the marriage of Mirza Kaus Shekon."

"Zauq, the poet, read some verses composed by himself to His Majesty and in return His Majesty favoured the poet with some verses of his own composition."

"Sukhanand, astrologer, presented an *arzi* (petition) stating that there was to be an eclipse of the moon on Thursday and begged that the usual alms might be distributed. His Majesty gave orders to bring a weighing machine....His Majesty weighed himself against seven kinds of grain, butter, gold, coral, etcetera, and then distributed the result among the poor."

The flower festival at Mehrauli was another popular event at the end of the Mughal era. Zafar and his family attended it regularly. Hindus performed their rituals at the Jog Mayaji temple and Muslims offered prayers at the shrine of Qutb al-Din Bakhtiyar.

This was the twilight of the Mughal empire and, it is said, the candle's dying spurt is always its brightest. The new imperial power moved the capital of India to mercantile Calcutta and Delhi diminished.

It was much later, after George V was proclaimed Emperor of India in 1911 at a grand coronation ceremony, that the British declared their intention of moving the capital back to Delhi. They were the natural successors to the Mughals and decided therefore to conduct themselves accordingly. However, in an act of monumental hauteur the British created a New Delhi, designed by Lutyens, with huge edifices to house the viceroy and his vast retinue, the legislature, the offices of state, the supreme court and the dozens of government departments. The bungalows had acres of gardens with servants' quarters tucked away behind screens of trees and vegetation. Straight avenues, in the Roman style, were lined with massive evergreens and the squares and gardens were adorned with statues of British monarchs, worthy viceroys and victorious generals. A very large circular shopping complex, named after one of Victoria's sons the Duke of Connaught, served the patrician requirements of senior civil and military personnel. New Delhi was the place from where the rulers ruled. But there was no art. Whatever survived lingered on in the dingy environment of the old city of Delhi whose walls were crumbling. At the time it was the courtesans and dancing girls who became the custodians of culture; a fact now nimbly avoided by current scholarship.

After independence things have changed rapidly and New Delhi has become a different Delhi. Not only is the city the new republic's centre of political power but, since it is the capital of a union of states, it attracts artistic talent from all over the subcontinent. Moreover, with India's enhanced industrial and economic status, the capital is teeming with foreign delegations, diplomats and cultural organisations. It is now largely an international city.

Nehru's vision is reflected in the renaming of some roads, which in their Hindi reincarnations have become *margs* and *paths*. And so there is a Josip Broz Tito Marg, a Max Müller Marg and even a Copernicus Marg. Though Irwin Road (after a viceroy then a mere baron but later to become the Earl of Halifax) has been renamed Baba Kharak Singh Road, for some unknown reason there is still a Wellesley Road. This is amazing since the Wellesley brothers (one became the Duke of Wellington of Waterloo fame) were responsible for the bloody demise of Tippu Sultan (the 'Tiger of Mysore') who is now being lauded as a great Indian hero. One would have thought that in their nationalist fervour the authorities would have turned Wellesley Road into Tippu Sultan Marg. No one, certainly not the British government, would have objected.

What is mysterious is the fact that even today New Delhi has roads named after Babur and Aurangzeb, the two Mughals widely regarded as unmitigated villains in present day India. But what is stranger is the following: In the old city of Delhi which has a sizeable Muslim presence with many Urdu speakers, both Muslim and Hindu, there are hardly any road signs in Urdu, that is, the Persian script. Whereas, in New Delhi, the road signs are in four scripts: the Roman, the Hindi (Devnagari), the Punjabi (Gurmukhi) and the Urdu (Persian). I have no doubt that in this respect India's capital is unique; not one of the world's other great cities proclaims street names in four distinctively different scripts. Interestingly, not many Muslims live in New Delhi which is increasingly becoming polyglot with Punjabis, Haryanvis, Uttar Pradeshis, Bengalis and Bangladeshis, Tamils, Keralites, Himachalis, Maharashtrians, Biharis, Gujaratis, Kashmiris, Nepalese and others from far and wide. Most Indian states have their 'Bhavans' (not embassies, but 'houses') in the capital and several have state-owned emporia which sell the particular products of each state. There are, moreover, over a hundred foreign embassies, trade missions and international organisations based in New Delhi. Several embassies represent important Muslim countries (such as Indonesia, Egypt, Iraq, Saudi Arabia, Iran and the United Arab Emirates apart from, of course, Pakistan) and it probably makes sense to use the Persian script on the road signs and to retain the detested names of Babur and Aurangzeb. It is perhaps a diplomatic way of telling these countries of the crescent that India with its genius for pluralism has not turned its back on its Muslim heritage.

In today's multinational and multicultural ambience New Delhi is the very epicentre of dance activity. There are, it is true, loud protests and laments from Chennai (Madras), Mumbai (Bombay), Kolkata (Calcutta), Bangalore,

Mangalore, Ahmedabad and other cities and towns. It is claimed, and not without some truth, that the central ministries and bodies such as the Indian Council for Cultural Relations and the Sangeet Natak Akademi, the national academy of music and dance, exercise their patronage too lavishly in favour of Delhi based dancers. Awards and honours, it is alleged, are handed out to favourites and networkers. In short, if you want to make it, make for New Delhi. *"Dilli chullo!"* ("On to Delhi!") is not a new cry in India.

There is, it must be said, the convenience of proximity and the law of demand and supply is, as always, the deciding factor. If, for example, an embassy wishes to lay on at short notice an evening of Indian culture for a visiting trade delegation all the ambassador's social secretary has to do is to make a few phone calls. Within a very short time an array of classical dancers and musicians will have been lined up for the event. There is, undoubtedly, a lot of work available and always the opportunity of making valuable contacts which could lead to lucrative foreign tours. This is the reason why a number of India's leading dancers and dance teachers are drawn to Delhi. They come from all regions of the subcontinent and represent many distinctive styles. It is not a question of being mercenary; dancers, like the rest of us, have the right to eat.

Birju Maharaj, the doyen of Kathak, has always lived in Delhi though his style of dance is named after Lucknow for it was in Lucknow, then ruled by Shia *nawabs*, that his forefathers fashioned and honed the repertoire. I was in New Delhi in February 2002 when Birju Maharaj, most ably assisted by his partner Saswati Sen, produced a Kathak festival at the Kamani Auditorium. It was a memorable experience. Dancers from other Indian cities were invited as were Pratap Pawar and Gauri Sharma Tripathi from London. The former, assisted by his Delhi based daughter

Asavari, dwelt on a Sufi theme that mapped the progress from adolescence to old age while the latter presented the riotous colours and joyous movements of Vasant, the celebration of spring.

The inclusion of two celebrated musicians, Zakir Hussain (tabla) and Girija Devi (singer), was a great bonus especially when they appeared with Birju Maharaj. The rhythmic fireworks between dancer and percussionist were stunning and the sensitive visual interpretations of the enchanting verses were unforgettable. Birju Maharaj is a master of *thumri andaaz*, the difficult art of conveying poetry and abstract ideas through hand gestures, arm movements and *nigah*, eye expression. That night in Delhi with Girija Devi singing and Birju Maharaj performing *thumri andaaz* will surely rank as a rare and treasured experience.

The first dance festival was soon followed by another in honour of Achhan Maharaj, Birju Maharaj's late father. It was billed as a festival of choreographies in Kathak. A galaxy of dancers, choreographers, scholars and critics participated. Those taking part included Maya Rao Natarajan, Rohini Bhate, Munna Shukla, Chetna Jalan, Kumudini Lakhia, Prabha Marathe, Bhaswati Misra, Jai Kishan Maharaj, Aditi Mangaldas, Arjun Mishra, Navtej Johar, Shanta Serbjeet Singh, Rita Ganguly, Saswati Sen, Swapna Sundari, Sunil Kothari, Uma Sharma, Leela Samson, Keshav Kothari, Leela Venkataraman, Madhavi Mudgal, Shovana Narayan, Singhajit Singh, Rajiv Chandran, Astad Deboo, Maya Krishna Rao, Shama Bhate, Shashidharan Nair, Veenapani Chawla, Renuka Narayanan, Prerna Shrimali, G.S. Rajan, Ashok Vajpeyi, Kamalini Dutt, Preeti Patel, Mangla and Raghav Bhatt, Ein Lal, Nirupama and Rajendra, Prashant Shah, Surendra Saikia, Madhurita Sarang, Parwati Dutta and Ashimnabdhu Bhattacharjee.

Apart from the presentation of some notable creative choreography there was discussion and debate on subjects such as *Movement decontextualised—Dancer neutralised: the challenge of choreography* and *How do you ensure classicism in a contemporary choreography?*

Rina Singha, who is based in Toronto, was also in Delhi during the February 2002 dance season. On the occasion of the Indian National YWCA Convention she choreographed and danced a piece titled *Am I my sister's keeper?* which concerned the clash of tradition with identity. There were many Biblical references and, significantly, Mrs Narayanan the wife of the President of India was the guest of honour. Seeing Rina Singha dance after a very long time I was struck by her loyalty to the style of her teacher Shambu Maharaj (Birju Maharaj's uncle) who taught her in Delhi at what was then the Bharatiya Kala Kendra. She has, nevertheless, extended the subject matter of Kathak into a completely non-traditional area.

Another dancer whom I first saw as little more than a girl in London has made a huge reputation in India. Kiran Segal, daughter of the celebrated thespian Zohra Segal, trained in the Odissi style of Orissa in eastern India but teaches and dances in Delhi. She has become a popular cultural envoy and has toured several countries. In Delhi she has a band of devoted students from various backgrounds and nationalities. The other established Odissi artists in Delhi are Sonal Mansingh and Madhavi Mudgal.

The famous Bharata Natyam dancer Yamini Krishnamurti directs a busy dance academy in Delhi as do the Kuchipudi experts Raja, Radha and Kaushalya Reddy. It was also a pleasure to see Shovana Narayan at New Delhi's Habitat Centre where she danced for the Indian Cancer Society. Miraculously she has fully recovered from a serious illness and is busy creating dances dealing with themes such as social and women's issues.

Another old friend whom I was glad to meet was Uma Sharma who heads the Bharatiya Sangeet Sadan which is located in a district called East of Kailash, a name with resonances. Her dance drama *Stree* portrays the many manifestations of womanhood and is packed with powerful references to the Hindu female pantheon. Appropriately the chief guests were women: Sushma Swaraj, India's Minister of Information and Broadcasting, and Sheela Dixit, Chief Minister of Delhi. Men in India are learning to take the back seat.

Leela Samson, like Yamini Krishnamurti a product of Rukmini Devi Arundale's Kalakshetra Academy in Madras, is imparting first rate training to her handpicked students. Her dance demonstrations interspersed with well prepared lecture notes were a joy to attend and the venue, the theatre of the India International Centre, was ideal. The products of her academy gave me a strong impression that the south Indian Bharata Natyam dance style is safe and flourishing in north India as, indeed, are all the other styles.

I am aware of the fact that foreign students from as far afield as Korea, Canada, the United States, Britain, France, Germany, Italy, Sweden and many other countries now flock to Delhi in search of *gurus* and well run schools. Very often, because of a lack of information and poor advice, they are disappointed and frustrated. This book might be of some use to them. However, it is the established first rate dancers and dance teachers of Delhi who merit greater recognition both in India and abroad for the marvellous work that they are doing. Also, up and coming dancers need to be noticed, commented upon and encouraged. In the hard, competitive world of the performing arts it is most often the young who are the first casualties and yet, ironically, the future itself is in the hands of the next generation. I believe that it is the critic's duty to extend assistance to those on whom the future depends.

In future volumes it is my intention to focus on dance practitioners and fresh talent in Mumbai, Chennai, Kolkata, Ahmedabad, Bangalore and other important dance centres.

For the general reader, both in India and abroad, the early chapters of this book provide a background to the aesthetics of Indian dance and the basic facts pertaining to the major classical styles. The history of the styles, their repertoire and training techniques are discussed, as are the methods of the great *gurus*. The dance enthusiast is also told what to expect during programmes of particular dance styles. There is as well a short account of India's immensely rich folk dance tradition and a glossary of dance terms covering the various styles.

CHAPTER 1

INDIAN CLASSICAL DANCE: THE BACKGROUND

*M*an is not alone in wanting to dance. Many birds and animals appear to dance at some time or other: the peacock and the lyre-bird for instance are famous for it. Like them, man also has probably danced from the earliest stages of evolution. He experiences pleasure as well as satisfaction in rhythmical movement, since this exercises his body and, at the same time, releases inner tensions. Moreover it can induce hypnotic trances. This may have led to the belief that dance has magical powers, and so it came to be used in early cults and rites for propitiating the gods and driving away evil spirits. By dancing man expressed himself in a way which he conceived as the most powerful and eloquent of the means at his disposal. He celebrated by dancing, he gained courage by dancing and often, like the birds and animals around him, he courted with the help of dance.

Dance is found among all men whether in primitive or advanced societies. Its functions vary in these societies from religion to pure entertainment. So in all probability, dance goes back as far as man himself but its styles and forms are many—some very new, or at least seemingly so, and others of great antiquity.

Indian dancing, even in its classical styles, is one of the most ancient forms still surviving. It has of course altered, but its basic elements would appear to be much as they were over two thousand years ago.

The earliest civilizations discovered in the Indian subcontinent are those of Mohenjo Daro and Harappa in the Indus valley, and are dated at about 6000 B.C. It would appear that by that time dance had achieved a considerable measure of discipline and it is likely, but not certain, that it was connected with religion. In any case it must have played a part of some importance in society, for one of the finds at Mohenjo Daro was a beautiful little statuette of a dancing girl. Not surprisingly however, almost nothing is known of the dance technique of this early period.

Around 2000 B.C., the Aryans came to the subcontinent through the passes in the North-West. They were a fair-skinned race whereas the indigenous inhabitants were dark. They were a close-knit society of people and were easily able to subjugate the Dravidians. So as to establish themselves permanently, they set about organizing a new order by instituting the caste system which was initially based largely on colour. The Sanskrit word *varna* means both caste and colour. At the same time they introduced their own culture and religion and in turn adapted some indigenous customs and even gods. This was made easier by the fact that they settled down with the intention of co-existing with the original inhabitants of their new homeland.

The caste system would never have survived so long, had it not been accepted by all. Military pressure could not have sustained it. Although caste was a form of segregation or apartheid, it was worked out in such great detail and so interlocked with religious, social and economic conditions that it operated without creating any tensions. It brought about a division of labour in a way which eliminated the need for slavery, and consequently this institution was never widespread in ancient India. Part of the success of the caste system lay in its great diversity. Apartheid as practised in South Africa was crude by comparison because it entailed the use of force, increased tension, and ignored the realities of contemporary conditions.

The caste system allowed for many gradations in the social scale and each had a vast spread. A certain amount of social intercourse was permissible between adjacent castes and in rare cases it was possible, though difficult, to step one stage higher in the caste structure. The scale went up gradually through many sub-castes and yet all were members of the same body politic. The Brahmins were the intellectuals and the head of this body. The Kshatriyas were the arms, the military caste which defended the whole. The Vaishyas were merchants who provided for physical needs and were likened to the stomach. Last of all came the Shudras who did manual labour and were compared with the feet of the body. The sub-castes within each of these four main castes were related to professions or occupations. For example, there were sub-castes of physicians, archers, money-lenders and cobblers. In the arts there were certain castes which specialized in music, in painting and in dancing. All of these functioned as hereditary guilds.

The caste system is now breaking up because the conditions which brought it into being and sustained it, no longer exist. Discrimination on the basis of caste has been made a legal offence, but the idea has penetrated deep into the consciousness of the people and will take time to die out completely.

The Aryans produced great scholars who studied everything in a scientific manner. Strangely enough, they never wrote any histories; instead all subjects, including history, were clothed in the garb of mythology and given religious sanction by being associated with the gods. They had a great pantheon of gods and goddesses, each of whom was responsible for some aspect of life. There were various degrees of gods as well as demons and there are stories of constant battles between the two in which the gods are always victorious.

Religious sanction always makes ideas much more invulnerable, and so legends grew around the history of the Aryans and their coming into India, beginning with the *Rig-Veda* and culminating in the two epics of the *Ramayana* and the *Mahabharata*. All learning was embodied in books called *shastras*. Each shastra covers its subject in detail and represents, obviously, not the sudden inspiration of a single man, but the accumulation of a tradition codified in one volume, sometimes by one whose name is known, sometimes by a person or persons whose names are not recorded. In the same way, the works of Homer could not have been produced out of the void of a barbaric society, but represent the acme of a long tradition of culture.

Brahmin teachers considered that the highest knowledge was not suited for all men and were anxious to pass it on only to those who were worthy of it and capable of using it with discrimination. This meant that such knowledge was preserved exclusively for the Brahmins themselves. To make quite sure that it would not fall into the wrong hands it was expressed in allegorical terms and complicated verses or *mantras* which had to be interpreted by experts, rather like the Greek oracles and the books by mediaeval alchemists and astrologers. Thus the Brahmins became the intellectual leaders of society and the custodians of religion.

The sacred scriptures consisted of the four principal vedas—the *Rig-Veda*, the *Yajur-Veda*, the *Sam-Veda* and the *Atharva-Veda*, and several minor ones. These, together with the two epics and the various *Puranas* or legends concerning the gods, have a close connection with the classical dance. There was, of course, a shastra for dance and drama and the respect for these arts was such that some regarded the *Bharata Natya Shastra* as the fifth veda.

When the sage Bharata was asked by his fellows to explain the origins of this veda, he replied that after the Golden Age and during the Silver Age the people of the world had strayed from a righteous path, and become subject to greed, jealousy and anger, so that 'their happiness mixed with sorrow'. The gods then asked Brahma, the Great Father, to devise a fifth veda which could be seen as well as heard and which would belong to all the people, since the shudras were forbidden to listen to recitations of the four vedas. Brahma, therefore, agreed to create a fifth veda which would induce 'duty, wealth, as well as fame, and contain good counsel...', which would be 'enriched by the teaching of all the scriptures and give a review of all arts and crafts'. So he took recitation from the *Rig-Veda*, song from the *Sam-Veda*, histrionic representation from the *Yajur-Veda* and the sentiments from the *Atharva-Veda*, and with a combination of these created the new *Natya-Veda*.

Brahma then asked the god Indra to teach it to the other gods and give a performance according to its principles. But Indra said that the gods were unable to do this since they would neither understand it nor interpret it skilfully enough. He suggested, instead, that the sages were better fitted for the task. Brahma, therefore, taught the veda to

Bharata and asked him to make ready a drama. Bharata in turn instructed his hundred 'sons', by which is probably meant men who followed him in becoming authorities on music, dance and drama. They then prepared for a performance. Brahma asked Bharata to include the graceful style in his play, but the sage said that this style was unsuited to men. So Brahma created from his mind *apsaras* or nymphs for this purpose. The drama was finally staged during the Banner Festival of Indra which was held in honour of his victory over the enemies of the gods and which was itself the subject of the performance. The gods were extremely pleased and rewarded the players with many gifts. However, certain demons who had sneaked in took offence at the dramatization of their defeat and saw to it that the actors lost their memories and their powers of speech and movement. Indra divined what had happened and, taking up the finest banner staff, battered all these demons to death. He then gave this staff, or Jarjara, to the players for their protection. But other demons came and continued to harass the actors until Brahma advised Bharata to build a playhouse. This done, its various parts were protected by different deities. All the actors and actresses too were given patron deities to protect them. Brahma himself protected the middle of the stage and this is why flowers are symbolically scattered on it at the beginning of every performance.

Brahma also tried to reason with the demons and spoke to them saying, that they were not the only ones to be shown to disadvantage in drama, but that drama would show all manner of people, gods, as well as demons, in every condition. 'There is no wise maxim, no learning, no art or craft, no device, no action that is not found in the drama.' It would instruct as well as entertain. Every man would find in it something of relevance to himself.

In Hindu drama, therefore, expression was achieved through music and dancing, as well as through acting, so that a play could be a combination of opera, ballet, and drama, in which none of these was given more prominence than the others. The *Natya Shastra* examines in detail every conceivable aspect of production: the ideal playhouse, metrics, prosody, diction, types of characters and appropriate costumes and make-up, intonation, the representation of sentiments, emotional and other states, style in acting, movements of every limb, the setting and construction of a play, conventions of time and place, and even the canons of criticism and assessment. It also deals with music, both vocal and instrumental. These instructions apply equally to acting and dancing for the two professions were combined. An indication of this is the fact that the word for drama, Nataka, derives from the word meaning 'dance'.

The date and authorship of the *Bharata Natya Shastra* are both in dispute. The book has been variously dated from the 2nd century B.C. to the 3rd century A.D., but there is even less certainty about the author. 'Bharata' originally meant a dancer-actor so that the title could mean simply 'A Shastra on Drama for the Dancer-Actor'. On the other hand 'Bharata' is also a name, and so it is possible that the title means 'A Shastra on Drama by Bharata'. However, for practical purposes, whatever his real name might have been, the sage of the *Natya Shastra* is called Bharata.

The dance gurus based their teaching on this treatise but it was handed down to their *chelas* (disciples) practically and by word of mouth. In any case, they reserved the most precious secrets of their art for selected chelas only who, in their turn, guarded them carefully.

European Sanskritists knew of the *Natya Shastra* from references to it in other books but believed that all manuscripts had been lost. It was only in the latter half of the 19th century that, while working on a mediaeval work on drama, Hall came across a manuscript of the *Natya Shastra*. This led to others being discovered and much work was done by the German Heymann, and by the Frenchmen Regnaud, Grosset and Lévi. In 1894 Pandits Shivadatta and Kashinath Pandurang Parab brought out the original Sanskrit text. Further interest was aroused in the early part of this century, by the discovery of a commentary by Abhinava Gupta. In 1950 Manomohan Ghosh made the first translation of the *Natya Shastra* into English, which was complete except for the part devoted to music. This was a major work of scholarship and original research.

A subject as rich and complex as Indian dancing has several aspects. Just as the precisely cut facets of a rare diamond combine to reveal its myriad beauties so, with Indian dancing, its full beauty is revealed only when all its many aspects are united in perfect balance. In order therefore to be able to appreciate this balance, it is necessary to have some idea of its constituent parts.

Dance was classified as either *margi* or *desi*. That which was sacred to the gods and danced for them was margi, while the dance for the pleasure of humans was desi. It was further defined as either *tandav* or *lasya* in character.

Tandav was first danced by the god Shiva, Lord of the Dance, who then conveyed this art to mortals through his disciple Tandu. Shiva is the symbol of procreation and it is because of this that tandav is often regarded as a male dance. To assume this, however, is to limit its field. Tandav covers all dance which expresses actions and feelings with strength and vigour, whether danced by men or women. When it is danced without facial expression it is called Prekashani tandav, and when it includes facial expression it becomes

Bahurupa tandav. There are seven generally accepted types of this tandav said to have been danced by Shiva:

Ananda, expressing joy.
Sandhya, the evening tandav.
Uma, the tandav he danced with his consort Uma.
Gauri, the tandav he danced with his consort Gauri.
Kalika, which he danced when he slew the demon Kalika.
Tripura, which he danced when he slew the demon Tripura.
Simhara, his dance of death which symbolizes the release of the soul from the prison of Maya or illusion.

Lasya is that element of the dance which is graceful and delicate and expresses emotions on a gentle level. It is usually associated with the dance of women because Parvati, the consort of Shiva, taught it to Usha, the daughter of the sage Bana, who then passed on the art to the women of India. However, since love is the predominant sentiment in lasya, it is also danced by men when their dance expresses this sentiment. For example, Krishna's dance with the *gopees* (milkmaids) is in lasya.

There are three main components, *natya, nritta,* and *nritya,* which together with their subsidiaries make up the classical dance.

Natya is the dramatic element of a stage performance. There are three main points of resemblance between natya and classical Greek drama. Bharata defines natya as 'a mimicry of the exploits of gods, *asuras* (demons), kings, as well as of householders of this world'. This is very similar to

Aristotle's description of tragedy as 'an imitation of some action that is important, entire and of a proper magnitude'. In both cases there is a purpose beyond pure entertainment. For the Greeks, tragedy effected, 'through pity and terror, the correction and refinement of such passions', the Natya Shastra maintains that drama will teach and, in addition, 'give courage, amusement, as well as counsel'. Aristotle's drama comprised fable, manners, diction, sentiments, music and decoration. Bharata also enumerates six parts namely decoration, postures, gestures, words, representation of temperaments and music.

Here the similarity ends, for to the Greeks tragedy was the highest form of drama, and tragedy in the Greek sense did not exist in Hindu drama.

In Greek drama the emphasis was on hearing, hence Aristotle was primarily concerned with the fable or plot and the poetry in which this would be expressed. For the Hindus the impact was mainly visual and so Bharata gives detailed attention to the manner of presentation.

Unlike Aristotle, Bharata does not forbid the representation of violent action, even death, on the stage, provided always that it is shown with control and beauty, however terrible.

Hindu drama was not bound by the unities of either time or place quite as strictly as was Greek drama and its idea of the unity of action too was somewhat different. The aim was, rather, towards a general unity of impression.

Nritta is the rhythmic movement of the body in dance. It does not set out to express a mood or sentiment or tell a story and therefore uses no facial expression. It visualizes and reproduces music and rhythm by means of abstract gestures of the body and hands and by extensive and precise use of footwork.

Nritya is that element of the dance which 'suggests *ras* (sentiment) and *bhava* (mood)'. Both ras and bhava are conveyed through facial expressions and appropriate gestures. The most important book on nritya is the *Abhinaya Darpanam* of Nandikeshvara, who is thought to have lived in the 2nd century A.D. As with Bharata, his identity is difficult to ascertain. On the subject of nritya, there are some differences between these two authors on points of detail, but the general outline is the same in both books.

Nritta, then, is concerned solely with rhythmic movement in dancing and is therefore loosely termed 'pure dance'. The object of both natya and nritya, on the other hand, is to depict ideas, themes, moods and sentiments. This they do by using *abhinaya*, which derives from the Sanskrit 'abhi' meaning towards, and 'ni' meaning to carry. The word thus signifies 'a carrying to the spectators'. The practice of

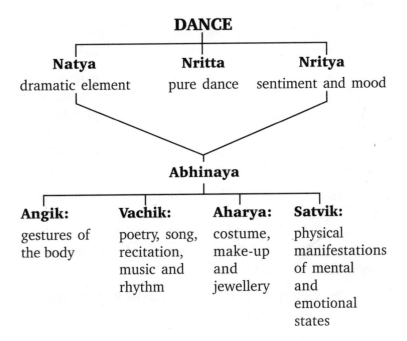

DANCE

| **Natya** | **Nritta** | **Nritya** |
| dramatic element | pure dance | sentiment and mood |

Abhinaya

| **Angik:** | **Vachik:** | **Aharya:** | **Satvik:** |
| gestures of the body | poetry, song, recitation, music and rhythm | costume, make-up and jewellery | physical manifestations of mental and emotional states |

abhinaya involves four techniques. These are known as *angik, vachik, aharya* and *satvik.*

Angik abhinaya is the term used for all gestures of the body and comes from the Sanskrit word 'ang' which means body. The analysis of the various gestures in the *Natya Shastra* is truly remarkable. There are thirteen gestures for the head, thirty-six glances, seven movements for the eyeballs, nine for the eyelids and seven for the eyebrows. The nose, the cheeks, the lower lip, each have six gestures and the chin has seven. There are nine gestures for the neck. The *hastas,* hand gestures, are sixty-seven in number. Twenty-four of these are for one hand, thirteen for both hands, and thirty are nritta hastas, belonging to the realm of pure dance. Hence these thirty are used exclusively in dancing, whereas the others may also be used in drama. There are three movements for the belly and five each for the chest, waist, sides, thighs, calves and feet.

Besides these there are thirty-two *charis,* which are movements for one foot and include the calf and thigh.

There are four ideal postures of the body in movement. Ragini Devi, the dancer and critic, describes them admirably as 'the deviations of the body from the central plumbline, or equipoise of the figure. These bends are called *abhanga* (slightly bent), *samabhanga* (equally bent) i.e. equilibrium, *atibhanga* (greatly bent), and *tribhanga* (thrice bent).'

A unit of dance which includes the postures of the body, and hand and foot movements, is called a *karana.* There are one hundred and eight of these, all of which are carved into the four gateways of the great temple of Chidambaram in South India.

The vachik aspect of abhinaya deals with the dancer's use of poetry, song, recitation, music and rhythm. The *Natya*

Shastra specifies certain tempos for particular sentiments, as for instance, 'In the comic and erotic sentiments the speech tempo should be medium, in the pathetic slow and in other sentiments a quick tempo is appropriate.'

Aharya abhinaya covers the use of costume, make-up and jewellery. There are special provisions for the appearance of every type of character, so that the race, caste, social status and sex of any character is at once obvious. For example, goddesses had green costumes and their ornaments were of lapis lazuli and pearls. The demonesses had black costumes with sapphires in their hair. These conventions were necessary because no stage sets were used in Hindu dance or drama.

Satvik abhinaya represents physical manifestations of various mental and emotional states. These are paralysis, perspiration, hair standing on end, change of voice, trembling, change of colour, weeping and fainting. Now in real life these manifestations are produced involuntarily, but the dancer, using satvik abhinaya, has to induce them voluntarily. This means supreme control of the mind, so that the dancer can not only turn the tap on, so to speak, but is also able to turn it off at will.

The *Natya Shastra* also enumerates eight rasas, which are sentiments or emotional states. Associated with each of these is a presiding deity and a colour:

Name of Ras	Nearest equivalent	Deity	Colour
Shringar	Love	Vishnu	Light green
Hasya	Humour	Pramatha	White
Karuna	Pathos	Yama	Ash
Rudra	Anger	Rudra	Red

Vir	Heroism	Indra	Light orange
Bhayanaka	Terror	Kala	Black
Bibhatsa	Disgust	Shiva as Mahakala	Blue
Adbhuta	Wonder	Brahma	Yellow

Some later authorities mention a ninth ras, Shanta or serenity. The presiding deity here is Narayana and the colour is the white of the lightly fragrant kunda flower.

Nandikeshvara gives this hint as to how a dancer or actor might attempt to evoke ras:

'Where the hand goes, there also should go the eyes,
Where the eyes go, there should go the mind.
Where the mind goes bhava should follow,
And where bhava goes, there ras arises.'

Since all the gurus based their teaching on the same shastras and because of the close link between religion and dance, the style of dancing must originally have been much the same throughout the land. But as the knowledge was passed from teacher to pupil it changed a little in transmission to suit the circumstances of the dancers and the customs of a particular area. People in a large country like India vary a great deal in habit, custom, temperament and language, and because of this dance took on a distinct character in each region. Dance terms acquired different meanings in different language areas and sometimes different words came to be used to indicate the same thing.

We have already said that castes were subdivided according to occupation and this applied to dancers as well.

The type of people in each dancing caste also considerably influenced the form of the art.

In the extreme South, for example, dancing girls were dedicated to serve the gods and it was they who preserved the tradition. Their dance was therefore feminine and suited to solo performances in the temple and later, the court. In the South-West the dancers were generally warriors of the Nayar caste and, quite naturally, their dance was masculine and emphasized the bhayanaka and vir rasas (the emotions of terror and valour). In the North it was the cultured patrons who were largely responsible for the elegance and allusiveness of the dance style. In the North-East the people are gentle and restrained by nature and this is reflected in the soft and delicate movements of their dance.

By the latter half of the 19th century dancing had generally come to be regarded with reservation. This feeling intensified into hostility. There are many reasons for this which stem chiefly from the decline of aristocratic patronage and the consequent fall in the status and reputation of the dancers. There was also in India at about this time an upsurge of Victorian middle-class morality which sapped the creative energies of the people. It was only the efforts of anti-philistines like Tagore, Vallathol, Menaka, E. Krishna Iyer, Rukmini Devi and Uday Shankar and the inspiration of Western dancers like Pavlova, that finally led to the resuscitation of this ancient art form.

Today, although dancing has been firmly reinstated, gurus and dancers are faced with the task of extending and enlarging the classical repertoire to include subjects which will be relevant and meaningful to the twenty-first century. Blind orthodoxy endangers authenticity. The classics must, and always will be a source of inspiration and instruction, but even these cannot come to life without being informed with the integrity of contemporary creative experience. Experiment and innovation are essential to the survival of a tradition. Bharata himself was aware of this several centuries ago and in comparatively recent times Tagore has written, 'There are no bounds to the depths or to the expansion of any art which, like dancing, is the expression of life's urge....Genius is defined in our language as the power that unfolds ever new possibilities in the revelation of beauty and truth....Greatness, in all its manifestations, has discontent for its guide....'

CHAPTER 2

DASI ATTAM

The home of Dasi Attam is in the South, in the area covered by the States of Tamil Nadu, Andhra and Karnataka. Like all the other classical dances of India, Dasi Attam too has its roots in the *Natya Shastra* of Bharata. It derives its name from its chief exponents in ancient times who were the devadasis or women in the service of the gods, and so Dasi Attam means 'the dance of the devadasis'. Relatively recently the term 'Bharata Natyam' has come into general use for the dance hitherto known as Dasi Attam. This change may well have been made in an attempt to dissociate the art from the devadasis who had come to be regarded as disreputable practitioners. The words 'Bharata Natyam' mean 'Dance according to the principles of Bharata', a term that could, indeed, apply to any of the chief schools of classical dance in India, since all of them are based essentially upon Bharata's work.

The most southerly parts of India have, throughout the history of that subcontinent, been the least affected by foreign influences, that is, with the exception of Aryan influences which were profound. This is due chiefly to the geography of that area, for it is divided off from the North by the vast plateau of the Deccan and the mountain ranges and forests of Central India. Invaders came always through the passes in the mountains far away in the North-West, and traders came to the western shores of India. So it is in the south of India where the largest numbers of the pre-Aryan inhabitants of the country are found. This is because the Aryans who came to the South had not come as invaders, but were pioneer settlers who had gradually filtered in, while others had come as missionaries. They were thus far outnumbered in their new homeland, and in order to preserve their identity they had confined themselves strictly to their own society, and built up a rigid caste system. Since they were both learned and wealthy, they very soon became considerable landowners, and thus superior to the indigenous population both educationally and economically.

In order to retain this superiority they applied the caste system extremely strictly and allowed no inter-marriage with the Dravidians. At the same time they applied the rules of their society in such a way that in time these came to be accepted generally as the mores of their adopted country. The Dravidians were separate but nevertheless indispensable units of society. Each caste had its duties, which were essential to the well-being of all. Mixing of the castes would blur the clear definition of these duties, and this would lead to a disruption of the smooth running of the community as a whole. Since religion too was bound up with this idea of society, as it was with feudal society in Europe, Aryan beliefs and with them Aryan culture were also gradually introduced, until the majority of the people of South India became Shaivite Hindus, for Shiva was the god of the Aryan Brahmins. He was the creator, the preserver, and the destroyer, and also Lord of the Dance.

The famous figure of Shiva as Nataraj (Lord of the Dance) shows the dynamic aspect of this god and embodies all his attributes. In his right hand he holds the *damru* (small drum), the symbol of creation. The idea of creation by means of sound has its roots in the belief that there are two kinds of sound, the struck and the unstruck. The struck is audible to us since it is a vibration of air, but the unstruck is a vibration of ether and inaudible to us. In the same way, with the Pythagorean theory, the music of the spheres could not normally be heard by humans. Whereas the sound we hear dies away, the other 'forms permanent numerical patterns which lie at the very root of the world's existence'. It is 'the principle of all manifestation and the basis of all substance'. Shiva the creator, then, holds a symbol of sound in his right hand. Balancing this on the other side, his left hand holds the fire of destruction. His other right hand is held in an attitude of reassurance—he will give protection—and his second left hand, with the arm held straight across the body, points to the left foot, which is raised in benediction and grants bliss to all who come to him. His right foot rests on a demon of evil which he has defeated. The Nataraj is an exquisite study of balance and symmetry, of movement and at the same time of stillness. To Rodin it represented the highest sculptural concept of body movement known to the world.

That the original Dravidian inhabitants of the subcontinent were already fond of the arts, dancing included, is now proved by the excavations of pre-Aryan sites and the discovery of dances which were purely Dravidian in origin, such as the tullals and devil dances of Kerala, and the dances of the aboriginal hill tribes. So with the aryanization of India, dance naturally continued to play an important part in the lives of these people, especially as it was so closely connected with religion.

There are numerous other representations of Shiva in the temples which display his different aspects singly. His static and generative aspect is worshipped in the form of a phallic symbol or lingam. This is a short column rounded at the top and mounted on a decorative plinth. Offerings of flowers and sweetmeats are placed at the base by the *pujarees* (worshippers).

Of the many temples dedicated to Shiva in South India, several date from the revival of Brahminism which came after the great Buddhist period. Buddhism had started in the North as a puritanical faith, not greatly interested in employing the arts to its service. Temple dancing was, however, regarded as particularly unnecessary, especially in view of the fact that some devadasis performed services of an immoral nature in addition to their temple duties. The kingdom of Ashoka, the great Buddhist, had covered almost the whole of the subcontinent, but even then the southern tip was not under his rule. Buddhism, therefore, never really captured the popular imagination in this area, as it did in the North, and the gods continued to be served as they had always been—the devadasis continued to dance for them with the same perfection and devotion as ever before.

Buddhism, unlike Hinduism, was a proselytizing religion and spread to the countries to the east and northeast of India where it took much more permanent root. With it also, of course, went the culture of India, its painting, its sculpture and its dance. In these countries it was adapted to suit the genius of each people. The dance, particularly, was bound to be affected by this transference. Without the shastraic literature which kept it alive and gave it the basis upon which it could develop, its form gradually petrified, its *mudras* (hand gestures) lost meaning and dropped out of use. Now, although still very beautiful, the dances of Bali and Cambodia bear only a superficial resemblance to the Dasi Attam which was their initial inspiration. In the theatre and dance of Japan there are now only traces which connect them with the dance of India.

As with most religions which begin with severe simplicity so it was with Buddhism. When it became firmly established, its austerities were relaxed one by one and its temples too were adorned with statues and paintings. Eventually, the Lord Buddha was accepted as one of the ten *avatars* or incarnations of Vishnu and Buddhism was thus absorbed into Hinduism.

The reassertion of Brahminism and its concrete expression in the form of magnificent temples, meant, of course, that the devadasis were more than ever in demand for service in these temples. Large numbers of them were attached to each one. The temples themselves were highly ornate structures, every possible surface profusely and painstakingly decorated with friezes, bas-reliefs and sculptures, not only of gods and goddesses and their exploits, but with figures of the heavenly nymphs or apsaras and their dance. The most famous of these temples dedicated to Shiva is that of Chidambaram in South India. On the four gateways of this are carved the 108 *karanas* or postures of the body in dance, which are described in the *Natya Shastra*.

A number of these are still in use, although the more acrobatic ones are no longer seen.

Throughout this time South India had been more or less left to itself, while the North had seen invasion after invasion. The Greeks, the Bactrians, the Scythians, the Kushans, the Huns and all the succeeding powers to the north and north-west had come in their turn.

In the twelfth century came the rise of Vaishnavism. It spread from the North and had an immediate appeal wherever it went. People turned to it as a more comprehensible expression of their faith and many temples were dedicated to it.

Because of constant upheavals and consequent re-adjustments, the people in the North rarely had the leisure to build enduring temples. The influx of influences was varied, some were artistically enriching while others totally inimical to artistic development. On the other hand the South, free from the fear and destruction of war, had both the time and the means to give rein to artistic expression. Their temples were abiding anchors which kept their religion as well as their arts from floundering. Since they were permanent, those attached to them had a firm and unbroken tradition. This applies especially to dance, where the temples were not only enduring records of the art, but also supported a living tradition in the persons of the devadasis and their musicians called *nattuvanars*.

Of the Vaishnavite temples those at Belur and Halebid have an important significance for the history of Dasi Attam. They are of course decorated with sculptures of Vishnu and the many stories and legends about him, but they also keep alive for ever the name of a very remarkable queen. This royal lady, Queen Santala, is said to have been the greatest of dancers, and it was in these temples that she danced. Sculptures depicting her are among the most beautiful there, and have been a constant source of inspiration to succeeding generations of dancers.

As in the North, so Vaishnavism enriched the poetry, the music and the dance of the South. And since the god Krishna was one of Vishnu's avatars Dasi Attam added to its repertoire a new store of songs and stories based on Krishna's love for Radha.

With the Muslim invasions in the twelfth and thirteenth centuries, Hinduism was again under stress in the North, and even in the South the Hoysala power was destroyed and the Pandyan kingdom was reduced to its former limits. This disruption, however, did not last very long and certainly did not have any very great or lasting ill-effects on Dasi Attam, for a century or so later the South was again re-united under the Vijayanagar Empire. This was a period of great splendour and extravagance. Vijayanagar flourished and Dasi Attam, through the devadasis, was at its height. The Muslim rulers to the north of the powerful Empire were under constant threat from it, and it was not until a confederacy of the Sultans of the Deccan destroyed it in the middle of the sixteenth century that Vijayanagar finally fell. Although much of the richness and splendour were undoubtedly gone for ever, the threat to Hinduism and its dance in particular was by no means overwhelming; for the Deccani Sultans themselves were great patrons of the arts. Consequently Dasi Attam went to their courts as well, and it is at this time that terms from Muslim usage like 'salamu' and 'tillana' were added to Dasi Attam. Both of these are adaptations of Persian words. In this way Dasi Attam started on a new phase of secularization, for up to this time the secular functions of the devadasis had always been performed among Hindus. They had danced for the king or highly placed patrons, they had helped in the celebrations of domestic festivities and taken part in religious functions. Now with the Muslims in power, even tolerant Muslims, some modifications were inevitable. The changes were not drastic and amounted to somewhat more emphasis on pure dance and, where abhinaya or expression was concerned, a greater use of love songs which could be interpreted in both human and divine terms.

Even during the height of the Mughal Empire, when it stretched into Mysore and Karnataka, the continuity of tradition in the South was not disrupted. Such struggles, as had arisen, had been largely dynastic and comparatively short and had not greatly altered the manner of living. Pressures from outside had not been strong enough to leave very profound marks. Social and religious life had been integrated and the caste system had been a stabilizing factor, the effects of which are still stronger there than anywhere else in India, even though officially the system itself no longer exists. The South Indians have, therefore, always been attracted to and occupied with aesthetic and intellectual pursuits, and in all they do, they exhibit a certain solid and definitive quality. Why is it, then, that they should have allowed so beautiful an art as Dasi Attam, to all but die out? The blame cannot rest on any one cause, it was, rather, an unfortunate combination of factors which led to the general decline.

By the last half of the nineteenth century the devadasis, once highly valued members of society, were falling into disrepute. They were already a caste unto themselves and by the end of the century this caste had come to be thought of as low. Because many of them prostituted themselves, their dance too lost the spiritual and devotional quality which made it great, and therefore also lost the following it once had. The Dasi Attam which a hundred and fifty years ago had been defined anew by the four brothers Chinniyah, Punniah, Vadivelu and Shivanandan of Tanjore came to be known fifty years later as 'Tanjore Nautch'. Shaivism itself, under the impact of the new materialistic machine age, had lost its religious fervour and its forms were reduced to mere ritual, so its dance also no longer aroused the same interest. British rule brought with it, not only the machine age but also Christianity. The missionaries who first came to India were not encouraged by the British Government, but nevertheless they came. They set up printing presses, hospitals and schools, and preached that all men are equal under God. They worked with the poor and the outcast, and converted many. This was the first real challenge to the caste system in

South India. Even the lowliest saw that given the opportunity, he could better himself.

The Hebraic faiths, Judaism, Christianity and Islam have never connected religion with dance. Music, sculpture, painting, architecture, literature and even drama had all been used by the Church, but dancing was something only the pagans employed in connection with worship. It was beyond the conception of the Victorian Christian to imagine that faith could be expressed through so immodest and voluptuous a medium as the 'nautch dance'. They were of course right so far as the 'nautch dance' was concerned, the idea was indeed impious—but Dasi Attam was not 'nautch'. To ladies who were used to quiet English parishes and tea on Sunday with the vicar, who were single-mindedly dedicated to the idea of service, these exotic movements must all have seemed alike: when Radha danced her longing for Krishna they found it hard to see this as an expression of the soul's longing for God—and dancers had such a bad reputation. They felt it their duty to do all they could to stamp out the practice. They were not alone and would never have succeeded so well if they had been. The Indians themselves had lost sight of the true nature and value of their heritage and allowed it to deteriorate. This was probably partly due to their eagerness to precipitate themselves into the 'modern age' and partly perhaps because they were dazzled by the new western culture. It all seemed so much better than their own, besides it was so much easier to 'get on' if they could meet European culture on its own terms.

By the beginning of the last century dance survived in only a few obscure places. However Rabindranath Tagore, Uday Shankar and Menaka had already begun to try and revive interest in the dances of the North. In the South, E. Krishna Iyer decided to reawaken the interest of his countrymen in the real Dasi Attam. Eventually he was joined

in his efforts by others. There were discussions in magazines
and newspapers as to the merits and disadvantages of the
dance. Public interest was aroused and in the early 1930s
some of those who had nursed Dasi Attam through its period
of disgrace, were able to perform again in public. Yet even
now the dance was still in the hands of its traditional
custodians.

Rukmini Devi was the first great dancer of South India
who was not a devadasi, and who, since she was from a
respectable Brahmin family, opened the way for the future.
She studied ballet under the supervision of Pavlova and in
1920 married the Theosophist Dr George Arundale. Her Dasi
Attam guru was Meenakshi Sundaram Pillai. She founded
the famous Kalakshetra and was chiefly responsible for
'Brahminizing' Dasi Attam into 'Bharata Natyam'. After her,
many other high caste families allowed their daughters to
take up dancing as a profession. Shanta, Kamala, and
Kausalya formed the nucleus of the new movement.

This new-found acceptability is a long-delayed echo
of the status of dancing in earlier times. Queen Santala
herself danced in the black marble-pillared halls of the
temples at Halebid and Belur nine hundred years ago, and
so became the inspiration of dancers of the future. Now,
once again dancing has become respectable, so much so
that it is an essential social accomplishment which everyone
is flocking to acquire. This can be regarded as a healthy trend
since it has aroused a consciousness of the dance, and so
given Bharata Natyam a wider field of appreciation both at
home and abroad, and in addition given recognition and
employment to the old nattuvanars. But there is,
unfortunately, a danger that the art may become diffused
by being so freely handled by amateurs. In recent years the
mushrooming of 'Academies', 'Schools', 'Colleges', 'Institutes'

and 'Societies' run by teachers of doubtful quality, is a serious threat to the true Bharata Natyam and its devotees. However, the exodus of the dance from the temple to the theatre and the home is in harmony with the spirit of the times in which we live.

CHAPTER 3

A DASI ATTAM PERFORMANCE

*T*he introductory piece of a Dasi Attam performance is always the allarippu. A dancer may begin the recital with her feet together, body leaning slightly forward and palms joined above her head. Indians always use joined palms for the namashkar, that is, when they greet anyone, but the position in which they are held indicates the status of the person greeted. When, as in this first position, they are held above the head, the greeting can only be addressed to a deity or a person who is deeply venerated. The custom is also found in areas where Hindu influence has been marked, for instance, at his coronation the King of Sikkim was greeted in this way by his subjects. The first action of the dancer, then, is to salute the deity. As the music begins, she glides her neck in subtle movement from side to side. Her eyes follow the neck in a triangular movement—up, right, left, and back to normal. This is repeated a few times and then the shoulders and hands join the movements of the eyes and neck. This combination is known as *rechakas*. The dancer's face lights up with joy and there is almost a smile on her lips, which flickers briefly into life at moments of emphasis.

This gliding of the neck from side to side indicates deep pleasure and, in a modified form, is a part of the natural vocabulary of gesture of Indians in general; since they, in common with the Latins, make abundant use of gesture to support speech.

Throughout the allarippu no accompanying song is used, and the only vocal accompaniment employed is in the form of dance syllables or *sollukuttus*. Each sequence is executed at slow, double and quadruple time. The next phase of the allarippu constitutes the salutation to the learned in the audience, though in former times it would have been addressed to the patron or the special guests. The palms are again joined, but this time they are held in front of the face. Again, other beautiful movements of dance follow. In the last phase the dancer takes up a half-kneeling position, the knee never quite touching the ground, and from here greets the whole audience, to the right, to the left and in front.

We saw earlier that the allarippu introduces, as it were, the recital which is to follow and shows some of the basic positions of Dasi Attam. The chief among these is one where the dancer stands with knees bent and with feet at an angle of about 120°. The arms are held on a level with the shoulders and parallel to the ground. The elbows are slightly bent and the hands are held so that the fingers bend up backwards. There are many slight variations to this position, for instance, the knees may be bent even further so that the dancer is almost sitting, or the hands may be held in front of the chest with the fingers in other specified positions, or the left arm may be extended to the side and the right held in front of the chest, both palms up and the head turned so that the eyes are on the left hand. It is from such positions that the adavus flow and, as with ballet, dancers must learn to achieve them with ease and maintain them comfortably.

After the allarippu comes the jatiswaram, which is again an item consisting entirely of pure dance. The rhythmic patterns are of paramount importance here, for the success of a jati depends entirely upon the interplay between, and the accomplishment of, both dancer and drummer. Between them these two create dynamic variations to the accompaniment of the vocal passages of swaras and sollukuttus. The dancer begins with feet together and the back of her wrists resting on her hips and marks time with her foot before beginning a jati. The jatis to be danced are never pre-arranged between dancer and drummer and the speed with which each apprehends the other's intentions indicates an almost uncanny rapport between the two. The tension is exactly the same as that created between the soloist and drummer during a recital of Indian music. When both performers are of the first order, each seems to challenge the other to a greater display of mastery. It is by no means essential for the dancer and drummer to confine themselves to the same jati, indeed the dynamic tension is much greater when one is counterpointing the other, for both must conclude on precisely the same beat. This obviously indicates great skill, knowledge of time measures and a mathematical ear, and requires lightning calculations on the part of both performers. But the dancer has more than these calculations to think of, because while her feet are occupied with the rhythmic patterns, her body must give abstract expression to the swaras, one beautiful pose melting rapidly into the next. The really expert dancer appears to picturize the music with her arms and body as with her feet she measures and improvises intricate jati patterns. The elements of pure dance movement seen in the allarippu are here greatly added to and elaborated.

The two items up to this point have been of pure dance only. The next introduces nritya for the first time. The shabdam opens with a pure dance piece in the form of a tirmana and then goes on to an interpretation of the *sahitya*, the literary content, and the actual words of the song which follows. The abhinaya at this stage is not very elaborate, for this is merely a brief introduction to it, and gives a foretaste of what is to come later in the performance. The sahitya is, however, interrupted occasionally by tirmanas which form an interlude. The possibility of a double meaning in the words of a shabdam is quite clear from the following example, which is in fact addressed to Shiva.

'O Thou, Beautiful One, Favoured of the Goddess
of Fortune, praised at all times by those learned in
the arts, Giver of plenty, to Thee I bow.
When I wait for Thee, who alone art my guide, is it
fair that Thou shouldst favour another with Thy
presence?
O Great Lord, I tremble with love and devotion
for Thee.
I cannot bear the flowery arrows of Manmatha,
the god of love. O Thou with the third eye in the
middle of Thy forehead, I seek Thy protection and
bow to Thee.'

As always the shabdam ends with a salutation.

All the elements of Dasi Attam have now been introduced and next comes what is perhaps the most exacting part of the whole repertoire, for all the elements are now brought into play in a single item, the varnam. The rendering of a varnam calls for all a dancer's virtuosity in nritya. Both alternate throughout the varnam which can last anything from forty-five minutes to over an hour. The music and poetry of the song too have a particularly high quality, so much so that at times they almost vie with the dancer for attention.

The varnam opens with a tirmana at single, double and quadruple speeds. Then follows the song which is punctuated by brilliant pure dance pieces. The songs of the varnam are always in some way connected with love and the precise nature of the mood is brought out in the opening statement. For instance, the mood may be one of religious love where the devotee is shown to be in love with the god Shiva. In the rest of the song she describes the torment and anguish she suffers as a result of her devotion to him. Not all the songs are necessarily connected with religious love. They can be purely erotic and these usually involve a *sakhi*, the name used for the confidante of the lovelorn maiden. In ancient times, a third party or go-between seems always to have played an important role in affairs of the heart. These songs usually tell of the maid confessing her love to her sakhi and begging her to arrange a meeting with her lover, or of the sakhi making a plea to the lover on behalf of her friend and telling him of her pitiable state. Sometimes the song is not one of unqualified praise for the lover extolling his beauty and virtues, but one reproaching his unfaithfulness or deriding his taste in the choice of a new love. Another song may tell of a conversation between a mother and her daughter who tends to become too easily involved with strangers.

The dance reaches a climax in the charnam, and although in this, as throughout the varnam, nritta and nritya alternate, it is the nritta which stands out for its beautiful and varied adavus and jatis.

After the speed and excitement of the varnam's conclusion, comes the complete contrast of a number of slow and lyrical padams. A padam has to be slow because it is exclusively abhinaya, interpreting in detail, as it does, the words of a song through facial expressions and hand gestures. All padams deal with the theme of love and the dancer is represented as the *nayika* or beloved longing for the *nayaka* or lover. This is an expression of the love and longing of the human soul for union with the divine spirit. Hindus regard love as one of the dominant and root sentiments; the other three being anger, heroism and disgust. This being so, they express their religious longing in the form of an analogy which is at the same time highly expressive and comprehensible to the simplest of souls.

The padam allows for an exhaustive exploration of every possible meaning of a phrase, and each phrase is repeated several times in order that the dancer may interpret every shade of meaning. It follows, then, that the greater the understanding of the dancer, the richer the colour she is able to give to any phrase; for example, in the padam which begins with the words 'Krishna come quickly...' the dancer can demonstrate the word Krishna in many ways, each time pointing one of his many attributes, qualities, or things associated with him.

We have already seen that the texts of the padams can be given a highly erotic interpretation. Here are two examples chosen at random:

'O friend, why does He hide from sight, the Lord Gopala of Muvapuri, and hidden, cast glances at me?

This is indeed an auspicious day.

Tell Him He will be royally welcome.

O friend am I not His?

When He comes, my behaviour will not be such as to make Him think I am childish.

How can I ever desert Him, He who is full of compassion for me?

Have I ever annoyed Him with talk of others?'

'O Krishna, I am on my way to Mathura to sell buttermilk.
Please let me go!
I shall come in the evening I assure Thee—do not hold so fast my skirt.
This is the King's highway, dally not with me here.
The milkmaids will soon join me; let me go.
O Krishna, I implore Thee, do not tease me now.
Please let go my hand! Why art Thou so impatient?'

Both of these, as it happens, concern Krishna, but in some songs the god is not actually named, so the dancer has to indicate the deity through her abhinaya. There was a time, however, when she used to make it quite clear that she was addressing not a god, but a particular member of her audience. Since in a padam a dancer was allowed great freedom of interpretation, she was at liberty to be as flirtatious and as inviting as she wished. Unfortunately, there were many 'patrons' who were highly flattered by this and were only too glad to be the objects of such alluring advances. It was this kind of thing which brought classical dancing into such disrepute, until in the end all dancers were dismissed as indecent and immoral 'nautch girls'.

The meaning of the word love was not confined to its merely romantic aspect. According to the *Natya Shastra* it has two bases—union (sambhoga) and separation (vipralambha). Both, of course, arise from different causes and are to be expressed on the stage accordingly. Sambhoga is to be represented by such actions as clever movements of the eyes, eyebrows, glances, serenity of eyes and face, soft, delicate and graceful movements of the limbs, sweet smiling words and so on. Vipralambha is to be represented by, among other things, languor, anxiety, yearning, indifference, fear and jealousy.

Most padams would come under the second heading and there is a very wide range of them.

One tells of a wife who has been superseded by a new love. It is a very poignant song in which the wife, utterly broken, recalls the happiness of the days when she and her husband lived in perfect love. Yet others, tell of women who are not so resigned, and who vent their anger on the wayward man by taunting him, and by denigrating their rivals, by sarcastic remarks and other displays of jealousy.

There is another beautiful padam in a different vein which, assuming that Ranganatha (Rama), is exhausted after his labours, expresses concern for him, and recounts from the *Ramayana* some of his exploits. Here the dancer has the opportunity of showing her range and versatility.

Padams can be the most interesting part of the whole recital, especially for those who have some idea of the basic content of each one, for if the dancer is truly accomplished she makes the meaning of the words perfectly clear. Bhava, or mood, is common to all men and therefore within the understanding of all. It is something which speaks to the soul and has no need of words. We can all see whether a person is happy or sad without being told in so many words. We can appreciate a padam without necessarily understanding the actual words of the song, just as one can enjoy an opera sung in a foreign language; although in both cases an understanding of the words would obviously increase our enjoyment even further.

After the padams comes the tillana. This is a dance of pure joy and the dancer's face and whole body express delight. She is exuberant yet captivatingly feminine, and displays the whole range of the devices of allurement. She is by turns capricious, coy, flirtatious, inviting, and almost mocking in the confidence of her beauty. She performs her intricate jatis with an ease which belies her consummate skill. Each adavu is repeated at two or three speeds and punctuated with scintillating tirmanas. The repetition of the same musical phrase throws into relief the dancer's variations as she combines in delightful harmony the movements of eyes, hands, fingers, neck, shoulders, waist and feet. The sculpturesque quality of Dasi Attam blends, in the tillana, with the fluidity of Kathak, so that one sculpturesque pose melts rapidly into another. It is as if the frozen figures of Belur and Halebid had become vibrant with the sap of youth.

The performance ends on a quiet and serious note with the recitation of a sloka. The recitation is in the form of variations on a melody which is set in a particular raga. There is no rhythmic or musical accompaniment. The dancer expresses the meaning of the fairly simple words through abhinaya, at the same time providing the adjectives, as it were, herself.

CHAPTER 4

THE DEVADASIS

*M*en have always conceived their gods in anthropomorphic terms and this being so, it was only logical that these gods should be endowed with human frailties. The deities had to be appeased, more often than not through fear of the consequences of omission. So worship has ever involved sacrifices of some kind. Men offered the best of their possessions—the fruits of the field, the fatted calf and even humans. Abraham was prepared to sacrifice the only son of his old age.

The fertility cult seems to have existed in all ancient civilizations. The great Mother Goddess appears under different names, Mylitta, Isis, Ashtoreth, Astarte, Ishtar, Aphrodite, Venus, Bhagvati, Parvati and Ceres to name only a few. The function of these goddesses was reproductive. They ensured the cycle of the seasons which regulated the growth of crops. They were responsible for the increase of the livestock and the perpetuation of the race. The well-being of the city and the countryside depended upon the goodwill of the regional mother goddess.

The reproductive powers of the goddess were embodied in the female sex organs and it must have seemed proper that the gift which would be most acceptable to her, would be the virginity of a girl. This would, in addition, be an auspicious beginning to the girl's ability to bear children, since by being defloured in honour of the deity, she performed a pious act and thus acquired fertility and prosperity.

Herodotus says of the Assyrians, 'Every woman born in the country must once in her life go and sit down in the precinct of Venus, and there consort with a stranger....A woman who has once taken her seat is not allowed to return home till one of the strangers throws a silver coin into her lap, and takes her with him beyond the holy ground. When he throws the coin he says these words, "The goddess Mylitta prosper thee." (Venus is called Mylitta by the Assyrians.) The silver coin may be of any size; it cannot be refused, for that is forbidden by law, since once thrown it is sacred. The woman goes with the first man who throws her money and rejects no one. When she has gone with him, and so satisfied the goddess, she returns home, and from that time no gift, however great, will prevail with her....A custom very much like this is also found in Cyprus.'

Herodotus does not say whether these women had to be virgins, but St Augustine tells of a custom in Phoenicia, where the worship of Venus demanded an offering of virginity. Parents offered their daughters to the temple to be prostituted in the service of the goddess. When the fixed period was over the girls were married off and thenceforth led the ordinary life of a housewife.

Young girls and virgins were dedicated to the temples for a variety of reasons. In an account of his visit to Syria, Lucian records that he saw a great temple to Venus at Byblos. Here they performed certain ceremonies in mourning for Adonis, whom they believed to have been killed by a wild boar in their country. Consequently, they beat their breasts and observed mourning as for one who is dead. But the next day they behaved as if he were alive and shaved their heads, in the manner of the Egyptians when Apis died. Those women who were unwilling to sacrifice their hair had, instead, to sell themselves for one day and the money they thus obtained was given to the temple.

Sometimes the sending of girls to the temple had a double aim, namely, that of serving the deity while at the same time earning their marriage portions.

Girls were also dedicated as a result of vows. Strabo gives an instance of this when he says, 'Now Comana is a populous city and is a notable emporium for the people from Armenia; and at the time of the "exoduses" of the goddess, people assemble there from everywhere, from both cities and the country, men together with women, to attend the festival, and there are certain others, also, who in accordance with a vow are always residing there, performing sacrifices in honour of the goddess. And the inhabitants live in luxury, and all the property is planted with vines, and there is a multitude of women who make gain from their persons, most of whom are dedicated to the goddess, for in a way the city is a lesser Corinth.'

Of Corinth itself he says, 'And the temple of Aphrodite was so rich that it owned more than one thousand temple slaves, courtesans, whom both men and women had dedicated to the goddess. And therefore it was also on account of these women that the city was crowded and grew rich....'

There is ample evidence in the writings of Socrates, Apollodorus, Plautus, Arnobius, Justin, and Eusebius which tells of sacred prostitution in the Middle East, West Asia, Greece, Cyprus, Egypt and North Africa. Although comparatively little is known concerning the pre-Aryan Indus Valley civilization, which flourished about the third millennium B.C., it seems likely that dancing played an important part in the lives of these people. Many clay figurines of dancing girls have been excavated from the ancient cities of Mohenjo Daro and Harappa. It is possible that these dancing girls were connected with religious ritual. Professor Mackay says, 'It is still uncertain whether dancing formed a part of the religion of the inhabitants of the Indus Valley, although it is so important a feature of the ritual of certain sects in India today. A scene on a fragment of a faïence amulet showing a man beating a drum and people dancing to the music seems to suggest, from its appearance on a religious symbol, that the dance was a ceremonial one; but this suggestion, of course, cannot at present be verified....Another amulet from the same city (Harappa) shows the cult-object invariably associated with the Urus-bull, while by the side of it appears a figure which may be of a woman dancing; if this interpretation be correct, the dance must certainly be a religious one. In connection with the subject of ritual dancing allusion must be made to the wonderful figure of a dancing girl found by Rai Bahadur Daya Ram Sahni. The dancer, who from her features is obviously an aboriginal type, may represent the predecessor of the dancing girls (devadasis) who are attached to many temples in modern India....It is interesting to think that this bronze figure may represent very probably a temple dancer of Mohenjo Daro.'

But there is no evidence to suggest that these dancing girls, whether secular or religious, were in any way connected with prostitution. With the advent of the Aryan invasion of India in about 2000 B.C., and the consequent decline of the Indus Valley civilization, new religious practices were introduced into the subcontinent. The worship of the sun-god Surya (equivalent of Apollo) demanded the services of girls in the temples to sing and play instruments in honour of the god. In time their function extended to include dancing and sacred prostitution. The *Padmapurana*, which evolved much later with the resurgence of Brahminism, goes so far as to say that the dedication of a number of prostitutes to the temple of Surya is one of the surest ways of gaining Suryaloka, or the heaven of the sun-god. The fact that the gods were accustomed to having celestial nymphs or apsaras dance for them in heaven, would appear to lend divine sanction to this statement. For surely they would require the same devotion on earth that they received in heaven. This recommendation of the Padmapurana was obviously implemented by those dedicated to the worship of Surya, for in the seventh century the celebrated Chinese Buddhist pilgrim Huien Tsang notes a large number of sacred prostitutes at the temple of this god in Multan. Al-Barauni, the Arab historian, also confirms similar practices in India.

The spread of Buddhism seems to have checked, though not altogether abolished, this trend. There are numerous stories in Buddhist literature of how fallen women were reclaimed to a state of grace, and thenceforth led lives of asceticism. This is borne out by the existence of orders of nuns and almswomen, called Bhikshinis, instituted by the Buddha himself.

Both Kautilya, in his *Arthshastra* (circa 300 B.C.), and Vatsayana, in his *Kama Sutra* (circa A.D. 100), talk about courtesans in detail, but neither of them makes any mention of sacred prostitution. The accomplished ladies they talk about were rather like the Greek hetairae. In the case of the *Kama Sutra* particularly, this is a strange omission, as the whole book is devoted to the art of love in all its range and subtlety. It is unlikely, in view of his scientific approach to the subject, that Vatsayana would have left them out due to any scruples of conscience. It may be that technically he would have classified them under religion, and therefore regarded them as irrelevant to his treatise. But in any case, the fact that these two authors say nothing about sacred harlotry, by no means proves that the system could not have existed in India. We have already seen that it existed there before their time and certainly after their time, and that it also existed in Western Asia and North Africa during their own time. Some writers have suggested that because South India had mercantile links with the Eastern Mediterranean during the ninth and tenth centuries, the idea of temple dancers may have come from those lands. But this seems highly unlikely, because the puritanical influence of Islam had already been well established there.

The fourth century A.D. saw the rise of Brahminism. The Laws of Manu laid down the functions of the four castes; the highest of them being the Brahmins or priests, whose persons were holy and who monopolized all learning.

When the great temples were first built in India, dancing girls were attached to them as a matter of course. These not only performed services for the idol, but also provided an additional source of income for the shrine. The ninth and tenth centuries saw the most glorious period of temple architecture and it was at this time that the temples in South India, still famous today, were built. The richness of the decoration of these temples was fittingly complemented by the enchanting forms and matchless dancing of the devadasis, literally servants of god. We know from inscriptions that the Chola king Rajaraja installed four hundred devadasis in his temple at Tanjore. They were housed in luxurious quarters in the four streets surrounding the temple and were granted tax-free lands. Their social status was very high for they attended upon the god himself; they looked after his sanctum and danced before him. Invitations to royal occasions served to enhance this prestige even further. Such a high regard for these women was not surprising, for they had undergone a severe training in music and dance, were skilled in languages and had, moreover, been 'married' to the temple deity. This last ceremony took many forms, varying from region to region.

In the Coimbatore district at least one girl from every family of musicians was selected for temple service. After her dance training at home she was dressed in fine clothes and bedecked with jewels. She was made to stand on a heap of rice, and two devadasis, also standing on heaps of rice, held a folded cloth before her. The girl held the cloth while her dancing master grasped her ankles and moved them up and down in time to music. In the evening she was taken to the temple for the Tali (wedding necklace) tying ceremony. She sat down in front of the idol and the officiating priest gave her flowers and marked her forehead with sandalwood paste. He then tied the tali, which had been lying at the idol's feet, round her neck. Later on, after more training in music and dance, the marriage was consummated by a Brahmin, preferably rich, who represented the idol.

Among the Basava sub-caste the girl was married in a similar fashion, but to a khanjar (dagger). This was clearly a phallic symbol representing the lingam of the god Shiva.

At the Suchindram temple in South Travancore, the marriage of the devadasi to the idol was symbolic of the marriage of Parvati to Shiva. The priest lit the sacred fire, recited the mantras (sacred texts), and tied the tali round the girl's neck.

In other parts of India the dancing girls went through marriage ceremonies with trees, swords and flowering plants.

These marriages meant that the devadasi could never be a widow, and so she was considered lucky. Her presence, therefore, on auspicious occasions such as weddings and births was regarded as essential. Whenever possible she made talis for others and sometimes incorporated a bead or two from her own as a special favour.

We have two descriptions of the dancing girls in the kingdom of Vijayanagar from foreigners at the court.

The first is Domingo Paes, who was a member of the Portuguese Embassy. He talks about the idol which has the body of a man and the head of an elephant (obviously Ganesh). This idol was attended by dancing girls who fed it and danced before it, and also dedicated their daughters to it. He says that any high-born man might visit these girls without censure, that they lived in the best quarters of the town and were allowed to sit and even chew betel in the presence of the King's wives. Paes is wide-eyed with wonder at their wealth, especially their jewellery. Seeing them on one particular occasion he writes, 'Who can describe the treasure these women carry on their persons? Collars of gold thickly set with diamonds and rubies and pearls, bracelets also on their arms, jewelled girdles and anklets on their feet.... There are some among them who have had lands presented to them and litters and maidservants without number. One woman in this city is said to possess 100,000 parados, about £25,000, and I can believe this from what I have seen.'

Paes' description is vividly authenticated by murals, which can still be seen, at a temple near Conjeevaram. Fernao Nuniz, a countryman of Paes, gives similar descriptions of the institution of devadasis in Vijayanagar.

It is plain, then, that these devadasis were women of means. But this was not their only valuable possession. They were highly educated and polished in their manners and so able to provide their patrons with intellectual stimulation. This is the main reason why men of rank and learning resorted to them, as their own wives, being mainly confined to hearth and home, were sadly lacking in these qualities. It was, therefore, the accepted thing for these gentlemen to support such women privately, or to hire them from the temples. Moreover, their association with good luck meant that in time, the presence of dancing girls became more or less obligatory at celebrations of all kinds.

Methwold, who visited the Muslim kingdom of Golconda in the time of Elizabeth I, remarks upon the system of devadasis and their dance training from early childhood. These dancing girls 'whom the lawes of the country do both allow and protect', were invited to formal public functions where 'they danced gratis, but at all other meetings, as circumcisions, weddings, ships' arrivals, or private feasts, they assist, and are paid for their company'.

The institution of dancing girls became, therefore, an accepted part of Muslim society. Another Englishman, Mundy, informs us that the Muslims at Agra distinguished among various types of dancing girls and regarded them as distinct from the level of common prostitutes. These dancing girls from Agra, Delhi and Lucknow, known generally as *tavaifs,* were not devadasis, but highly sophisticated courtesans and repositories of culture and refinement. The sons of the upper classes were sent to them in order to round off their education. Though most of these tavaifs were professing Muslims and so had no connections with temples, their development obviously owes much to the devadasis. Their accomplishments, particularly in music and dancing, and their marriage to trees and flowering plants, compare exactly with the custom of the temple dancers. In both cases the preservation of classical dancing, particularly in the South, is due in large measure to these women.

A later picture of the life and customs of the South Indians, including of course the devadasis, emerges from an account of the Abbé Dubois at the end of the eighteenth century. He was well qualified to write *Hindu Manners, Customs and Ceremonies*, since he spent thirty years of his life in that country. Talking of the status of women in general, he says that it was not considered seemly for ordinary women to learn to read, sing, or dance. If any of them did by chance acquire any of these skills, far from exhibiting them, they would be ashamed to own up to them. This attitude was fostered by the fact that only dancing girls required the use of these arts. Later, this was to have a serious effect on the survival of classical dancing and indeed on the education of women in general. It is only comparatively recently that the education of women has become widely accepted.

From the eighteenth century onwards, there was an ambivalent attitude towards the devadasis. On the one hand they were fully accepted, indeed, according to Dr Shortt, they were an asset to the town in which they lived and were at the very centre of Hindu society. The wives of citizens neither saw any harm nor felt any injury when their husbands consorted with devadasis; on the contrary, they thought it perfectly honourable. Yet on the other hand, there was an implied censure in the fact that these very wives did not, for anything in the world, wish to have the accomplishments commonly associated with dancing girls. A possible explanation of this may lie in the structure of the caste system. The devadasis, although connected with the temples, were not Brahmins. They formed, as it were, a caste unto themselves. Their way of life was based on matrilineal law. Property passed from mother to daughter although sons were not exempt. In practice the daughters of devadasis, after the requisite training, also became temple dancers. If for some reason such as a physical defect, a girl could not take to her mother's profession, she was married off to someone in her own caste. The sons either became nattuvanars (musicians) and dance masters, or married outside their caste and left the community. There were occasional cases of the sons or daughters of the richest of the devadasis marrying into good Brahmin families.

Many nattuvanars took the surname Pillai or Mudali, which were regarded as respectable adjuncts to Tamil names. These masters have jealously guarded and preserved the art of dance music in spite of a grave danger, at one time, of it being utterly lost. The danger arose because many of them, being illiterate, had no access to the shastraic literature connected with the arts. However, some families tenaciously preserved the theoretical background and set a standard for both the practice and the theory of the music. The great musician Mattuswami Dikshitar and his pupils, the brothers Chinniyah, Punniah, Shivanandan and Vadivelu Pillai deserve particular mention for this work. Their families and their pupils have continued the tradition to the present time.

There were two main divisions of dancing girls, the valangai or right-hand and the idangai or left-hand. The valangai would only dance for or consort with the upper or right-hand castes. The idangai were not selective and were sometimes known as kammaladasis because they catered for the artisans, that is the kammalans or left-hand castes.

No devadasis, however, were allowed to have any dealings with the Untouchables. If they did, they were tried by their own Panchayat or caste court, and if found guilty were excommunicated.

As we have seen, all devadasis were temple dancers, but those who danced at court or for the nobles were called rajadasis and those who danced at weddings and social ceremonies of all kinds were known as alankaradasis. The name sanis was reserved for those in Telugu districts, and in the temple at Vizagapatnam they were called kurmakis. The devadasis also differentiated among themselves on the basis of language. In Southern Travancore the Malayalam-speaking dancers would neither marry into nor even eat with the families of Tamil-speaking devadasis.

Both the South Indian Princely States and the Madras High Court recognized their rights and status. They were legally permitted to adopt daughters from outside their profession or caste. These girls were entitled to their adoptive mothers' inheritance exactly as if they had been real daughters, but these rights were recognized in British India only in those areas which came under the jurisdiction of the Madras High Court. In some Princely States in other parts of India, the rights of temple dancers were also recognized, though in varying degrees from State to State.

The gift of a son from the gods is the greatest boon to an Indian family. If a marriage failed to produce a son, one of the daughters would be 'married' to the temple idol and serve a period there as a devadasi, after which she would return home and be given all the privileges and responsibilities of a son and heir. She would inherit her father's property; and at their death would perform the important religious ritual of applying the torch to the funeral pyres of her mother and father.

As mentioned before, the devadasis were averters of ill-luck, so the duty of performing the Arti ceremony was exclusively theirs. A small diva (oil-lamp) which burnt ghee (clarified butter) was placed on a salver. The subject was either the idol or a person. The devadasi would hold the salver at arm's length up to the subject's forehead, and describe a given number of circles with it. This Arti was performed twice daily for the idol and for anyone else from whom the evil eye or danger had to be averted. People going on a journey or about to encounter danger, in battle for instance, would get a devadasi to perform the Arti. This ritual was also used to avert the evil eye from new brides, pretty children and beloved sons.

Yet another function of the devadasis, which the Abbé Dubois describes, was connected with their reputation for bringing good luck. They were hired to accompany people when they went visiting, and it was considered most improper to go anywhere without a number of these attendant 'good luck charms'.

What appears to have surprised the good abbé most of all was the modesty of these women. He admires their cleanliness and their good taste in clothes, their dignity of deportment and the civility of their language. 'Indeed,' he says, 'they are particularly careful not to expose any part of their body.' He concludes that this probably arises from their sophistication in the art of seduction, the unseen being more tantalizing than the seen.

In 1870 Dr Shortt, a surgeon in South India, read a paper before the Anthropological Society of London, entitled 'The Bayadéres; or Dancing Girls of Southern India'. He describes how these girls started their training from the age of five or thereabouts. Before sunrise they had instruction for an hour each in singing and dancing, and the same again in the afternoon. After three years they were allowed to perform in public, but their training continued throughout their career. He notes several kinds of dancing which the girls were supposed to master. They were paid a token salary by the temple authorities, but their riches were accumulated through the munificence of their admirers. He, like the Abbé Dubois, praises their beauty and their culture and is not at all surprised that so many European officers took them for mistresses.

At the beginning of the 20th century Thurston encountered many devadasis in the temples of Madurai, Conjeevaram and Tanjore, and in his book *Castes and Tribes of Southern India* he gives a detailed description of how a devadasi retired from her profession. 'When a dancing woman becomes too old or diseased, and thus unable to perform her usual temple duties, she applies to the temple authorities for permission to remove her ear-pendants (todus). The ceremony takes place at the palace of the Maharaja. At the appointed spot the officers concerned assemble, and the woman, seated on a wooden plank, proceeds to unhook the pendants, and places them, with a nuzzar (gift) of twelve fanams (coins) on the plank. Directly after this she turns about, and walks away without casting a second glance at the ear ornaments which have been laid down. She becomes immediately a taikkizhavi or old woman, and is supposed to lead a life of retirement and resignation.' The pendants were later returned to her, but she never wore them again.

One of the main reasons why the devadasi system fell into disrepute was that young girls were sometimes abducted to swell the numbers in the temples. This led to a concerted effort on the part of the British Government, the Indian States and some Indian social reformers, to put an end to the system. The Princely States of Mysore and Travancore both stopped the dedication of devadasis in 1910 and 1930 respectively. But in 1927 there were still 200,000 temple prostitutes in the Madras Presidency alone, which was a part of British India. In that same year Gandhi wrote, 'There are, I am sorry to say, many temples in our midst in this country which are no better than brothels.'

Katherine Mayo in her books *Mother India* (1927) and *Slaves of the Gods* (1929) presented a false and one-sided view of Indian society, but succeeded nevertheless in stirring the conscience of many people both in India and abroad. There was a hue and cry against the system but it is difficult to say how far these attempts were successful, since it was not easy to get accurate and consecutive assessments of the numbers of devadasis. In the census of 1931 the point was made that many did not return themselves as such, but regarded themselves as married women by virtue of their 'marriage' to the temple god.

Although there are no devadasis as such in India today, there are many good dancers, dance teachers and musicians who come from the devadasi caste. It is they who are the custodians of the tradition, the discipline and the feeling of reverence for music and dancing, nurtured through hundreds of years. Their approach to these arts has retained an attitude of dedication which only professionalism can engender. Whatever else may have been said about them by well-intentioned puritans, it is undeniable that their art was an integral part of their religion and as such pure and untained. It is to them that we owe the survival and preservation of one of the oldest classical dance forms in existence today.

CHAPTER 5

KUCHIPUDI

The earliest dance-drama of South India, which unfortunately cannot be dated with certainty, was the *Shiva-Lila Natyam*, which consisted of plays based upon legends about Shiva. By the tenth century, inscriptions prove the existence of other religious dance-dramas which were called Brahma Melas. Later, Vaishnavism made inroads into the traditional Shaivite cults and the worship of the god Vishnu brought into being new art forms and new themes. These were, of course, concerned with Vishnu and his ten avatars. Of the ten the one who attracted most popular devotion, was Krishna; for he, in the *Bhagavad Gita*, introduced a new concept into Indian religious thought, the idea of a personal God. For the poor peasant it was Krishna who made possible the love between God and Man and the bond of devotion one for the other. This gave rise to the Bhagti movement, and the bhagtas who followed its precepts roamed the countryside with its new message of love. These bhagtas, known in Andhra as Bhagvatulus and in Tamil Nadu as Bhagvatars, used poetry, song, music and drama for the propagation of their faith and beliefs. In Andhra their dance-drama came to be called Kuchipudi and in Tamil Nadu, Bhagvata Mela Nataka.

The first book to refer to these new dance-dramas is the *Machupalli Kaifiat* of 1502. The people of Siddhavattam were sufering great hardship under the local tyrant Gurava Raju. They presented their grievances in the form of a play, ostensibly as entertainment for their king, Immadi Narasa Nayaka. Their diplomacy bore fruit, for we are told that the king read between the lines and liberated his people. Even at the end of the sixteenth century, by which time the mighty kingdom of Vijayanagar had declined, the learned Pandita Radhya Charita remarked on the high standard of the art in South India.

Kuchipudi and Bhagvata Mela Nataka have a common origin. Both have Vaishnavite themes and use Telugu, the language of Andhra. Moreover, the dancer-actors in each case are Brahmin men. It seems, nevertheless, that Kuchipudi was the first to evolve. It grew in Andhra, an area comparatively near North India which was the home of Vaishnavism.

Sidhyendra Yogi, a saintly Telugu Brahmin, can be called the founder of this dance-drama as we know it today. He was a devotee of Krishna and the lord appeared to him in a darshan or vision and asked him to write a play on the Parijatapaharana. This legend tells of how Krishna was asked by Rukmini, his wife, to obtain for her the Parijata tree from the garden of the god Indra. Krishna, with the help of Narada Muni, the sage, succeeded in getting the tree for Rukmini. Now, Krishna's love Satyabhama became extremely jealous when she heard of this episode. She taunted Krishna, nagged at him and became more and more sarcastic about the lord's relationship with Rukmini. If he cared for her at all, he would have to prove it by bringing her the tree as well. Krishna had no alternative. He set out for Indra's garden and the quest began....

When Sidhyendra Yogi finished the play, he was confronted with the problem of staging it. Nowhere could he find actors who were sufficiently competent to play it or people willing to back him. Eventually, he arrived at Kuchelapuram, the village of his wife's family, which lay on the banks of the river Krishna about twenty miles from the city of Masulipatnam. Here the Brahmins, who were Krishna worshippers, agreed to help him. Young men and boys learnt their parts and their families supported the scheme enthusiastically. It was a great success, and after this the villagers put on the play every year as a part of their religious festivals. The neighbouring villages, Kappatralla, Alampur, Marampali and Mandapetta, also took up the idea. In 1675, the Nawab of Golconda, Abdul Hassan Tahnisha, saw a performance of *Parijataparana* by the Kuchelapuram Brahmins. He was so impressed that he granted the village and the surrounding lands to the dancers, with the stipulation that the tradition of the dance-dramas should be carried on. This grant was inscribed on copper plate, which was the custom in South India symbolic of authority and perpetuity. This is an interesting example of how a Hindu religious art was not only tolerated, but actually fostered by a Muslim prince.

Through the years Kuchelapuram village came to be called Kuchipudi, and it is this name which attached itself to the dance. Although none of the other villages perform the dance-dramas any longer, Kuchipudi has, in spite of many vicissitudes, carried the tradition down to our own day.

Tirtha Narayan Yati's famous dance-opera *Krishna Lila Tarangini* is a work much favoured by Kuchipudi artistes. It deals with Krishna's life from childhood to marriage. Each part of this work is interspersed with the rhythmic dance syllables known as sollukuttus. Since the *Krishna Lila Tarangini* is a very long dance-opera, it often happens that selected pieces from it are danced or sung as solo performances. A popular item is the very first section, 'Balagopala Tarangam', dealing with the childhood of Krishna. It has five stanzas of poetry set to music, and sollukuttus between each stanza. A very unusual feature of the 'Balagopala Tarangam' is that the artiste has to perform various balancing feats while still dancing. With an ornate brass pot resting on his head, he improvises a few rhythmic patterns within the given time scale, or he may have to do the same thing on the spherical shape of a large earthen pot placed upside down on the ground. This illustrates the high technical virtuosity required of a Kuchipudi dancer.

The greatest contribution towards the abhinaya, or expression, of this dance was made by Kshetrayya of Muvvu, a veritable genius in the writing of padams. He wrote 4500 of them although only 700 are extant and danced today.

The well-known play, *Golla Kalapam* of Ramiah Shastri, and the *kritis* or dance-songs of Thyagaraja are further material used by the Kuchipudi dancers. The kritis of Thyagaraja are addressed to Rama who, like Krishna, was an incarnation of Vishnu. Apart from these, the themes used are the epics and puranas, especially the *Bhagvata Purana* and Jayadeva's *Gita Govinda*. The last work gives the Kuchipudi dancer-actor twenty-four hymns or ashtapadis to interpret through abhinaya. The first ashtapadi is the Dasavatara, very commonly enacted, which gives an account of the ten avatars of Vishnu and their births. After acting out one, the dancer assumes a pose associated with the avatar and pauses before going on to the next. Thus, he starts with Matsya (the fish), the first incarnation, carries on to Kurma (the tortoise), Varaha (the boar), Narasimha (the man-lion), Vamana (the dwarf), Parasurama (the wielder of the axe), Raghurama (Rama), Balarama (Krishna), Buddha (the enlightened one), and last of all Kalki (the horseman of destruction), who is yet to come.

The Kuchipudi artistes are well versed in Telugu and Sanskrit and have an understanding of the literature of dance and music. Since they themselves provide the vocal music, they have to be singers as well.

The nritya elements (representing moods and sentiments) of Kuchipudi are padams, varnams, shabdams and slokas.

Padams are danced in exactly the same manner as in Dasi Attam. The most popular authors of padams are Jayadeva, Thyagaraja, Sarangapani, Kshetrayya and Maganti Subba Rao.

Varnams too are danced as in Dasi Attam.

Although many shabdams are similar to those of Dasi Attam, Kuchipudi has a few special varieties. The Vinayaka Kavita, the Mundaka Shabda and the Abhishekam form part of this group. An abhishekam takes about ten minutes to unfold and describes a deity from birth to glorification. There are abhishekams about Rama, Prahlada, Sita and other important mythological characters.

Slokas are verses which, like shabdams, are rendered in solo abhinaya. They are, however, pure poetry and as in the Thumri Andaaz of the dance-style Kathak, the dancer sits throughout his recitation of them and gives full scope to shringar bhava, the expression of love. How this North Indian influence found its way into the repertoire of Kuchipudi would be an interesting subject for investigation. In the nritta or pure dance part, too, a strong Kathak element can be seen. It is possible that Kuchipudi absorbed these influences during the Mughal period when Andhra was a part of the empire and Kathak at the peak of its popularity.

The pure dance or nritta of Kuchipudi consists of adavus, jatis, jatiswarams, tirmanas and tillanas. These are similar to the nritta of Dasi Attam, but Kuchipudi has one type of pure dance, namely, kannakole, not found in Dasi Attam, Bhagvata Mela Nataka or Kuravanji, all of which employ the same basic techniques. The kannakole is mainly footwork. While the musicians play the syllabic beats, the dancer executes patterns within the tal or time-measure (pronounced 'taal'). In the saptatal of the kannakole the dancer improvises variations on seven different tals. This particular technique of footwork is very much like the layakari of Kathak in which the dancers of Jaipur and Lucknow excelled and which we shall discuss later.

The music of Kuchipudi is Karnatic and the chief musician is the nattuvanar who recites the dance syllables, at the same time clapping them out with his hands or playing them on a pair of small brass cymbals. There are three other musicians, a mridangam player, a clarinettist and a violinist.

Each male character wears a *dhoti* (loin-cloth) with a jacket, and jewels and crown if the part requires them. He may also wear a beard and moustache. The female characters, played of course by men, wear the normal sari and choli with false plaits or other more elaborate coiffures. Nowadays the sari is being replaced by the fan-fronted costume worn by Dasi Attam dancers. The facial make-up is quite simple.

Kuchipudi dance-dramas are performed only at night. A temporary open-air stage is constructed in the temple courtyard, but if more people than the courtyard could possibly hold are expected, the stage is put up at the end of a street. In this case the street itself would be the auditorium and the balconies of the houses on either side serve as stalls and private boxes.

The audience begins to congregate hours before the show. Little boys reserve the best places, people talk and gesticulate and babies add to the general clamour. There is, underlying it all, an air of expectancy. The stage has no curtain to be rung up so there is no hint whatsoever that the proceedings are about to begin. Suddenly Hasyagadu appears. Appropriately attired as the Fool, he jumps, staggers, capers and makes faces. His function is to draw attention towards the stage, to make the people settle down and prepare themselves for the good things to come. After his exit there is an invocatory prayer by the artistes off stage. This is usually from the *Gita Govinda* and invokes the blessings of the gods. The musicians led by the nattuvanar, now take their place on one side of the stage. They play a short rhythmic piece on the mridangam and cymbals, and after this the nattuvanar sings a prayer in honour of Balatripurasundari, the goddess of the Kuchipudi temple. He follows this with a long sloka explaining the meaning of the dance-drama, its significance to the lives of the people and their moral duty to listen patiently and learn from it.

The important characters perform an introductory dance called a *daru*. This involves the holding up of a sheet of white cloth by a pair of volunteers. The artiste comes on behind it, showing only his head and feet. He does a few dance movements and when the sheet is whipped dramatically away, he comes forward and dances more elaborately. The audience knows by his gestures whom he represents and he demonstrates his skill at considerable length.

There are many kinds of darus. They are not improvised but form an integral part of Kuchipudi. Later, as the dance-drama progresses, the onlookers are regaled with extemporized snatches of comic relief known as Pagati Veshamu. These come after the longer movements and are more in the nature of intermissions. Much the same thing took place in the mediaeval mystery and miracle plays in England, where it became customary for actors to insert unscheduled slapstick into didactic religious drama.

Unfortunately, encroaching modernism, in the form of the gas lamp, has now appeared in Kuchipudi. This has destroyed the other-world atmosphere created by the oil-fed divas, the tiny-tongued lights licking into the night. Now we have the incessant hiss of gas and the vigorous pumping of lamps, sometimes during the tenderest part of the drama.

The most important Kuchipudi artistes of modern times were Lakshmi Narayana Shastri and Chinta Krishna Murti, both Brahmins from the parent village. The products of a long tradition of the art, they were experts in every sense of the word. Lakshmi Narayana Shastri was in his time justly famous for his role of Bhama in *Bhama Kalapam*. He trained some excellent pupils, the famous dancer Balasaraswati being among those whom he instructed in the rendering of padams. It is sad indeed that for many years this master was neglected by the public and the State.

Chinta Krishna Murti organized a permanent dance company in the village. Its repertoire included the classics of Kuchipudi, and when invited, they would go on tours of the surrounding villages and towns. However, they too were in a neglected condition and their finances were precarious. The art is being kept alive mainly through the faith of a few people like the Reddys.

In recent times women too have begun to learn Kuchipudi, but they mainly perform only short extracts from the dance-dramas as solo items. Kuchipudi is therefore better known today through these performances than through the actual dance-dramas which are rarely, if ever, performed outside the local villages.

CHAPTER 6

BHAGVATA MELA NATAKA

*T*he King of Tanjore, Achutappa Nayak (1561–1614), one day inadvertently ate a betel leaf with his left hand. Now, why should this seemingly innocent action have led to the establishment of an important school of dance-drama? A short explanation of the customs of India is here clearly called for. The betel is the heart-shaped leaf of a climbing plant, smaller in size than a man's hand. It has a mildly pungent taste and possesses some medicinal value, especially as a digestive aid. The leaf is thinly coated with a touch of slaked lime and the refined sap of the katha tree, and then folded into a neat triangle containing finely chopped areca nut, cardamom, scents and other herbal preparations. The triangle is secured with a single clove. Very often, in sophisticated circles, the betel or *paan*, as it is called, is covered with silver leaf and sprinkled with rose water. Although the paan was chewed after meals to counteract the richness of the food, it later became a social habit, until today, paans are an addiction with some people, particularly with those who take refined tobacco with them. The mouths of such habitués are permanently stained a rich reddish-brown. In the best houses paans are offered to guests on silver salvers with a certain amount of ceremony as in the West one would be offered a choice liqueur.

The paan, however, was only incidental. The real culprit was the left hand. The king should have used the right hand, since the left hand, which performs the duties of personal hygiene, is regarded as unclean. It is probably due to this that the term 'left-hand castes' arose in South India, because these were the low castes which carried out all the menial and unpleasant tasks. Achutappa's conscience was so burdened that he sought ways of expiating his guilt. A gift to the holy Brahmins seemed the best means of expiation. Now, it happened that at this particular time there was a group of Brahmin refugees in Tanjore who had come from Andhra. What is more, among these were some dancers, musicians, and others who were devoted to the religious arts. Since the king was a patron of the arts, here was an eminently suitable opportunity. He therefore granted, about ten miles from the city, a house, a well and a portion of land to each of the 501 families. The king's desire was, that they should continue their cultural activities and develop them. In gratitude the Brahmins named their village Achutapuram, after their royal benefactor. The village has now come to be called Melatur and ever since its inception, dance-dramas have been performed at the local Varadaraja Perumal temple. The dancers are Bhagvatas, men servants of the gods, and their dance is known as Bhagvata Mela Nataka.

About 200 years ago, Venkatarama Shastri wrote a dozen dance-dramas which became Bhagvata Mela favourites. They are *Usha Parinayam, Rukmangada, Golla Bhama, Rukmini Kalyanam, Sita Kalyanam, Dhruva Charitram, Harishchandra, Kamsavadha, Shivarathrivaibhavam, Bhasmasura Vadham, Markandaya* and *Prahlada Charitram*. All of them have Vaishnavite themes and are written in Telugu. They have great literary merit and integrate acting, dancing, music and singing with great success.

Natesa Iyer was the next great Bhagvata. Although he did not write any plays, he was an actor famous for his female roles and, as a teacher, he produced actor-dancers of the calibre of Bharatram Nallur Narayanaswami, K. Subramania Iyer and Kodanda Rama Iyer. Natesa Iyer had no sons but his adopted daughter, Padmasini Bai, learnt from him and became a well-known Harikatha or devotional singer. His house at Melatur is a place of pilgrimage and it has become customary to end every dance-drama by going to it in procession and singing the closing chorus there.

The leading figure of recent times was Balasubramania Shastri. He was both an organiser and source of inspiration. His group included K. Subramania Iyer, P.K. Subbier, R. Nagarajan, N. Venkataraman and G. Swaminathan. Every year in May or June, during the Narasimha Jayanti festival, they presented the dance-dramas to the public. A cycle of four is now performed annually, *Prahlada Charitram, Harishchandra, Markandaya*, and *Usha Parinayam*.

The roles in these dance-dramas are handed down from father to son and are cherished as family inheritances. To be worthy of this great tradition and because of the religious significance of the plays, the dancer-actors prepare themselves by penance, prayer and fasting. The spirit of love and dedication which infuses the players in the Passion plays of Oberammergau bears a striking resemblance to that of the Bhagvatas.

The technique, music, costume, make-up and stagecraft are, in the main, similar to those of Kuchipudi, although there are some significant differences. The main characters introduce themselves with the daru, and the adavus, jatis and varnams are rendered in the Kuchipudi manner. The satiric and comic interludes are in Tamil, the language of the area, whereas the dance-dramas themselves use Telugu. While in Kuchipudi, solo dances are given considerable freedom, an example being the Dasavatara, in Bhagvata Mela solo dances are only permitted if they form a part of the main action of the drama. In the past, lighting was provided by placing earthenware oil lamps, divas, on the trunks of banana trees. Today, electric lights are used. For the stage itself, drop scenes and curtains have recently been adopted. These are rather crude innovations and one wonders whether they add anything to the atmosphere of the art.

The chief play, *Prahlada Charitram*, is always the first to be performed, since it concerns Narasimha, the man-lion incarnation of Vishnu, to whom the temple is dedicated. The legend tells of the destruction brought on by hubris. The demon, Hiranyakasipu, wanted to be immortal. Therefore, in order that he might obtain this gift from Brahma, he undertook to repent of his sins by embarking on penances and fasts. Brahma, benignly and perhaps a trifle naïvely, granted the boon. Hiranyakasipu would henceforth be preserved from death by day and by night, indoors and in the open, in heaven and on earth; he could be killed by neither man nor beast. The demon was delighted, his self-importance knew no bounds. In his foolishness, he challenged the supremacy of Brahma himself. Hiranyakasipu now decided that in future all the people should worship, not Brahma, but himself. They were compelled to recite hymns in his honour and tell their beads to the accompaniment of his name. But there was one who refused to obey. It was Prahlada, his own son. The boy was a devotee of Vishnu and nothing could persuade him to transfer his allegiance. His father argued with him, threatened him and even tried to kill his own son, but the hand of Vishnu protected the boy and no harm came to him. One evening in the palace,

Hiranyakasipu was raging at his son. Prahlada maintained that God was omnipotent and omnipresent. His father, beside himself in his wrath, struck a mighty blow with his sword at a nearby pillar, hacking at it as he screamed, 'If he's everywhere, he must be in this too!' 'Yes, he is,' said Prahlada. At that moment, Narasimha, the man-lion Vishnu, sprang out of the pillar and, clawing Hiranyakasipu, dragged him to the doorstep. It was now the time between the end of day and the beginning of night, the precise time when the demon was not immune from death. He lay on the doorstep, neither indoors nor out. His body was neither on the earth nor in heaven. It was thus that Narasimha, who was neither man nor beast, destroyed the demon.

The mask of Narasimha, which lies encased within the sanctum of the Varadaraja Perumal temple, is of mysterious origin and said to be possessed of inexplicable powers. No one knows how it came to Melatur, or for what precise length of time it has been in the temple. When the *Prahlada Charitram* is staged, the mask is taken out and worn by the actor who plays Narasimha. Normally, no masks are worn for either Bhagvata Mela or Kuchipudi, and even in the special case of *Prahlada Charitram*, the man-lion dons it for only one scene in which he has a verbal duel with another character. At the climax of this scene the actor enters a trance-like state and becomes, as it were, Narasimha himself. This condition of complete identity is attributed to the sacred mask and the people of Melatur believe that once every year the god Narasimha manifests himself to them through the body of the Brahmin actor. Immediately the play is over the mask is returned to its place inside the temple.

The inducement of hypnotic states through dancing is by no means uncommon. It exists among the dervishes of the Arab countries, the tribes of Africa and those of African descent in the West Indies and America, to mention only a few. In the West it is clearly seen in the contemporary popular dances so widely prevalent among young people. Unfortunately, these dances and the rhythms which go with them, have been assimilated into the cultures of Europe and North America without regard for their original context and value, so that here they no longer have their intended therapeutic effect. Something of the same pattern has occurred in the opposite direction, especially in the field of music. The avidity with which certain Indian musicians took to the otherwise worthy European harmonium, has created untold havoc with a musical tradition which is, by its very nature, unsuited to such an instrument.

During the actual performance of Bhagvata Mela there are two departures from Kuchipudi. The jewelled statue of the Lord Narasimha is placed in the main entrance hall of the temple and the doors are left wide open so that he may see the dance-drama and hallow the proceedings with his presence. The second difference is the entrance of the elephant-headed god, Ganapati or Ganesh, the remover of obstacles. In Bhagvata Mela, an actor representing Ganapati appears after the exit of the musicians who perform the invocatory duties.

Although Bhagvata Mela may be performed only by men, it is becoming increasingly fashionable for some women dancers to present short excerpts from these dance-dramas to form the abhinaya items of their Dasi Attam performances. There is, of course, no harm whatsoever in this, so long as it does not misrepresent the original renderings of the dance-dramas.

Bhagvata Mela Nataka used to be performed in five other villages in the neighbourhood of Melatur. At Theperumanallur and Nallur the tradition died out about 80 years ago, and a little later also at Oothkadu. The last dance-drama at the village of Soolamangalam was performed in 1950 through the efforts of E. Krishna Iyer and Rukmini Devi, but in spite of their attempts to resuscitate the art it has died out in this village too. The only village of the five where it is still performed is Saliyamangalam, but even here the performances are sporadic.

CHAPTER 7

KURAVANJI

$\mathcal{T}$he Kuravanji is a folk dance of South India based upon the free use of Dasi Attam techniques. The dancers are usually young women and belong to a hill tribe called the Kuravas. They are well known for their good looks and their cheeks are often tattooed with motifs made up of small dots. These marks may serve three quite different purposes. They may be used purely as beauty spots to enhance the looks of the girls. On the other hand, there is another theory about beauty. Extreme perfection, it is thought, is likely to invite admiration or even jealousy and hence, the evil eye. If, however, some tiny mark is added which mars absolute perfection the cause of the original jealousy is removed and the evil eye is averted. The 'evil eye' is a superstition taken very seriously in India. Whenever complimentary remarks are made, it is a matter of course to indicate that no envy is felt, by adding a short phrase such as 'By the grace of God' or 'May the evil eye be far from you'. There is also another custom, whereby the evil eye is averted from anyone who is likely to be admired, by making a small black mark with kohl behind one ear. A possible third reason for the tattoos on the faces of the Kurava women may be, that by this means they disfigure themselves permanently, and so are unlikely to tempt the gods to take them away from the earth while they are in the prime of their beauty and youth. The gods of India, like the gods of Greece, were sometimes susceptible to the attractions of the daughters of men.

The Kuravas are a nomadic gypsy people. The menfolk are snake-charmers, acrobats and tumblers, the women usually fortune-tellers. Their living is necessarily precarious and they have acquired a reputation for petty thieving and pilfering. There are many wandering tribes in India, all of whom are beyond the pale of society and the caste system. They represent the unassimilated elements of the original Dravidians who could not or would not be incorporated into aryanized society. It is possible also that among these tribes a certain number is made up of those who had been expelled from their own castes, and therefore had no place in a settled community. One of the ways in which this could happen was a transgression of the Laws of Manu concerning marriages and sexual misdemeanours. These were tolerated between men of one caste and women of a lower caste but not the other way round. If a woman had any relationship with a man of a lower caste than herself, or was even suspected of this, she, together with the children of such an alliance, was turned out of her home and village with great ignominy. She would then have no alternative but to either become a prostitute or join a group of wandering gypsies.

The very great similarity between Dasi Attam and Kuravanji makes the theory all the more plausible that it was such women who introduced this dance-form to the Kuravas. The Kuravas were, as we have seen, complete outcasts and excluded from all social and religious functions, and so would have no other means of seeing and imitating Dasi Attam. This seems the only possible explanation for the influence of a highly sophisticated dance like Dasi Attam on the primitive folk-art of a nomadic tribe. There is no doubt that Dasi Attam does contain some elements of the pre-Aryan dances, but these do not now stand out as distinct from the whole, and would not account for the resemblance between the two dances.

The Kuravas, then, are an example of those non-caste tribes which were forced into coherent units through the will to survive and out of sheer economic necessity. These tribes were ostracized by Hindu society and later the British government exacerbated the situation by classifying them, and stigmatizing them, as 'criminal tribes', the members of which could not enter the municipal limits of cities or towns, and were not allowed to own property or enter government service in any capacity no matter how humble. The only friends these tribes had were the missionaries who did what they could for them by way of medical care and education.

It was only after the Independence of India that these 'criminal tribes' were given constitutional and legal rights. The state and welfare organizations took an interest in the social uplift of these people and it was discovered that they had rich and fascinating folk-lores.

The legends of the Kuravas always revolve around fortune-telling and romantic episodes. There is a well-known story among them about Subramanya, the son of Shiva, who fell in love with Valli. This beautiful dancer was the daughter of a hunter. All Subramanya's eloquence and powers of persuasion could not win the heart of this maid of the forests. The rejected lover finally appealed to the wise elephant-headed Ganesh and they decided upon a plan. Ganesh transformed himself into a fully grown elephant. The two then concealed themselves in strategic positions near the path which the girl was in the habit of using. As she approached, Ganesh suddenly appeared. Valli was frightened and started to run but the rogue elephant followed fast. Subramanya, of course, 'rescued' the distraught maiden from the terrifying elephant. After this she could hardly spurn his appeals and she succumbed to his charms.

There are many other stories which tell mostly of a forest girl's love for a prince or a temple deity and how this true love was returned.

The Kurava women dance these themes in the form of a folk-ballet. Six to eight dancers take part in a Kuravanji performance. The Dasi Attam movements become fluid and lively and sometimes passionate in intensity. There is no time limit, the duration of the ballet depending upon the inspiration of the dancers and their audience.

Like Dasi Attam, this dance was often Shaivite in inspiration. One of the earliest known Kuravanjis is the *Thirukutrala Kuravanji*, composed in honour of Shiva as Thirukudanthar. The other well-known ones are the *Chitrambala* and the *Kumbesara*. All of these are performed during Shaivite festivals. There is, however, one Kuravanji, the *Azhagar*, which is danced for the god Vishnu.

M.D. Raghavan, a Madras University anthropologist, states that in recent years the Kuravanji dancers have usually been men made up as women, symbolizing the consorts of Shiva and Vishnu. They dance and sing, each group trying to outdo the other in proclaiming the superior qualities of its own god. This seems to imply that it is only recently that the Kuravas have felt the full impact of Vaishnavism and that the rivalry between this and Shaivism still occupies an important part of their consciousness.

Shanta Rao has often incorporated Kuravanji dances into her programmes with considerable success. In her ballets for the Kalakshetra troupe Rukmini Devi also used Kuravanji, especially the *Thirukutrala*. Other choreographers have followed this lead.

In 1986, Kuravanji was presented to a mass audience in India when Padma Subramanyam, Chitra Visveswaran and Sudharani Raghupathy appeared in a full-length Kuravanji dance-drama on Doordarshan, the state run Indian television network.

CHAPTER 8

KATHAKALI

$\mathcal{K}$athakali has a comparatively short history, but as such a complex art cannot, it is obvious, come into being suddenly and out of nothing, it is worth while to examine the conditions which made it possible. The home of Kathakali is Kerala, one of the smallest states of the Indian Union. It lies in the extreme south of the peninsula, and occupies a narrow strip of land facing the Arabian Sea stretching right down to Kanya Kumari (Cape Comorin) at the southernmost tip of India. The state is composed of the two erstwhile princely states of Travancore and Cochin. Its smooth white beaches with coconut palms, its quiet backwaters and picturesque paddy fields create an atmosphere of calm beauty.

This is where traders from other countries first came, for the Malabar coast has the longest history in India of contact with other lands. Phoenicians, Greeks, Romans, Arabs and Chinese all came here for spices, hardwood, gold, peacocks, apes and ivory. Jews took refuge here after the second sack of Jerusalem and Thomas the Apostle, it is claimed, brought Christianity. Many settled here and most left some mark of their visit. The square fishing nets of Cochin and the temple architecture are both the legacy of the Chinese. The Arabs brought slaves and the influence of Islam and seem to have settled happily. There is a powerful and wealthy community of Christians here, who take pride in the ancient origin of their Church and regard the Protestant and even Roman Catholic Churches as more recent offshoots.

Nevertheless, for all this history, geographically this is a comparatively new land, and shouldered its way out of the sea by underwater volcanic action some time before the Aryan incursions into India. This scientific fact has been absorbed into the mythology of the country with that remarkable aptitude for an explanation of events, in which the Aryans excelled, especially when such an explanation could be turned to their own advantage. It is said that the Brahmin warrior Bhargava, who was an avatar of Vishnu, had in error committed the terrible sin of matricide. To atone for this hideous offence he undertook many austerities and penances. When he felt sufficiently cleansed from his sin, he flung his axe far out into the sea in an act symbolically renouncing violence. The gods were pleased and the waters receded to the point where the axe had fallen and so this new land was born out of the primaeval depths of the ocean. In those days, as often today, it was thought proper to make offerings and gifts to holy and learned sages in order to rid oneself of the stain of sin. Such practices have been encouraged by all religions from time immemorial. Accordingly, Bhargava granted this new kingdom to the Brahmins in a final act of expiation. This legend was doubtless propagated by the Nambudri Brahmins as a justification for their riches and vast land holdings.

How the Nambudri Brahmins actually came to Kerala is not known with any certainty, but what is known is that they came very late in the history of Kerala. One theory is that they were Aryans who had filtered into South India many centuries after their settlement of Northern India, probably about the third century B.C., and after subjugating the local tribes had established their supremacy in matters of both state and religion. The other, and more plausible theory is that although some may well have come this way, the majority of Nambudri Brahmins came very much later than this; not in fact, until the latter part of the Middle Ages, when Muslim power in the North extended up to the borders of Assam. To escape conversion or subjection, some high-caste Brahmins of Bengal, like the Pilgrim Fathers, set sail from Bengal. Hugging the coastline, they sailed past Ceylon and right round the peninsula, choosing for their settlement the hospitable shores of Kerala. With them they brought Sanskrit and a rich heritage of learning, their wealth, and that most important of their assets, a power over men's minds. This theory gains added weight from the observations of anthropologists, who have noticed similarities between the cultures of Brahmin Kerala and Brahmin Bengal.

Every legend has its symbolism and inner meaning. An example is the story of Parasurama and the snakes. The name means Rama-of-the-Axe and is another appellation of Bhargava. After he had given Kerala to the Brahmins, they found it difficult to settle there and abandoned the country. Some time later they came back, determined to colonize it, but found that the snake people, the Nagaloka, had taken possession of it. There was, naturally, a battle between the two, for the Brahmins regarded the land as theirs by right and the Nagaloka as usurpers. The Nagaloka were eventually defeated, but Parasurama, in a rare peace overture, stipulated that although the land was to be parcelled among the Brahmins, they were, nevertheless, to accommodate the Nagaloka by setting apart a small portion of their land for the use of the conquered people. This portion of land, moreover, was on no account to be touched or tamed in any way. Now, this legend clearly indicates how the Aryan

Brahmins came to be the chief landowners in Kerala, but not being able to exterminate the Dravidians, took them on as junior partners or relegated them to the forests.

The indigenous Dravidians were worshippers of Bhagvati, the Earth-Mother goddess, and it was only natural that they should venerate the snakes who lived in the earth. The legend clearly identifies the dark-skinned Dravidians with the black cobras so common in Kerala. Later, after the Nambudris' supremacy had been established, the custom of each household actually setting apart a small grove in the compound for the habitation of snakes, became universal. These snake groves are common even today and women and children set milk offerings in them for the nagas (snakes) who, far from harming anyone, are said to protect the household.

This veneration of snakes resulted in one of the oldest dance-forms of Kerala—the ceremony of Pampin Tullal, or the dance of the snakes. This is a ceremony performed by members of the Pulluvan caste in order to propitiate the household snakes. An important centre for the worship of snakes is at Mannarsala, where special snake-dance festivals are held. These dances are of Dravidian origin, as were others such as the ritualistic dances connected with the ceremonies of Bhagvati and the various devil dances. All these were early influences which helped towards creating the climate for the composite art of Kathakali. Many of them involved the use of fantastic costumes, masks or make-up which, although they do not bear a direct resemblance to those of Kathakali, can at least be regarded as having created the conventions which allowed the representation of super-human beings to be associated with an extravagant appearance.

Kathakali is, in fact, the result of a marriage between the pre-Aryan Dravidian dances and the later ones which were introduced by the Brahmins. It combines the consciousness, the religious practices and the techniques of these two cultural streams in perfect harmony and balance. The Dravidians were a gentle, peaceful people, worshippers of nature and devoted to Bhagvati, the benevolent Mother Goddess of the earth, who provided them with all their needs, spiritual and material. She brought forth the fruits on the trees and the grain in the fields, and protected them from evil demons. It was because of their unwarlike disposition that the Dravidians were swamped by the aggressive Aryans and driven into the forests and mountains. Some survive still as aboriginal tribes, mainly in the states of Orissa and Bihar. These children of the forest are known as Adivasis or aboriginals, and their way of life, as described by anthropologists such as Verrier Elwin, gives us some clue as to the nature and character of the original inhabitants of India. Dance for them was truly a part of their life. Their deities were extremely important to them, and through dance they did honour to these deities, propitiated them and celebrated their triumphs. One of these dances, the Bhagvati Pattu, is in honour of the triumph of Bhagvati over Daruka, the king of the demons. It still just about survives, as do Tiya-attam, Mutti-yettu and Tiray-attam. All these dances were accompanied by the *chenda*, a cylindrical drum which is held upright and struck with two slender sticks. This instrument is now an important part of the orchestra which accompanies Kathakali.

The coming of the Brahmins resulted in the inevitable changes which always occur with the influx of alien elements. When two or more peoples live on the same soil, there must needs be a considerable amount of give and take, and social and religious synthesis. The warrior caste, the Nairs, who claimed to be the equivalent of the Kshatriyas in other parts of India now came into being. Racially they were half Aryan and half Dravidian, so it was natural that in them should repose the music, the dance and the religious mores of both races. They combined with the culture of the Dravidians the sophistication of the Aryans, whose approach to everything was analytical and academic and who defined their laws, artistic, social or religious, by meticulous attention to every possible detail. The Brahmins, moreover, encouraged the Nair caste who protected, by force if necessary, Brahminical rights and privileges. Nowhere else were the Brahmins so much in rapport with the warrior castes. In fact, nowhere else in India is there a caste system quite like that of Kerala. Inter-marriage was permissible with the Nairs, although not for the eldest son. He alone was obliged to marry a Brahmin girl. The others, if they chose, might marry either within the caste or be found a wife or, more likely, a concubine from among the Nairs.

In time the benevolent goddess Bhagvati became identified with the mother goddess of the Aryans, who was the terrifying and bloodthirsty Kali. The Nairs adopted Kali as their patron goddess and an image of her is still to be found in every Kalari.

The Nairs were a highly organized military caste and, justifiably, very proud of their prowess in wielding weapons of war. This skill was scientifically taught and careful attention was paid to developing those qualities which would produce the desired results. They began their training while they were still small boys. They were given special massages and exercises which developed their suppleness, agility and strength. Training took place in sunken gymnasia known as Kalaris, beginning at about three o'clock in the morning and ending late at night, with breaks in between. During their long and hard apprenticeship they learnt not only the skills of the art of war, but also how to gain a psychological advantage over their opponents—what we would nowadays call psychological warfare. This was achieved through training in mime, gesture and acting. A Nair's very deportment and mien were calculated to portray his own superiority and confidence and to arouse fear and uncertainty in his opponent. His miming skill was said to be so great that he could pretend to throw a lance or spear and do it so convincingly that the enemy would actually feel the pain of his body being pierced. A part of the training was given in the form of martial dances and combat exercises. Some of these dances still survive, especially the dagger dance and a dance with a long incredibly flexible, snake-like sword. The sword dance is particularly spectacular and dangerous-looking, since once the sword begins to twist and hiss through the air with lightning speed, the smallest error in judgement or split-second delay in reaction would almost certainly prove fatal not only to anyone within range but to the man wielding it as well.

Hand to hand combat was highly stylized in ancient times. The rules were strict and respected by both parties and, as with most forms of physical combat, this codification led to aesthetic qualities appearing in the form of the contest. Gradually, as these qualities were realized, it became a pleasure simply to watch the procedure and appreciate the finer points of the skill of the combatants. This happened in Europe, for example, with fencing and the Graeco-Roman style of wrestling, and in Japan with the war dances of the Samurai. All of these evolved into entertainments from being, initially, serious arts of war. Indeed so great was their aesthetic appeal, that even now, when they are otherwise redundant, they survive solely because of their inherent beauty and skill.

Gradually the need for the Nairs to fight diminished, but they preserved their knowledge, kept themselves in practice through dancing and made Kathakali their own preserve. To this they brought all their traditional skill and training techniques. Even today the exponents of Kathakali are mostly Nairs. They retain the name Kalari for their practice place together with most of the exercises and methods of massage they used as warriors. The basic stance of a Kathakali dancer is a logical extension of the natural position adopted for any form of hand to hand combat. The flexed knees help to absorb the shock of landing and the wider apart they are held, the greater the freedom of movement in any direction. The one curious thing is that the weight of the body is taken by the outer edges of the feet. There are said to be two reasons for this, namely, to reduce further the shock to the spinal column and to make dancing for long periods less tiring to the feet.

The Aryan influences on Kathakali come from the vast store of art forms codified and embodied in the Sanskrit shastras of the Brahmins. One way they could propagate and keep alive the wisdom of the gods was in the form of stories and legends. These sacred texts were recited in the temples, which were forbidden to the lower castes. This form of recitation was known as Chakkiyar-kuttu, because the reciter belonged to the Chakkiyar caste. The Chakkiyars claim descent from the Sutas of the *Mahabharata*. This may or may not be true, but they certainly have existed for a very long time, for they are mentioned in the second-century Tamil epic, *Silappadikaram* or the Epic of the Anklet. A platform known as the Kuthambalam existed in most temples for their use. The Chakkiyar would sit or stand on this platform with his accompanists. First he would offer prayers to the temple deity and after this recite a selected Sanskrit verse. He would then go on to expound his text. The language of the exposition was always the vernacular of Kerala, Malayalam, albeit a Sanskritized form of Malayalam. An obvious comparison of his function is with that of a preacher giving a sermon from the pulpit, particularly if that preacher is of the old fire and brimstone type. The Chakkiyar, too, brought in topical analogies and situations to illustrate his text and was not above censuring particular members of his 'congregation'. However, unlike the solemn preachers of the past, he held his listeners' attention by trying to make his discourse as amusing and entertaining as possible. This he accomplished through witticisms and frequent use of mime and gesture to bring his story to life. This abhinaya or expressionistic aspect was later absorbed and considerably emphasized by Kathakali.

The Chakkiyar was accompanied on a large copper drum called a *mizhavu*, by a drummer who was always of the Nambiar caste, and also by a woman who played a pair of small brass cymbals. She was of the same caste but was known as a Nangiar. She beat out the time solemnly, for she was expected to remain serious and straight-faced, no matter how amusing the performance of the Chakkiyar. This solo performance had two other names, Prabhand-kuttu and sometimes Kathaprasangam Manthrakam.

At one time the Nangiar herself stopped being a mere accompanist and took over the Chakkiyar's role. This Nangiar-kuttu became quite popular, but for some reason has now died out.

Later on, three or four Chakkiyars performed together and this new form became known as Kudiy-attam, which was really the forerunner of the dance-drama which later developed in Kerala, for they had already begun to incorporate excerpts from the plays of Kalidasa, Bhasa and Harsha.

The performers in Kudiy-attam, unlike those in Kathakali, were both men and women, which clearly indicates that there must have been a greater element of lasya here than in Kathakali. The plays were long and performed at night. Particular role-types had different costumes and special make-up colours. All these conventions were later to be absorbed into the Kathakali tradition.

Faithful patrons of Kudiy-attam were the kings of the Perumal dynasty, especially Kulasekhara who died in 430 A.D., Bhaskara Ravi Varma and Cheraman.

A third type of dance, the Pathakam, was very similar in form. This gave much greater importance to Malayalam, although the subject matter of the plays came from the same Sanskrit sources.

Vaishnavism had, in the twelfth century, given birth to Jayadeva's *Gita Govinda*, which had come to be recited and danced in most parts of India.

Some time around 1650 or perhaps a little later, the Zamorin of Calicut introduced to Kerala a dance-drama modelled on Jayadeva's work. Like so many important happenings in India, there is a story attached to this event as well. It is said that the Lord Krishna himself once honoured the Zamorin by appearing before him and giving him a peacock feather. These divine visitations or darshans were accorded to the selected few, and in commemoration of his vision the Zamorin wrote a drama. This play, written in Sanskrit, was performed in a technique already known and used in the plays of that time. The name given to the work was *Krishnapadi*, and when it was staged with actors, music and dance it was called Krishna Attam. To this day the performers of Krishna Attam wear a symbol of the Lord Krishna in the form of a peacock feather. It was a long play and lasted for eight nights. During these nights the life of the Lord Krishna was unfolded in detail—his childish games and encounters with the demons, his escapades with the maidens of Mathura, his going out into the world to fulfil his mission, his darshan to Arjun as his charioteer, and the famous discourse in the form of the Song Divine, the

Bhagavad Gita, and finally his return to heaven when his task on earth had been accomplished.

With the passage of time Krishna Attam became a religious tradition. Performances acquired a sanctity, and the people who attended them believed that they earned special blessings by doing so. Krishna Attam is still performed at the temple of Guruvayur during the festival of Krishna Jayanti, which celebrates the birth of the god. The technique and manner of presentation have undergone no change over the years. The make-up, costumes and jewellery are very similar to those of Kathakali. However, in Krishna Attam, Brahma, some monkey characters and demons wear painted wooden marks. This is obviously a legacy of the exorcistic rituals of the devil dances and the rites of the Kali cults. Although abhinaya plays an important part, it is not as exhaustive as that of Kathakali and nritta or pure dance is given more emphasis. On the other hand, there are some beautiful movements in Krishna Attam, which no longer survive in Kathakali. The musical instruments of the two dances are the same, except that Krishna Attam does not use the chenda. The convention of using singers to deal exclusively with the text is a significant innovation which Kathakali took from Krishna Attam. This left the dancers free to apply all their energy and concentration to the interpretative dancing for which Kathakali is famous.

With the popularity of the dance-drama as an art form, rivalry developed amongst the rulers of Kerala as to who could maintain the finest troupe. Now, as the fame of the Zamorin's Krishna Attam had spread far and wide, the ruler of Kottarakkara became curious and asked his neighbour to lend him his troupe. But the Zamorin was proud and jealous of the high standard of his dancers. He refused. Not only did he refuse, but added insult to injury by sending a message to the effect that there was no point in sending a troupe to a court where none was learned enough to appreciate the subtleties of Krishna Attam. Naturally, the Raja was mortally offended at such condescension. He determined to prove that he could vie with the best so far as cultural matters were concerned. To this end he wrote a play on the life of Rama.

For the performance he enlisted the help of another ruler, the Raja of Kottayam who was a brilliant actor-dancer. He also got the help of two Nambudri Brahmins. They were of immense help to him because it was the sympathetic attitude of the Brahmins which had resulted in the emergence of drama in the first place. These two priests, learned in the scriptures, were therefore also well versed in the exposition of the sacred texts through dance.

By the end of the seventeenth century, Raman Attam had come into well-defined existence. It used many of the techniques of Krishna Attam, but also introduced some changes.

Raman Attam too was performed over eight nights. The custom of using singers was retained as it now became more than ever impossible for the dancers to do their own singing. This was because the chenda was added to give more volume, vigour and excitement to the drama, which meant that the dancers had to save all their breath and energy for the increased tempo and agility of the dance movements.

Another addition to the Krishna Attam practice was that the text was interpreted much more fully. To do this the abhinaya was extended, particularly that of the face, *mukhabhinaya*, and that of the hands, *hasta-abhinaya*. In order to give full expression to mukhabhinaya, masks were done away with altogether and replaced by more elaborate and varied make-up. New costumes were designed for different role-types, traditionally by the Raja of Kottayam who, it is said, saw them in a dream. However, he gave the same voluminous skirts to all the chief protagonists, because his dream, sadly for Kathakali, revealed only the top half of the characters. But the greatest innovation of all was in the language of the play. The Raja of Kottarakkara took the daring but astute step of writing his play in Malayalam. Hitherto the language of culture had been Sanskrit and no literature of classical stature had been produced in the vernacular. The Raja thus no doubt laid himself open to further taunts of lack of refinement from his rival at Calicut. Nevertheless, Chaucer-like, his confidence gave a new status to the common tongue. Because the drama could be understood by everyone, there now existed no reason why it should not be performed outside the confines of the temple. The lower castes, being prohibited from entering the temples, had not been able to hear the Chakkiyars or see Krishna Attam. Now they could wonder at the exploits of Rama, see the episodes of his life from his romantic marriage to his exile. They could see the abduction of his lovely wife, Sita, by Ravana the King of Lanka, and Rama's search for her. Finally they could share his triumph over the demon king, and the joy of his reunion with Sita.

Raman Attam gained tremendous popularity and very soon all the episodes of the *Ramayana* had been dramatized. Plays were written with themes from other sacred works such as the *Mahabharata*, the *Shiva Purana* and the *Bhagavad Purana*. The name Raman Attam now became unsuitable because of this widening thematic range and so the name Kathakali or story-play was substituted in its place.

However, some scholars tend towards the conclusion that this sequence of events is merely legendary, and that in actual fact Krishna Attam did not come into existence first. One estimate of its date places Raman Attam in the fourteenth century. Krishna Attam, according to this theory, originated almost three hundred years later, that is, in the seventeenth century. But the date of Krishna Attam itself is in dispute, although the earliest date given to it is still later than that given to Raman Attam. Some have suggested that the mid-fifteenth century is a more likely date for the *Krishnapadi*, even though the work itself indicates that it was written about 1650.

Nevertheless, the dates of these two dance-dramas do not make any difference to their contribution to Kathakali. Kathakali, as we know it today, is a comparatively recent dance form when considered in the context of the history of dance in India, although its roots reach right back into pre-Aryan times. Its merits are not increased in any way by the attempts of its misguided admirers to give it a greater age than that which it has.

The development and encouragement, if not the survival of art, has always owed much to the aristocracy and the wealthy. Only those who had the means could satisfy their aesthetic drives. Kathakali was no exception. Although it became popular with rich and poor alike, it was the rulers of Kerala who nurtured it with their scholarship, their talent and their wealth. Not only did they support permanent troupes, but many of them took an active part in the performance and even wrote new plays.

The first of these was the Raja of Kottayam whose four plays were all based on the *Mahabharata*. Later, the Maharajas of Travancore played a similar notable part in the history of Kathakali. Karthika Tirunal who was Maharaja at the end of the eighteenth century wrote no less than seven plays; but his interest extended even further and he wrote a treatise on dance called *Balarama Bharatam* under his own name, Balarama Varma. This book remains a classic among its kind. His younger brother who followed him to the throne, although he wrote only one play, encouraged the art greatly.

Prince Asvathi, the grand-nephew of Karthika Tirunal, was a famous composer and wrote four plays. Music was the chief passion of another Maharaja, Swathi Rama Varma, who surrounded himself with musicians from many parts of the country and himself composed 75 padams for Kathakali.

Apart from these royal patrons, there is another name which deserves mention. It is that of the poet Irayimman Thampi (1783–1863), who wrote three new plays. He had a daughter Thankachi, who continued the poet's tradition and wrote another three plays.

The eighteenth and nineteenth centuries saw great development and activity in Kathakali. During this time the dance-drama was at the height of its achievement and collected an immense repertoire of plays.

By the mid-nineteenth century, British power, which had been increasing over the years, had become firmly established. In 1877, Victoria was proclaimed Empress of India, and European influences and ideas spread rapidly. The Victorian age was a time of supreme self-confidence for the British nation. The empire builders and the colonial administrators who followed them felt perfectly justified in adopting a policy of aloofness from the peoples they governed. There were some British scholars who took an interest in the culture of the country, but the administration was, for the most part, indifferent.

Naturally enough, those Indians who were educated in the atmosphere of British supremacy came to accept the values which their mentors instilled in them. Yet there were some who still cared about their own heritage. Kathakali might well have faded into oblivion had it not been for the efforts of one such man, the Malayalam poet Vallathol Narayana Menon.

Vallathol's love for Kathakali began at an early age, when his father used to take him to see the dance-dramas. When he grew up, he realized that it would not be long before the art died out. He felt that it was his destiny to preserve Kathakali from the decline that had set in. There still lived many good gurus and musicians, but these had few pupils, as young men found more lucrative occupations elsewhere. Vallathol's plan was to bring these teachers and musicians together in one place and systematically engineer a revival by rousing the conscience of the Malayali people. He experienced great difficulty in raising funds and had to resort to the expedience of a lottery. This was highly successful and he collected seventy-five thousand rupees. With this he was able to establish, in 1930, the centre upon which he had set his heart. To his Kerala Kala Mandalam (The Kerala Institute of Arts) near Shoranur, he brought the greatest masters of Kathakali, Mohini Attam and Ottan Tullal—men like the late Ravunni Menon, Kavalapra Narayana Menon and Kunju Kurup. The Institute attracted the attention of the public and the Government; students were given grants to attend and the great revival of Kathakali was well under way. He took his troupes on tour in India and abroad and with the profits from these tours, the Kerala Kala Mandalam was able to have its own buildings at Cheruthuruthi near Shoranur. These highly successful tours, in addition to providing much needed finances, had created a demand for Kathakali. To the Institute came students from various parts of India. It produced artistes who are today leading Kathakali dancers.

By 1941, the Kerala Kala Mandalam had proved its worth enough for the government to be concerned about its survival and well-being. It was taken over by the state and Vallathol appointed its director.

The Kerala Kala Mandalam now gets a grant from the Sangeet Natak Akademi, India's national academy of music and drama, and the Institute is among the most important in the country. However, the International Centre for Kathakali in Delhi is now also doing excellent work. In Kerala itself there are other worthy Kathakali institutes.

Gopinath and his partner Ragini Devi are two names which cannot be omitted from a history of Kathakali. They pruned the length of performance, simplified its techniques and adapted it to modern stage conditions. Uday Shankar made use of Kathakali's vocabulary of mime in the creation of his ballets as did Rukmini Devi and Mrinalini Sarabhai, and Ram Gopal adapted and presented Kathakali in most Western countries. Krishnan Kutty, Madhavan and Ananda Shivaraman contributed to the renaissance of the art. Shanta Rao is an outstanding dancer of Kathakali and has proved that the more intricate and difficult tandav aspect of the dance is not necessarily beyond the capabilities of a woman dancer.

Now that Kathakali has been firmly re-established, it is interesting to see how choreographers are presenting Kathakali successfully in the contemporary theatre.

CHAPTER 9

MAKE-UP, COSTUME, HEAD-DRESS AND JEWELLERY OF KATHAKALI

$\mathcal{U}$nlike the make-up of the other schools of Indian dance, Kathakali make-up is a complex art, the application of which requires between two to four hours. Usually it is the Patukaran or reciter who specializes in this aspect of the drama and because of its importance he is one of the most highly-paid members of the company. The make-up artist begins his work early in the morning. He prepares the paints afresh for each performance and begins by grinding to a fine powder stones of various colours, green, blue, orange, yellow, red and black. He then mixes each, on a smooth surface, with oil. The fine patterns of the make-up are made with a long flexible piece of bamboo with never a tremor to blur the outline.

There are three main types of characters, the Satvik or virtuous beings, such as gods, kings or heroes, the Rajasik, characters with particular vices such as lust, greed or vanity and the Tamasik, or out and out evil characters such as demons.

Kathakali make-up is in no way natural, indeed at first sight, may seem rather terrifying or at least grotesque for it deliberately sets out to alter the normal proportions of the human face. But then nothing about this dance-drama is natural, which seems fair in view of the fact that the characters are for the major part super-human and those which are mere humans or play only a minor role, have much simpler make-up and costumes. With continual acquaintance, however, the make-up and costumes begin to appear less strange and eventually appropriate and even necessary, for the characters look so different from human beings and behave in a manner which would appear so exaggerated in ordinary people, that it becomes far easier to accept them as supernatural beings. Moreover, the long preparation, the ritual of applying the new 'face' and putting on the costume, also undoubtedly gives the actors time to discard their own personalities and think themselves into becoming super-beings.

The Satvik characters such as Krishna, Rama, Arjun and Nala wear what is known as the *Paccha* or light-green make-up. The face is first painted green, and the eyebrows and eyes exaggerated and elongated in a stylized form with black. The lips are bright red and look as if smiling and caste marks are painted on the forehead. Finally the chutti or rice paste is applied in rows, to frame the cheeks and chin. It looks like layers of white paper each coming out beyond the one above it. Some actors do in fact use paper but those who are particular about everything being authentic, still insist on rice paste. The chutti is shaped so that it completely alters the normal structure of the face, widening the jaw-line considerably and narrowing again at the chin. It takes a long time to put on, since the shapes must be cut to fit the face and the outline be exactly the same on both sides of the jaw. Once on, it takes over an hour to dry. The Rajasik characters, such as Ravana, the demon king of Lanka, wear the *Katti* or knife make-up. This too has a green base but the green is broken by red patches at the sides of the nose. Above the eyebrows from the bridge of the nose are drawn two broad, flat-ended curves in red and outlined in white. Above these are white lines across the forehead with an inverted capital 'A' between them and the bridge of the nose. Another red and white oval patch is painted on the nose. Above the upper lip is painted a stylized red moustache which curls over the cheeks. This too is outlined in white. The finishing touch is added with two off-white pith knobs, called *chuttipuvvu*, on the tip of the nose and in the middle of the forehead. The more wicked a character is, the larger is the size of these knobs, which are symbolic warts or disfigurations. Fangs are inserted under the upper lip.

The bearded characters are of three kinds and are distinguished by the colour of their beards. The Veluppu Tadi are the white beards and are of good omen. The Karuppu Tadi or black beards are barbaric forest hunters, brigands and robbers. And the Chokanna Tadi are the demonic characters and have red beards.

The Veluppu Tadi make-up is for beings like the monkey-god Hanuman and the monkey character Vivida. For Hanuman for instance, the area around the eyes is painted black, the inner edge sloping away from the eye along the nose and diagonally down along the cheek, then up to the outer edges of the eyebrows and across them at the top. This black area looks very roughly like two triangles within which the eyes are enclosed, and is edged with a white line which curls over the cheeks on either side. The lower half of the face is of a reddish colour. A red line along the ridge of the nose is outlined in white, and red and white are again used to decorate the chin and forehead. The pattern on the forehead gives the impression of two 'eyes' set very high and close together on the face. The chutti layers are crescent-shaped and may be fixed in scallops down the sides of the face, and in this case, a white decoration is drawn above the upper lip. Sometimes, however, one set of crescents are fixed from above the upper lip and around the mouth to the chin. This has the effect of considerably narrowing the lower half of the face. The mouth is painted thin and black and has ivory fangs inserted into it. The overall result of this make-up is to give the face a long narrow look like that of a monkey. The white beard he wears is round and flat and is made of wool or cotton thread.

An example of the use of Karuppu Tadi or black beard make-up is the role of Kirata the hunter, a disguise which the god Shiva assumes in order to test the fighting skill of Arjun. The basic colour of the face is black, and patterns in red below the eyes are outlined in white, as are similar curved patterns on the forehead. He too has a white wart-like knob on his nose and wears a thick black beard. But the most demonic and terrible make-up in Kathakali is the red beard or Chokanna Tadi of which Dushasana and Bali are fine examples. For this the top half of the face is painted black and the lower half is reddish. These two areas are divided by two serrated layers of chutti extending from the upper lips to the temples, the total effect being that of a rectangular shape. Designs of red and white are painted on the forehead and nose and two pith knobs are added. Fierce-looking fangs are placed in the mouth and the lips are painted thin and black. A very full red beard completes the make-up.

The wicked female characters are usually ogresses and she-demons such as Surpanakha and Putana. Their basic make-up is called Kari and is black, including the lips, but is relieved on the cheeks and forehead by bright red crescents which are outlined with white dots, as is the whole face. A red and white pattern embellishes the chin and the tip of the nose. These characters too have fangs. She-devils also have large black breasts. The fifth type of make-up is called Minukku. The basic colour of this is natural, that is, a sort of pale beige. All female characters such as heavenly nymphs like Urvishi, queens, goddesses, heroines and even evil ones in disguise, and minor male characters such as holy men, Brahmins, charioteers, messengers and so on, use this make-up. The women's eyes are outlined in black and eyebrows emphasized with a graceful curve. The lips are given a lovely shape in red, and sometimes the cheeks are adorned with a curved line of white dots which are repeated on the forehead and chin. A dusting of finely powdered mica imparts a soft glow to the skin.

However, in addition to all these there are some characters who have their own particular make-up, for example, Nagaraja the king of the cobras has a make-up which suggests figuratively the head of a snake; Ravana's evil sister, who is a she-demon, has a special black make-up with a large bundle of feathers in her head-dress; Bhima, when he appears in his famous battle of vengeance with Dushasana, has the characteristics of Narasimha the man-lion, and accordingly his make-up is lion-like. Narasimha himself too has a special hairy lion-like appearance.

COSTUME

The costume of Kathakali is no less remarkable than its make-up. It is as far removed from the ordinary clothing of the people of Malabar as is its make-up from resemblance to the natural face. Whereas the Malabari dresses in ordinary life with the minimum fuss and ornament, restricting himself to spotless white muslins, in Kathakali he goes to the other extreme. Normally, because of the mild climate, the men find a mundu or sewn loin-cloth with a vest or shirt quite sufficient, and when they go to the temple even this is reduced, for they may not be covered waist upwards. The women wear a sari and in rural areas they often do without a blouse or a petticoat since a sari alone is adequate to cover the body completely. But in Kathakali not only is the body more covered, but covered with a multiplicity of layers. It has been suggested that the costume has been influenced by various foreign elements. This is a plausible explanation since the coastline of Malabar has been an important meeting place of many races since pre-Christian times. The full skirts and the hats of some of the characters bear a striking resemblance to the costume of the early Portuguese who came to Malabar.

The chief male characters all wear up to three or four long-sleeved, high-necked jackets all of which fasten at the back, where there is an opening. This allows the back to be cooled by fanning when the actor becomes too hot from his exertions. The colour of the jackets varies with the type of character. Traditionally, Krishna wears a dark blue jacket, and those who oppose the gods wear red. All demons are in black except the wickedest among them who wear red jackets which have a rough, shaggy surface symbolic of a hirsute body. Hanuman wears a white jacket of fur. The only actors in Kathakali with a bare torso are the male characters who wear the Minukku make-up, the Brahmins and sages among these having the sacred thread over the left shoulder and under the right arm. The female characters too have coloured jackets. All the major characters wear extremely full skirts which have been compared to farthingales. They are indeed similar in general outline, the main difference being that the Kathakali skirts reach just below the knee and are not held out by hoops. The skirts consist of several layers of white cotton cloth draped over a waist-band which is then secured round the waist. The skirt is thus partly held out by the quantity of material gathered into the waist. This is double at the top, because of the tuck-in of material which forms a frill on the inside of each layer. The flare is further assisted by the position held by the dancer, his splayed knees holding it out sideways and the outward curve of the base of his spine causing a bustle-like effect at the back. The length of the 'underskirts' is shorter than the topmost layers, and whereas the others are more or less plain, the top layers have borders of stripes in bright colours as well as gold. They also have sunray pleats although these are not, of course, graduated in width from waist to hem. Over these again are two strips of coloured material, again with rich borders, which are added on either side. The whole skirt is then finally secured at the waist with a sash under another narrower strip of material. The skirts of demonic characters are often black or of a dark colour. All other skirts are generally white.

The Minukku characters, if they are male, wear a simple loin-cloth which is long in some cases, short in others. The females have full-length skirts which have extra fullness in front. These are usually white with borders, but not always, and demonesses generally wear black. The skirt again consists of a long piece of cloth. This is tucked round the waist so that it forms a fan-like frill of pleats in front and the whole is fastened with a golden girdle.

HEAD-DRESS

There are several kinds of head-dress in Kathakali and as with the make-up they go with the types of character, but the two which are most splendid are the Kiritam and Mudi, both of which are made of wood.

The Kiritam is used by the most important role-types. It looks rather like a tiered crown, surmounted by an orb with a point, the whole being backed by a halo. Both the crown and the halo are richly worked in colours of red, green, white, gold and silver. Although occasionally the jewels are real, the majority of companies are too poor to afford such luxuries and the inlaid work is done with imitation jewels of glass, pieces of mirror, beetles' wings which are green when they catch the light, silver beads and gold foil. The patterns on the halo are arranged in concentric circles, making the resemblance to a halo more marked. But, of course, its significance is not quite the same as that of the halo in Christian connotation, because it does not symbolize holiness. Indeed the biggest halo, almost three feet across, is worn by the red-beard characters, an indication that the size of the halo is related to the dimension of character of this role-type and has nothing to do with 'goodness'. The red-beard must inspire fearsome awe and it follows that in order to do this the actor must be as tall as possible. A man of average height or, worse still, a short man would run the inevitable risk of appearing ridiculous. Natural endowments, therefore, are usually more important in casting this role than acting-dancing ability.

The back of the halo is almost always plain, but occasionally it may be decorated. The whole magnificent but nevertheless cumbersome head-dress is firmly secured to the head by means of cloth bands. It is regarded as a very precious item, even revered, for an actor never puts it on without saying a prayer first.

Of the Mudi head-dress there are three main types. One is worn by the Paccha make-up types such as the gods Krishna, Vishnu, Rama and his two sons Lava and Kusa and certain high-minded and noble characters. If its basic form is not made of wood, it is constructed with cane, fibre and cord. This basic frame is covered with red felt which is then decorated with silver bands from which hang rows of sparkling silver droplets. The top of this dome-shaped head-dress is finished off with a crown of peacock feathers trimmed short.

The second kind of Mudi is worn by the Kari role-types as well as the she-demons and Karuppu Tadi characters such as Kirata the hunter. This is tall and cylindrical but gradually widens out towards the top and ends again with a thick edging of peacock feathers still trimmed but a little longer than those of the other Mudi. The basic colour of the head-dress is black but it is decorated top and bottom with bands of white peacock quills. Between these borders, placed side by side, is a row of thin, long silver leaves, which look like the long petals of a daisy which is half open.

The third kind of Mudi, known as the Vatta Mudi, is worn by Hanuman and other monkey characters. It looks a little like the hats worn by Italian priests—round crown and a flat, wide brim—except that the crown is surmounted by another smaller dome and a still smaller one which terminates in a point. Hanuman's hat is white and the underbrim is elaborately decorated with peacock quills and tiny silver pendants, which scintillate with the least movement of the head. All those who wear a Kiritam or Mudi, also have long black hair made of grass fastened to the back of the head.

All the other members of the cast wear comparatively simple head-dresses. Those playing female roles wear a cloth which is bound round the forehead and hangs down the back, so covering the whole head and rendering the use of a wig unnecessary. It is fastened by a decorated head band.

Brahmins in ordinary life do not cover their heads, but in Kathakali they wear a piece of plain cloth which is bound round the head and like the women's head covering falls a little way past the waist. This material is somewhat softer and does not look as neat and even as that of the women.

Other male Minukku characters often wear turbans. Sages wear a head-dress which looks like matted hair piled high on top of the head in a bun.

Characters other than the main ones and the Tadi role-types may also wear long beards of dyed hemp.

JEWELLERY

Jewellery and ornament too are extravagant in Kathakali. All those actors who wear jackets have breastplates and necklaces of multiple strands of golden beads. Women have breastplates with the breasts covered with coloured material and necklaces. Unlike the rounded breasts of the ordinary women the breasts of the she-demons are large, black and pointed.

Most of the characters, both male and female, wear large disc-like ear-rings, some concave and some convex, inlaid with bright jewels. These may be worn in single pairs but another smaller pair may be added above the main ones. In addition, a pair of enormous discs are often held by an unseen helper on either side of the face of a rakshasa or demonic character.

Wrists and forearms have bracelets and decorated shoulder pieces are added at the top of the upper arm.

In addition to the many stranded necklaces the principal characters also wear what are known as Uttariyam. These are long white scarves with bordered ends, which are hung round the neck. Each is bound at intervals and ends in a tassel-like shape, so that it looks like a bell on a thick rope. One pair of these 'bells' has mirrors set in it, so that the actor can, if he wishes, check on his make-up. Actors manipulate these stoles to great effect during the performance. The last two items which complete the make-up and costume of the Kathakali dancer are a set of long silver-coloured nails which are worn on the left hand, and bells, which are tied not round the ankles as is usual in Indian dancing but just below the knees.

This description is enough to give a general idea of what the various role-types look like, but of course there are variations from company to company.

Arguments have been put forward for the reform of both make-up and costume in Kathakali with some justification. The make-up, it is said, hides the marvellous movements of the face. But it is an indispensable part of the whole and modifications necessary for a stage performance would have to be carried out so as not to destroy its essential character. Oil-bound paint does not dry very quickly, yet since it is worn for so long there is a danger that it might crack. The more vulnerable part, however, is the chutti. Some actors already substitute paper for this, but with modern resources there is no reason why a synthetic material should not be used, which would at the same time be more lasting and more flexible. It would be a pity to discard the present form of make-up completely, since it gives a highly imaginative verisimilitude to the characters, for it really only emphasizes the facial characteristics of certain role-types, in an extremely stylized manner. This is not only visually exciting, but was, undoubtedly, positively necessary—because of the very large audience and limited lighting arrangements.

So also with the costume, which certainly lends style and grandeur to the dancing, but at the same time must, by its very nature, be a great burden on the dancers. The use of a single jacket would possibly make the body of a dancer seem too small in comparison with his voluminous skirt and immense head-dress, but a thick lining which is both light and porous would surely overcome this difficulty. The skirt itself too could be made lighter and more comfortable by using modern fabrics.

In view of the present revival and popularity of Kathakali, changes are sure to be made, and it is unlikely that they will be rash, now that so many truly great and dedicated artistes are taking an interest in this dance-form.

CHAPTER 10

MOHINI ATTAM

*M*ohini Attam is named after the seductress supreme of Hindu mythology who appears in several stories. But the original, far from being a mortal woman, was in fact the god Vishnu who had assumed feminine form.

The gods and asuras, it is said, once churned the oceans, in order to extract Amrita, the elixir of life. All went well until the elixir had been extracted, but then there arose a dispute as to who was to have it, the gods or the demons? Since the gods considered that the demons were being unfair, Vishnu decided to take the matter into his own hands. Accordingly, he assumed the form of the most beautiful woman imaginable. This Mohini had the graceful curves of a vine, her limbs shone with the full golden bloom of youth, her face enchanted all who looked upon it. As soon as the asuras saw Mohini they desired her. She fled and they followed. In this way the asuras were enticed away from the Amrita and the gods carried it off.

This legend was danced by Menaka in her ballet called *Deva Vijaya Nritya* (Victory Dance of the Gods). There is also a sequel to the story.

When the god Shiva was told of Vishnu's stratagem, he wanted to see Mohini; so Vishnu obliged. Immediately, Shiva too conceived a passion for Mohini. The result of this passion was that Shiva produced Shasta his son from his own thigh. It is this Shasta who is so beloved of the people of Malabar and there are many shrines to him in the countryside of that region, particularly in forests and at crossroads.

There is yet another story about Mohini, which is often danced in the Kathakali dramas. This concerns a king of Ayodhya, one Rugmangada. During one of his hunting expeditions into the forest, the king encountered a beautiful enchantress who was really a wicked ogress in Mohini's form. He fell so passionately in love with her that he completely lost all sense of proportion and was prepared to do anything to attain her. So much so that it did not strike him as odd that so lovely a creature should ask him to kill his only son for her sake. Although reluctant, he was just on the point of performing this terrible sacrifice when suddenly Vishnu appeared and stopped him.

From stories such as these, the name Mohini came to be synonymous with the essence of feminine beauty and allurement, and Mohini Attam is a dance which displays just such qualities. It is a solo dance, reserved exclusively for women.

Its history is not very certain. What is known is that it was patronized about 150 years ago by a prince of Travancore, and became very popular. In technique it lies somewhere between Dasi Attam and the lasya aspect of Kathakali. Because of its inherent qualities, Mohini Attam was eminently suitable for use by loose women, and was frequently used by them to attract would-be clients. This led to its unpopularity and eventual decline at the beginning of the last century. Nonetheless, when the Kerala Kala Mandalam was founded, Vallathol managed to find Kalyani Amma, a fine exponent of it, and engaged her on his staff. She began teaching it there, and then later at Tagore's Santiniketan. The demand for Mohini Attam grew, but the Malabaris had not forgotten its insalubrious associations. They finally managed to persuade the Maharaja of Cochin to ban it, and this ban was not finally lifted until 1950. The dance has since regained favour and Shanta Rao, Mrinalini Sarabhai and Roshan Vajifdar are among its best known exponents.

Mohini Attam is for the most part nritta although abhinaya is by no means absent. Its allarippu is similar to that of Dasi Attam, but is known as *solukattu*, and like Dasi Attam it has swarajatis, varnams and tillanas. Although their technique differs somewhat its movements are more graceful and alluring than those of Dasi Attam. It is always soft and gentle with no sudden jerks or heavy emphasis on tal with the feet.

Its music is Karnatic and the language of its songs is Malayalam. The nritya has many points in common with Dasi Attam, but the influence of Kathakali is much more marked here, especially in the use of mudras. Stories, such as those from the *Gita Govinda*, are danced in Mohini Attam, but most of its songs deal with the various situations connected with love. All these are exquisitely conveyed through gestures of the eyes and hands, expressions of the face, and voluptuous poses of the body.

In Dasi Attam the dancer is not obliged to sing all the time, but here she should really do so even if it is only with the singer among the musicians who accompany her.

There have never been any restrictions as to where or when Mohini Attam ought to be performed. As dancing is almost certainly a part of any celebration in India, Mohini

Attam was often danced at private festivities such as births, anniversaries and the like. In this sense it adapts more easily to the stage. It does not, like Dasi Attam, have to create an atmosphere of devotion. It is not handicapped on the stage by subtleties such as those in Kathak, and it does not have the staging problems of Kathakali.

Indeed, it requires nothing but to be danced. The costume is uncomplicated. A white sari with a traditional border is worn with a plain choli, which is a fitted blouse. The hair is gathered into a large smooth chignon on top of the head but to one side. This is decorated either with a circlet of jasmine or a traditional hair ornament. Jewellery of the traditional kind worn in Malabar adorns the ears, neck, wrists and fingers. A girdle of gold emphasizes the waist. The make-up is natural but highlights the eyes and lips. Ankle-bells are, of course, indispensable. Some dancers of Mohini Attam use the costume worn by the female characters in Kathakali.

Mohini Attam does, of course, require training, just as any other dance, but it is a dance which is learnt comparatively easily, since there is nothing in its technique which might cause extraordinary difficulties. This, together with its obvious charm and beauty, is attracting more and more girls to it, although a good artiste will always give to it the aesthetic quality often missing in the performance of amateurs.

Bharati Shivaji's fine rendition of Mohini Attam at the Edinburgh Festival in 2002 brought this style to the attention of an international audience.

CHAPTER 11

OTTAN TULLAL

*L*iterally Ottan Tullal means 'running and jumping'. It is a dance created by the poet Kunjan Nambiar who lived in the mid-eighteenth century. He can best be described as a people's poet. Such was his influence on the literature of Kerala, that he marks a milestone in its development, and a whole period of writing is named after him.

The Nambiars were a caste somewhat lower than the Chakkiyars and one of their functions was to play the *mizhavu* or drum during Chakkiyar-kuttu. There are two stories about Kunjan Nambiar, both of which relate how he came to devise Ottan Tullal. According to one, he was a member of a troupe maintained by the Raja of Ambalapuzha. For one particular performance he was, it seems, overlooked for a part which he felt was in accordance with his talent and experience. However, he satisfied his ego by taking an artist's revenge. On the day of the performance he stationed himself opposite the palace and began to sing at the top of his voice as he danced to the accompaniment of loud drumming. The content of his song was satirical in its criticism of the establishment. He attracted crowds, and Ottan Tullal was born.

In the second account, Kunjan Nambiar is said to have been playing the drum for a performance of Chakkiyar-kuttu and at one point made a mistake. The irritated Chakkiyar immediately showed his annoyance by making slighting remarks about the Nambiar. Embarrassed at this public rebuke, Kunjan resolved to prove his worth and redeem his good name.

The next day the Chakkiyar was performing as usual in his corner of the temple, with an attentive and admiring audience around him, but this time he had competition. In another part of the temple stood Kunjan Nambiar. He was dressed in an entirely new kind of costume, his singing and dancing too were quite different from anything the people had ever seen. At first they turned to him from sheer curiosity but gradually, as they listened, they became absorbed in this novel exposition until finally the Chakkiyar was left with hardly anyone to pay attention to him.

This perhaps was the very first performance of Ottan Tullal, and the pattern of the temple was repeated over and over, and its popularity proved phenomenal.

Ottan Tullal had many advantages over Chakkiyar-kuttu. The Nambiar had greatly simplified the Sanskritized Malayalam of the Chakkiyar. He used a language which was closer to the average man and understood by him without difficulty. Kunjan Nambiar also made the music more interesting. He 'borrowed' the Chakkiyar's immunity, and like him, made critical, witty and outspoken remarks about people and their foibles, social conditions, and anything else which appeared to need correcting. At the same time he was careful never to offend and always to preserve good humour. It was perhaps this which really protected him most of all, for unlike Chakkiyar-kuttu, which was confined within the temple walls and so had sacred protection, Ottan Tullal could be performed anywhere, in the temple, at a private house, for a festival or just in any convenient open space. Neither was it restricted to any particular time, although the afternoon is now most popular.

Encouraged by the success of the first tullal, Kunjan Nambiar composed about fifty more, all based on the sacred epics and puranas but all, nevertheless, made relevant to contemporary conditions.

Ottan Tullal has now come to be known as 'the poor man's Kathakali'. This is because, in comparison with that dance-drama, it is cheap to put on. There is only one performer, who plays all the parts in turn. The musical accompaniment is also simple, for it requires only one drummer, who plays on an elongated drum called the maddalam, one cymbal player who keeps the tal on his little cymbals, and sometimes a singer. This singer assists and occasionally takes over the singing from the dancer, who normally does at least some of the singing himself. The technique of the dance too is very similar to that of Kathakali but is not quite so formal and inflexible. There are neither settings nor props, not even a curtain. The make-up of the dancer is not very intricate and though the costume is colourful, it is not as elaborate as that of Kathakali.

A strong white line is drawn on the face, following the contours of the cheek-bones and the beard line of the chin. All the area within this is painted green. The eyes and eyebrows are emphasized with black. The lips are painted red, and around the caste-marks on the forehead is made a pattern in black and white. The eyeballs too, as in Kathakali, are made to look red. The head-dress is a crown with a large semi-circular frame and two huge discs like ear-rings. It is decorated with gold, silver and multi-coloured glass. The bare torso of the dancer is also richly adorned with multiple necklaces and a small breastplate. At the top of the upper-arm and cupping over the shoulders, he wears decorated wooden epaulettes, and on his wrists, two bracelets. The most interesting part of his costume, however, is his skirt. This is made up of strips of white and red cloth which are looped, so that they make a kind of skirt reaching to the knees. This 'ribbon-skirt' is bunched at the back and sides, while in front hangs a bright red cloth.

As in Kathakali the bells used by the dancer are tied, not round the ankles, but just below the knees.

A performance of Ottan Tullal usually lasts a manageable two hours. It is always preceded by an invocation to the lord Ganesh and Saraswati the goddess of learning and the fine arts. The dancer usually sings a verse first and then interprets it with mime and gesture, using his hands, face, eyes and body. He may, if he wishes, leave most of the singing to his musicians. The interpretative passages are interspersed with pure dance which, as the name implies, is energetic and full of life. If at any time the dancer wishes to get his breath back, he simply turns away from the audience and has a rest, while the musicians continue to play. The dance is quite informal and sometimes the dancer actually goes in among his audience and addresses members of it individually.

There are two other varieties of tullal, Seetankan Tullal and Parayan Tullal but neither of them are as common as Ottan Tullal.

They differ from it in the cadence and metre of the songs and in their costumes which are much simpler.

There are not many dancers of Ottan Tullal today, since there is little monetary reward for the hard work involved in the acting, dancing and singing which together make up this dance. Its greatest exponent of recent times was Malabar Raman Nair of Quilon.

This dance lies somewhere between a folk-dance and a classical dance. Its roots are certainly the same as those of Kathakali and, broadly speaking, it follows the same principles. At the same time it has a very close link with the people. It has played a large part in their relaxation and entertainment for it deliberately sets out to be non-academic. The common people themselves were particularly partial to it because it often championed causes near to their hearts, but its future now seems very uncertain. Even if it does survive Ottan Tullal will probably never regain quite the same old popularity.

CHAPTER 12

YAKSHAGANA

*T*he best-known form of dance-drama in Karnataka is Yakshagana. For its subject-matter it has about fifty plays based on the stories of the *Ramayana* and the *Mahabharata*. Most of the dramas present the dilemmas and conflicts of war and the dancing itself is always vigorous and masculine.

As with Kathakali the whole plot unfolds through dance, song and abhinaya. However, the abhinaya content is not as developed as in Kathakali and the dancers, who are always men, sing the verses and dialogues themselves. Also, since it is a rural dance, the dancing and make-up are somewhat simpler than those of Kathakali. The character-types which Yakshagana portrays are grouped under two categories only, the *sumya* or gentle, and the *rudra* or fierce.

There is a considerable comic element in which the spectators delight. This is introduced by a clown who appears on the scene with the other dancers. He mimes their singing, tries to dance even better than them, and makes stray impromptu comments about the characters. The dance is generally performed after the harvest has been collected, so the village audiences are in the mood for light-hearted buffoonery and merrymaking.

Yakshagana is enacted in the village square or common. It has no stage, is an open air performance and in the local dialect is often referred to as Bayalata, from 'bayal' meaning field.

CHAPTER 13

KATHAK

*H*istorically, Kathak dates back to Vedic times, when the epics of the *Rig-Veda*, the *Mahabharata* and the *Ramayana* were composed. The word Kathak, story teller, derives from 'katha' which means story. Communities of Kathaks wandered around the countryside conveying the stories of these great epics and myths to the people by means of poetry, music and dance, all three of which were closely linked. The chief aim of the Kathaks was to instruct the indigenous population of the subcontinent in the knowledge of the gods and mythology of the Aryans. This means of instruction has a parallel with the early Greek theatre and with the beginnings of English drama. Indeed, the link is more than superficial, for all Indo-European languages, myths, legends, rituals, superstitions and sex symbols can be traced back to the common Aryan source.

India's earliest contacts with the outside world were initially established through trade. There were regular routes along which caravans moved from China and Central Asia, through the Indus valley to Turkey, Iran and Egypt. These commercial links must surely have resulted, in some degree, in the interchange of cultural ideas.

In the fifth century B.C. there arose in North India a new religion which was, to begin with, very different from the Vedic religion then prevalent. It was founded by Prince Siddharta of the Sakya tribe who, forsaking riches and power, preached equality among all men and by his own example showed the path to self-realization. He came to be known as Buddha or the Enlightened One and his teaching spread in due course, especially under the saintly king Ashoka, to most of the countries of Asia. Buddhism was a spartan religion in comparison with the Vedic rituals of the Brahmins. It called for the simple life because according to it, the greater the detachment from the world and its temptations, the nearer was the source of enlightenment. This new religion involved no gods and no elaborate worship of them. Therefore, it did not need to employ the arts, all of which had hitherto been connected with religion. Buddhism was propagated through monks and nuns who had taken vows of poverty and chastity and who devoted their lives to social service with an almost Christian dedication. Religious dancing like that of the Kathaks was irrelevant to its needs. Nevertheless, Buddhism tried neither to stamp out Hinduism nor campaigned actively against the Kathaks, who continued to practise their art. It was not until much later, when Buddhism became almost a sect of Hinduism and the Buddha himself was enthroned in the Hindu pantheon as an avatar of Vishnu, that it used the arts of painting, sculpture, music and dancing.

After Alexander's incursion into India in 326 B.C., the northern part of the subcontinent was subjected to the invasions of the Scythians, the Kushans, the White Huns and the Gurjaras, all of whom came through the mountain passes in the North-West. Each of these peoples left the imprint of their racial and cultural characteristics on the population of Northern India. This constant influx was bound to weaken the structure of the caste system carefully laid down by Manu for the consolidation of Brahminism. The increasing struggle for dynastic power led to an emphasis on temporal and military matters, and for this reason the Brahmins did not exercise the same control over society as they were able to in the South. The patronage of the arts must also, to some extent, have passed from religious leaders into the hands of kings and princes, although the themes would undoubtedly still have found their inspiration in the scriptures of the Hindus.

The population of the Indo-Gangetic plain had by this time undergone considerable racial change and it is fair to assume that the classical dance of this area too must have been modified and enlarged according to the new characteristics of its ethos.

From the eighth century the new dynamic force of Islam appeared in the subcontinent. It was brought first by the Arabs and then, in a more permanent form, by Central Asian Turks. For over a millennium, in spite of the many invasions which had taken place during that time, Indian society had not been called upon to adjust itself to so radically new a situation. Here was the complete antithesis of the caste system. Islam preached that all men were brothers under One God, that there was only one path to heaven which lay through the teachings of the Prophet, and that it was morally dangerous to make representations of living things. This attitude was seriously to affect Kathak dancing, which was not only concerned with many gods and goddesses but also portrayed them in human form. This made the dance doubly sacrilegious to the Muslims and therefore it was vehemently condemned. The Kathaks had to find Hindu patrons, often Rajput princes of Central India, or disperse into the countryside where they could safely continue to dance in their traditional manner. With the passage of time, under less severe rulers, these Kathaks were to be permitted once more to dance with impunity.

Muslim society was based largely on merit and even slaves could aspire to kingship, but the caste system of Hinduism had at this time become stratified and effete. It had no equipment to counteract this new element of fluidity which was so rapidly forcing itself into society from without. The temper of the times had, however, long been conducive to new movements, both in the Hindu and Muslim religions. In Islam it took the form of Sufism and later, in Hinduism, of Bhagti. Both were mystical in intent, preached toleration, and practised devotion to God and service to humanity. The best minds in Islam were attracted to Sufism. It was as the indirect result of the tremendous influence of the teachings and poetry of the Sufis, that later Muslim monarchs became tolerant of, and even encouraged and fostered the Hindu arts. The Bhagti movement, on the other hand, which matured into fullness later than Sufism, strove to mitigate the inequalities of the caste system by stressing the brotherhood of man and of God's love for all human beings irrespective of religion, caste or social background. It was this great synthesis of the quintessential best in both Hinduism and Islam, that produced Bhagats like Kabir (1440–1518), who was born a poor Muslim weaver in Varanasi and who became the generative source of great poetry and music.

The Kathak dancers used much of the Bhagti-inspired poetry for the nritya parts of their performances. This poetry was intensely emotional and declared the poet's love for God in personal terms.

The rise of the Vaishnavite cult which came before the Bhagti movement, had an important bearing on the development of Kathak. This embodied the worship of Vishnu, the god of preservation in the Hindu pantheon. In his incarnation as Krishna he was the chief subject of music and dance. There are understandable reasons for the Lord Krishna's long-sustained popularity with the common man throughout India. His romantic love for Radha symbolized the love of God for Man in terms which were simple and immediate. He was, moreover, always depicted as an engaging young man of dark complexion, and as such represented a major concession by the fair-skinned Aryans to the original dark-skinned inhabitants of the Indian subcontinent. Krishna, therefore, represented the synthesis of the Aryan and Dravidian cultures. His warm human qualities made it possible for people to identify themselves with him without feelings of blasphemy or sacrilege. His mischievous audacity evoked delight not fear, love not awe, and so lent itself admirably to presentation in dance form.

The art of mediaeval India was dominated by the Krishna theme and legends about him became a permanent feature of the Kathak repertoire. As a child, Krishna was both playful and precocious. He constantly played tricks on his foster-mother Yasoda. He was particularly fond of milk and butter, and the story goes that as a child he would organize raiding parties of young friends. Together, they would steal into the house where the butter had been hung from the ceiling out of reach and carry it off in triumph. Once, when he was very small his mother thought he was eating mud. She made him open his mouth, and saw not mud, but all the world and its profound mysteries. This brought home to her that her son was no ordinary mortal. As he grew older, Krishna's interest turned from milk to milkmaids! Many are the stories of his dalliances with them in the glades of Vrindaban and by the banks of the sacred river Yamuna. In his role of Murli Manohar or Govinda (flute-playing cowherd) he would charm the gopees (milkmaids) from their mundane tasks with the ethereal music of his magical flute. Once when they were bathing in the river, he hid their clothes, and then watched their confusion from a tree-top. The chief target of his attention, however, was the beautiful Radha, and he would seek every opportunity of waylaying her. One of her daily household chores was to fetch water from the banks of the Yamuna and he delighted in teasing her, upsetting her pitchers and embarrassing her with his amorous advances.

The Krishna stories also have a serious aspect. In the *Mahabharata*, Krishna appears to Arjun as his charioteer and discourses with him on his duties as a warrior, as a statesman and as a man seeking the truth. Krishna's main teaching was that duty, however unpleasant, must come before all else and man must endeavour without hope of reward.

All these episodes were excellent subjects for poetry, music and dance, which, in Vaishnavism, were important means of worship. There are, therefore, many famous poets, musicians and dancers connected with this cult. It reached its culminating point in the twelfth century with the poet Jayadeva, author of the *Gita Govinda*, who composed numerous keertans or devotional songs, and whose wife expressed them through dance. Later the poet-musicians Chandidas, Tulsidas, Mira, Vidyapati and Surdas carried on this tradition. Much of their poetry incorporates actual dance-syllables known as *boles*. This clearly indicates that dance was an essential of such hymns and neither was complete without the other.

The Muslim religion, as we have seen, excludes such arts as sculpture, painting, music and dance as forms of worship and these arts have no place in Islamic religious ritual. So when the Muslim influence established itself in India, this attitude had a profound effect on the hitherto Vaishnav-dominated Kathak. Because of its religious connections the early Muslim rulers, regarded this indigenous form of dance as unsuitable for their patronage, but they were by no means insensitive to the pleasures of music and dancing when divorced from religion. The result was that they sent for musicians and dancers from Persia and Central Asia. These dancing girls were known as domnis, hansinis, lolonis and hourkinis. Each of them had their own distinctive style of dancing.

Now, as we have already seen, this was not the first cultural contact between India and the lands lying to the north-west. There had been rapport between them for many centuries. Musical modes from Persia such as Yamani and Kafi were incorporated into the Indian raga system at the time of Amir Khusro, who lived from the mid-thirteenth to the early fourteenth century. His genius touched not only music, but literature as well and so contributed towards the synthesis. Consequently the dancers and musicians were easily able to absorb those features of the Indian arts which they considered would be acceptable to their patrons. The few Hindu dancers who found their way to the courts were, in their turn, influenced by the new styles. This apparent secularization was to have a significant extension in the later Mughal period of Indian history.

The Mughals brought political unity, economic stability and social justice. They took an intensive interest in, and fostered the Indian arts. The flower which resulted from the Islamic seed sown in the rich soil of Hindustan, displayed the colour of both cultures. The lotus had met with the rose.

Akbar the Great had married a Rajput princess, with the result that Hindu dancers and musicians at long last performed in the royal presence and came under the Emperor's direct patronage.

Kathak now entered its golden era. Dancers, musicians and poets flocked to the imperial court and to the provincial courts of the Rajas and Nawabs.

With the growing stability in government came a new affluence which was reflected in every aspect of life. Dress at court was, of course, modelled on Persian styles and the court dancers too adopted the costumes of the day. In the last few years of Akbar's reign there is evidence that dancers, both men and women, wore an interesting new costume. The men wore a jacket, and the women a choli, a fitted blouse with short sleeves which leaves the midriff bare. Both had tight trousers called a 'chust pajama'. Over these they wore plissé skirts made of stiff material in three tiers the longest of which reached several inches above the knee. These skirts bear a remarkable resemblance to the tutu of Western ballet which was not invented until very much later. The women also wore, over their shoulders, a transparent scarf of silk or muslin, known as an 'orhni' or 'dupatta'. The head-dress consisted of a muslin turban.

In the time of Akbar's son Jehangir, the dancers adopted the dress which was popular in the early part of his reign. The popularity did not last long at court, but whereas the fashions of the nobility changed, the dancers retained this costume and it has been in use ever since. It consisted of the 'chust pajama' in a bright colour over which was worn a high-necked diaphanous dress called the 'angarkha'. The soft, flowing, bell-shaped skirt was of full length and, like the sleeves, was left unlined. For women, an embroidered waistcoat of rich satin emphasized the body line. Men wore a double-breasted 'angarkha' which fastened on the left, with their 'chust pajama'. The women also wore a gossamer 'orhni'. The palms of their hands and bare feet were dyed with henna. Numerous miniatures of the seventeenth and eighteenth centuries show dancers in this costume. Its advantages, so far as the Kathak dancers were concerned, were that the full skirt fanned out at every fast movement, accentuating the fluidity of the dance, and yet was transparent enough to reveal the outline of the figure and perfection of the pose when the dancer was still.

The themes of the dances were now no longer confined to the myths and legends of Hinduism. The wider repertoire included imperial, social and contemporary themes. In fact, under rulers less tolerant than Akbar, Kathak developed along purely secular lines. The dancers concentrated on brilliant variations of rhythm, the beauty of which was heightened by tantalizing pauses and lightning pirouettes.

The Dhrupad style of music is essentially religious and had been connected with Kathak since the late fifteenth century. It came to its peak with the genius of Tansen during the reign of Akbar. This mode is dignified and majestic and has no room for frivolous ornamentation. The poetry is chaste and uplifting, using similes of sixteen selected flowers, fruits, birds and animals, four of each. As these similes adorn the music, so in Kathak, they serve to embellish the bhava, which is the language of gesture for the expression of various moods. With the emphasis on nritta, however, and the absence of religious themes, this music was used less and less in later times, until it became the convention to use just a single phrase of music, called the *lehra*. The lehra was convenient because, as it was repeated over and over, it did not distract attention from the rhythmic variations of the dancer and drummer.

The decline of the Mughal Empire and the rise of European power saw the gradual decadence of Kathak. Most of the petty princes and warlords had little appreciation of the fine arts and so Kathak degenerated into voluptuous and sensual styles. Although there was an attempt to retain the basic graces of Kathak, the tendency was increasingly towards lasciviousness, and the performers became notorious as women of easy virtue. It was this debased form of Kathak which the European adventurers called 'nautch', which was a corruption of the Indian word 'naach' meaning dance.

This infamy touched even the temple dancers, and certainly did much to discourage girls from respectable families from adopting professional dancing as a career.

The true spirit of Kathak, however, survived in spite of these social stigmas. High caste Hindu girls, especially in Rajasthan and Bengal, had to be accomplished in the arts in order to make a good marriage. They were therefore tutored at home, often to very high standard, but their attainments were reserved exclusively for the pleasure of the family.

The first dancer of genius to break this embargo was Menaka. Her achievements were truly outstanding—trained under the best gurus, she revived Kathak as an entertainment worthy of public support and what is more, she gave to it the imprimatur of social acceptability in its homeland, and also introduced it to other countries.

Menaka first formed a residential school of dancing at Khandala in 1938, and gathered together some of the best teachers in each style. Her main interest was in exploiting the possibilities of Kathak in productions of ballets. In this she was helped by Dr Raghavan, Karl Khandalawala, Maneshi De, Ram Narain Misra, Vishnu Shirodkar and Ram Chandra Gangooly. She produced three ballets in which she employed pure Kathak techniques, discarding the lehra and using classical music skilfully blended to complement the ballet themes. *Deva Vijaya Nritya* is about Vishnu's transformation into the beautiful Mohini in order to rescue the Amrita or elixir from the demons. The second part of this ballet tells of how Shiva fell in love with Mohini and how he went into tapasya, meditation, so that he might regain his self-control. *Krishna Lila* deals with the life of Krishna in Vrindaban and how Radha fell in love with him.

The third ballet, *Menaka Lasyam*, is the story of the sage Visvamitra's attempt to gain immortality through tapasya, and of how the god Indra sent an enchanting apsara, named Menaka, to tempt him and so interrupt his meditation. Menaka's fourth and most important ballet was Kalidasa's *Malavikagnimitram*. In this she employed, for the first time, Kathak and Manipuri as well as Kathakali techniques. Her friendship with Pavlova was a constant source of inspiration to Menaka, and of great help to her in staging these ballets.

Today, there are two main branches of Kathak, named after the cities in which they took shape and flourished. These are the Jaipur and Lucknow schools. These schools or *gharanas* have their own distinct personality which was imparted to them by different gurus. Very often the traditions of the gharanas were sustained by succeeding generations of the same family. This gharana system also prevails in music, both vocal and instrumental.

The Jaipur style developed under the patronage of the Rajput rulers of Rajasthan and has a very strong religious flavour. One of the founders of this school was Bhanuji, a devotee of Shiva, who is said to have been taught by a saint. The greatest contribution to this style was made jointly by the brothers Hari Prasad and Hanuman Prasad, descendants of Bhanuji. Hanuman Prasad was a very religious man and it is said of him, that once at the festival of Holi he arrived late at the temple and the doors had been shut for the night. Nevertheless, his devotion was such, that he danced in the courtyard outside. At the climax of his dance, the temple bells within came miraculously to life and the doors burst open of their own accord. Even if this story is apocryphal, it is an indication of the power of this guru's dancing.

A more recent name is Jai Lal, another descendant of Bhanuji. Jai Lal started dancing at an early age and was highly accomplished in the two percussion instruments, the *pakhawaj* and the *tabla*. It was due to this, that his dancing was famous for its rhythmic quality. He included long *parans*, which are pure dance pieces set to subtly varying syllabic beats of the pakhawaj. His partiality for pure dance is evident to this day in the dancing of the exponents of the Jaipur gharana.

Sunder Prasad, the younger brother of Jai Lal, later became the guru of this school and taught at the Bharatiya Kala Kendra in Delhi.

There is a minor offshoot of Kathak not widely known, which appears to have been connected at one time to the Jaipur gharana. It was founded by Janki Prasad of Bikaner, but its adherents settled in Varanasi and Lahore. The main differences between this branch of Kathak and the two major gharanas are that it stresses clarity of line and execution even if this means sacrificing speed, and whereas, for footwork, the Lucknow and Jaipur gharanas allow the use of percussion instruments, here the dance syllables only are permitted. Its exponents were the brothers Sohan and Mohan Lal, Nawal Kishore and Kundan Lal.

The Lucknow gharana matured into a distinct and individual style in the time of Wajid Ali Shah, 'Akhtar', the last Nawab of Avadh.

By the end of the eighteenth century, the Mughal Empire had declined to such an extent that the Governors and tributary Nawabs and Rajas were independent in all but name. Delhi had been the centre of culture. All the arts had had full scope and flourished in rich profusion. With its decline, its poets, musicians and artists gradually began to leave. In Avadh the Nawabs now saw an opportunity to transfer its glories to their own capital, Lucknow. The migrants from Delhi were welcomed and given pensions and grants, and a new centre evolved. Lucknow became synonymous with elegance and aesthetic appreciation. When Wajid Ali Shah ascended the throne in 1847 at the age of twenty, the court circle already included artistic protégés of all kinds. He was by nature inclined towards the arts and resolved to outshine all his predecessors. The young Nawab devoted himself to this end with an energy which now seems suicidal. He spent twenty million rupees on building the famous Qaisar Bagh palace, the Imperial Garden palace. He established a centre for the training of dancers known as 'Pariyoṅ ka Khana' or 'House of Fairies', because all the girls were selected for their beauty. He surrounded himself with famous poets of the day who wrote in Urdu as well as Persian, and was himself a prolific writer of verse, a competent musician and a dancer. His dance guru was Thakur Prasad whom he respected so much that he elevated him to the highest seat in the court.

Wajid Ali Shah's palace always echoed to the sounds of music and dancing, and he himself organized many productions of Rahas which were based on Indian themes of the Ras Lila but were set in a Persian background. The scenarios set down, precisely and in minute detail, all stage directions and instructions as to how each role was to be played. These productions were lavish and reserved only for the court circle. The Rahas had most of the elements of ballet but were similar to pageants in that they were not produced on a stage. They were extravagant entertainments for a highly sophisticated audience, and were at a remove from the realities of life. The music was provided by his court musicians Sikandar Piya, Kadar Piya, Lallan Piya and Akhtar Piya whose fortes were *dadra, thumri* and *ghazal*, which are particular types of poetry set to music.

One of the important poets at the Nawab's court, Sayed Agha Hassan Amanat, wrote a dance-drama in Urdu verse entitled *Inder Sabha* or The Court of Indra. This is a significant work because it is the first drama written in Urdu and takes Hindu legend and clothes it in the rich poetic sensibility of Persia. The apsaras of India become the purrees (peris) of the Caucasus. Indra and his court are seen in Mughal dress and the whole atmosphere conjures up a dream world of every kind of beauty and luxury that the Persian poets associated with the pleasures of Paradise.

Inder Sabha, which resembles the Sanskrit classic *Vikramorvasia*, returned, perhaps unconsciously, to the original concept of Hindu drama, where poetry, dance, music and costume were equal members of the same body. The play also brought back to Kathak, after many centuries, its element of natya and led to a wide extension of bhava.

Wajid Ali Shah's passion for these arts was carried to a point where he neglected his state duties. This lack of interest in political affairs made it possible for the English to annex his kingdom and he was sent into exile.

Thakur Prasad's two sons Binda Din and Kalka Prasad succeeded him at the court of Wajid Ali Shah. The Lucknow branch of Kathak as it exists today is a direct result of the contribution made by these two brothers. Kalka Prasad's forte was a mastery of rhythm. Binda Din enriched the lyrical content with his own compositions of thumris, dadras and ghazals. Between them the brothers evolved a style which had lyrical grace as well as technical precision.

So, as we have seen, the Lucknow gharana at this point had all the elements of Kathak which are now extant, the last additions being thumris, dadras and ghazals. In fact, the thumri in both music and dance was invented, it is said, by the Nawab himself.

The last outstanding patron of Kathak was Raja Chakradhar Singh of Raigarh. He too was a dancer and musician and his patronage extended to all dancers irrespective of their gharana. Jai Lal of Jaipur and Achhan Maharaj, the eldest son of Kalka Prasad of Lucknow, both served him for many years. He encouraged and nurtured young talent wherever he found it.

The Raja's fate was almost identical with that of Wajid Ali Shah, and for the same reasons. He was forced to abdicate in favour of his son and deprived of the means to indulge his interests, died a broken man about a hundred years ago.

The present guru of the Lucknow gharana is Birju Maharaj, the son of Achhan Maharaj who died many years ago. The gurus Lachhu Maharaj and Shambu Maharaj, the younger brothers of Achhan Maharaj, have also passed away.

Lachhu Maharaj taught Kathak in Bombay and created many ballets, the most important being *Malati Madhav*, which the Bharatiya Kala Kendra invited him to choreograph and produce. It was first presented at the Sangeet Natak Akademi Dance Seminar in 1958. He was an outstanding choreographer and experimented with adopting Kathak for Indian films. He produced Kathak ballets in conjunction with the Dagar brothers, Moinuddin and Aminuddin, the leading exponents of the Dhrupad style of north Indian classical music.

Shambu Maharaj and Birju Maharaj taught at the Bharatiya Kala Kendra in Delhi, where many of their pupils were Government of India scholarship holders. This school was a result of the efforts of Nirmala Joshi, whose great dream it was to form an institution where the best teachers of Kathak and Hindustani music could train suitable pupils and, at the same time, experiment in ballet productions. She finally succeeded in 1952 when the Bharatiya Kala Kendra came into existence. It later became the Kathak Kendra.

Shambu Maharaj was a great exponent of bhava and revived many thumris and bhajans. He had the distinction of holding two of the highest awards in Indian art. Hundreds of dancers were trained by him, among the best known of whom are Bharati Gupta, Damayanti Joshi, Gopi Krishan, Kumudini Lakhia, Maya Rao and Sitara.

Birju Maharaj's efforts are directed towards adapting Kathak ballet for the modern stage. This presents an interesting challenge, for the theatres today contain a very much larger audience than was ever possible in either the temple courtyard or the intimate atmosphere of the *Mehfil*, the select company of connoisseurs. The choreographer must communicate delicate nuances and at the same time provide movement on the stage. The music for his highly successful ballets *Kumara Sambhava, Shan-é-Avadh* and *Dalia* was provided by the two Dagar brothers.

The stage settings and costumes were especially designed as these were period pieces. For ballets set in the early Hindu period the women wore a sarong-like skirt which was a little above ankle length. This allowed full freedom of movement and at the same time made it possible for the footwork to be seen to advantage.

Kathak dancers today have considerable freedom in their choice of costume, as a wide variety of permissible styles are in use. Broadly speaking these are either Hindu or Muslim inspired.

Among the Hindu costumes the oldest and that which is most generally used is the 'ghaagra and orhni'. The ghaagra is a long, very full, gathered skirt with a broad gold or silver border. Narrow silver or gold bands radiate all the way from waist to hem. The rich coloured silks used for the ghaagra must not be so heavy as to hinder the dancer during fast dance movements. The choli, worn with the ghaagra, is usually of a contrasting colour and has embroidered sleeve-bands. The light, transparent orhni is interwoven with gold patterns and draped over the head and left shoulder. The jewellery worn with this costume is rich and varied. Bracelets, armlets and necklaces are of gold. The heavy earrings, also of gold, are set with precious or semi-precious stones. Their weight is taken off the ear-lobes by fine gold chains or, more usually, ropes of tiny seed-pearls which hook into the hair. A jewelled 'tika' is suspended in the middle of the forehead.

Another costume which is becoming increasingly popular is the sari. The heavy silk sari has a wide gold border and pallav. This is the part which in normal wear hangs over the left shoulder, but for dancing is taken round the waist and allowed to hang down from it on the left side so as to show off its full beauty. An orhni is worn over the choli and draped over the left shoulder. The jewellery worn with the sari is much the same as that which goes with the 'ghaagra and orhni', the only addition being an ornate girdle or belt which emphasizes the slim line of the whole ensemble.

The Hindu costume for men consists of a silk dhoti with a brocade border. This is draped round the waist and between the legs to give a loose trouser-effect. A silk scarf is tied round the waist. The upper part of the body is left bare except for the sacred thread which is always worn, though sometimes a loose fitting jacket with short sleeves may also be worn. The jewellery is elaborate and consists of a wide gilt necklace with stones and a variety of smaller necklaces. Small pieces of gilt jewellery in a traditional pattern are mounted on cloth. These are tied round the wrists and arms.

The Muslim costume, as we have seen, was added much later, but has become so popular and so closely associated with Kathak that many people really believe that this is a Muslim dance brought from Persia by the Mughals. The costume is still essentially the same as it was in Jehangir's time, except that the skirt of the angarkha is now shortened to calf length. The jewellery worn with it is necessarily delicate and light, so as to be in keeping with the gossamer effect of the angarkha. The ear-rings are plain gold rings, each with a drop pearl and two smaller stones on either side. Two rows of pearls may be worn round the neck. Armbands and bracelets are of gold or silver filigree decorated with coloured stones. Sometimes an unusual hand ornament is worn. This is basically a circular jewelled ornament for the back of the hand and is kept in place by delicate jewelled links attached on one side, to a bracelet round the wrist, and on the other, to five rings worn one on each finger and the thumb.

A Jhumar or Chapka is an ornament for the head which may also be worn. This is a fan-shaped piece of jewellery which rests flat on the hair. The apex of the triangle lies near the parting and the delicate jewelled 'ribs' of the fan shape radiate forwards to rest flat on one side of the head.

There is no invariable rule about the details of a Kathak costume and dancers make adjustments to suit personal needs and preferences. For instance, there are many types of dhotis. The angarkha and waistcoat vary a great deal in style and cut. While some dancers wear a tight fitting bodice in the same colour as the angarkha and 'chust pajama', others prefer a contrasting colour. In the 'Kathak' dances of Indian films, the neckline of the waistcoat is cut below the bust to give a more alluring line.

Indian films have used dances which were supposed to be Kathak, but are best described as having drawn some inspiration from Kathak. The discrepancy arose not necessarily because the dancers did not know Kathak, for some such as Sitara certainly did, but because directors had to take into account the tastes of the 'groundlings' who are not interested in subtleties. Apart from a few exceptions

Kathak has generally suffered at the hands of film makers. Satyajit Ray's *Jalsaghar*, for instance, had a notable Kathak sequence which featured the remarkable Roshan Kumari.

A medium which should prove excellent for Kathak as a solo dance, is television. It is ideal for conveying to the audience the delicate bhava and abhinaya of the artiste. Skilful direction and camera work with close-ups of the eyes, the facial expressions, the hands and the feet could, possibly, add a new dimension to Kathak. Moreover, television functions in an intimate atmosphere and the dancer could easily produce the feeling among viewers that the performance was directed to each one individually.

As far as the theatre is concerned, on the other hand, it would seem that the future of Kathak lies in ballet, where its rich and varied repertoire of nritta, nritya and natya can be fully exploited. Uma Sharma's *Stree* (*Woman*), for example, is the direction in which Kathak is now moving. As a further experiment Birju Maharaj used seven dance styles in a Calcutta production in 1994.

CHAPTER 14

A KATHAK PERFORMANCE

A Kathak recital usually begins with the Ganesh Vandana. This is a salutation to the elephant-headed god Ganesh, who represents good luck and symbolizes the dispelling of misfortunes. There is a certain legend about him that explains these associations.

It is said that Parvati the consort of the Lord Shiva, took a great deal of time over her toilette. She would spend hours bathing, dressing and adorning herself. This meant that Shiva was kept waiting—something which went much against his dignity. His remedy was to burst in upon her unannounced and catch her in a state of unreadiness, whereupon he would proceed to tease her. Now Parvati was not to be outwitted so easily, and hit upon the idea of setting their son Ganesh on guard. Whenever Shiva was approaching, Ganesh would warn his mother. One day Shiva was so frustrated by the child's action that he cut off his head. Parvati, utterly distracted at her loss, completely withdrew herself from her lord. Shiva now realized that the only way to win back his wife's favours was to restore the child to her—but the head was lost. He therefore resolved to use the first available head he could find. This happened to be that of a baby elephant. Accordingly, he joined the elephant's head to the child's body. The situation was saved. The boy not only regained his life, but now had the added advantage of the elephant's wisdom and, not least important, Parvati was reunited with Shiva. From that time, Ganesh became the symbol of good arising from adversity and thence an averter of evil.

All religious ceremonies begin with slokas honouring Ganesh. Both the *Abhinaya Darpanam* and the *Sangeet Sara* lay down that all dance performances must be prefaced by this invocatory gesture.

In the Ganesh Vandana, the praises of Lord Ganesh have dance syllables blended in with the words. Although this invocation used to be the first item actually danced, the normal practice now is for it to be only played on the pakhawaj before the dancer enters.

The first item to be danced may be one of two pieces, the *rang manj ki puja* which is the offering to the stage, or the Muslim salutation called the *salaami*. In the rang manj ki puja the hands are cupped together above the head and the fingers open out like a flower in the *pushpanjali hasta*, as the hands come down towards the chest. They are then tilted forwards as if offering flowers to the stage. Then follows the water offering and obeisance to the presiding deity. This torah ends with a namashkar which is the Hindu salutation.

Before Kathak went to the Muslim courts this was, of course, the only opening item. Now, *puja* is a form of Hindu worship, so even though rang manj ki puja is purely nritta, its symbolic religious associations made it unacceptable to Muslim patrons. Consequently this was re-choreographed to embody the Muslim salutation or salaam and called the salaami. Nowadays either opening is permissible. In the salaami the right hand only is used and the left is kept at the side. The fingers are held together and very slightly bent. The thumb rests across the palm. The hand is then raised to touch the forehead while the head is bowed as a mark of respect.

The opening item is followed by the *amad*, which is the Persian word for 'entry' or 'coming'. The amad corresponds somewhat to the *alap* in Indian music, in that it establishes the atmosphere. It is always danced to a very slow tempo. The dancer is first seen in one of the characteristic Kathak poses. For example, the pose might be one where the left arm is extended horizontally with the elbow slightly bent and the palm of the hand facing downwards. The right hand is held above the head with the elbow again slightly bent and the palm facing the audience. In both hands the forefinger is bent at the second joint so that the thumb touches it. The left foot is crossed behind the right and rests on the ball of the foot, and the knees are slightly bent. The body from the waist upwards is then turned to face the audience. This produces the tribhanga, or three bends, in the body. The eyes exhibit shringar ras. The attitude is one of composed self-possession.

Very often the amad blends imperceptibly into the thaat, which is the next movement and means generally a decorative or graceful attitude. The neck glides subtly from side to side in time with the tal, and the tremulous fingers, wrists, and eyebrows heighten the beauty of the thaat. In the Lucknow gharana the thaat is performed on one spot, the only concession to movement being that the upper half of the body may be swayed very slowly from side to side. The disadvantage here is that the delicate subtlety of the movements can only be appreciated by those sitting fairly near the dancer. Originally, of course, the audience was very limited in number and so this type of thaat was quite possible, but in the comparatively vast auditoriums of today, it tends to be lost to most of the audience. The thaat of the Jaipur gharana is different, in that the dancer glides gracefully first to one side and then the other. The *sum* is beautifully marked by a sharp turn of the head. This is the key beat.

The thaat heralds the gaths. The tempo of the music is increased and the sarangi plays a faster lehra, but the dance itself is still performed at a slow speed. Gaths introduce nritya for the first time and the dancer takes up one theme after another. These need not be connected in any way or presented in any particular sequence. They are easily recognizable as each begins and ends with a sharp turn or *palta*. The first gaths to be danced take the form of gath nikas. These give only a thumbnail sketch of the story to be represented. After a palta the dancer takes a few steps forward and stops in one of the basic positions, the only movement a barely discernible undulation of the fingers and wrists, giving a hint of the energy held in check. There is a tantalizing pause and then she starts one of the beautiful gaits or gatis for which Kathak is noted. The gati clearly suggests the type and condition of the character portrayed. For example, to show a gopee fetching water from the well, the dancer may take four steps forward, bending to one side in the action of picking up a pitcher and putting it on her head. The gait which follows, together with the expression on her face, would show that a girl is moving slowly with a heavy pitcher on her head.

After gath nikas the programme continues with gath bhava. Even here the story is suggested in an allusive manner, for it is assumed that the audience is familiar enough with the legends to be able to follow them from brief references. In India, of course, this is perfectly justified as the people do know the stories, but outside India it is not so. This should not, however, deter Western audiences, for the stories to be danced are either in the programme or are explained before they are danced. Also, very often the dancers first show how each of the characters are identified. The Lord Krishna, for instance, is shown by the hands in the attitude of holding his flute, or by the appropriate gesture for the peacock feathers he wears in his head-dress. Shiva is characterized by the snake round his neck or the crescent moon on his head, and Radha by drawing the veil, the ghungat, over her face. The use of mime is very apparent here, and Kathak perhaps uses the technique of mime, without the help of words, to a greater extent than any of the other styles. There are numerous stories which might be danced as gath bhavas. One of the most popular is called the *Panghat Gath*. Radha is seen going to fetch water from the well. Krishna is following her. She fills her pitcher and starts on her way back. Krishna meanwhile is bent on mischief and shatters the pitcher by throwing a stone at it. Radha is drenched. She pretends to be angry with him, although perhaps secretly pleased to see him. Brushing him aside with mock indifference, she walks off, wringing her skirt as she goes. All this is shown by the one dancer, who changes from Radha to Krishna, Krishna to Radha, marking each change with a palta.

Up to this point the tempo or *laya* of the dance has been fairly slow, therefore nritya items like bhajans, ashtapadis, dadras, and thumris may be introduced at any point in the performance so far. It is not usual to add them later than this. The reason is that in Kathak the tempo of the dancing increases gradually as the performance progresses. Reduction in laya is regarded as a fault. All these are poems, so the dances accompanying them are, naturally, interpretative and bhava plays a very important part in them. It would be impossible to do justice to them later for two reasons: the laya would have to be reduced and the dancer's bhava would be impaired for lack of breath after the faster pieces. The nritta items which are to be danced are inserted at any time of the performance according to their laya.

The gaths over, the dance progresses into passages of pure dance in various complex rhythms. These take the form of tukras. Although at first sight all tukras appear to be similar, this is not in fact the case. The *natwari* type of tukras are usually danced first. Natwar is one of the epithets of Krishna the dancer, and the boles of these tukras are said to reproduce the sounds created when Krishna danced on the serpent Kaliya's hood. All boles with *ta-thei thut* and *tigda-digdig-digta* and their variations are classified as natwari.

The pace of the dance is now faster, and in the parans the nritta is danced to compositions played on the pakhawaj. The dancer has to reproduce the sounds of the boles with her ghungurus. The movements are vigorous and represent the tandav aspect of the dance. The dancer recites a phrase of boles and then dances it as the accompanist repeats it on the pakhawaj. The dancer then recites a longer and more complex phrase and dances this, and so on. Occasionally it is the other way round, and it is the pakhawaj player who calls the phrases. This may result in a friendly competition between them of 'going it better and faster than you'. Such a thing occurs more often between vocalists or instrumentalists during a recital of Indian music. In the days of the princely courts this competition was not infrequently vicious, each trying to prove his superiority over the other. The patrons encouraged this by giving costly gifts or titles to the one who should outdo the other. The defeated one, who had lost face, would either beg permission to leave the court and seek his fortune elsewhere, or would sulk for months, avoiding the company of his fellows. In the meantime, of course, he would be practising furiously, hoping to stage a comeback and regain lost favour. Indian history is full of stories of such rivalries between artistes, wits, theologians, chess-players and even gods and goddesses.

The next part of the recital is usually the paramelu, which is a little faster. The word is from 'para' meaning different and 'mela' meaning union, and in the paramelu the sound syllables of various percussion instruments such as the nakara, the pakhawaj and the tabla, are blended together with the Natwari boles. Paramelus are danced at great speed and come to a climax with the pure footwork of the tatkar.

The tatkar ends the recital. The rhythmic patterns are all-important. The dancer's body is held quite still and the arms are usually folded. Only the feet move, seeming to tread air. There may be an accompanying melody at the beginning but as the tatkar reaches a climax, no sound is heard except that of the drum and the ghungurus. There should be no stomping unless it is required to provide clear punctuation of the rhythmic pattern. The dancer begins with a simple rendering of a tal and goes on to progressively more complicated variations. Sometimes these match the drum beats and at other times they counterpoint them. Just as in a jati, so in a tatkar, the dancer must know within a beat what the drummer is going to play. As some sequences extend over a hundred beats or even more, and boles are not generally recited, the task of the dancer becomes exceedingly difficult. Nevertheless, the essential rapport and unity between dancer and drummer must be maintained without a single lapse. The pleasure lies in the pure aesthetic enjoyment of the rhythm. Tremendous excitement is generated by the sheer precision and clarity of the variations, for no matter how fast the tempo, every fraction of the beat is sounded separately and clearly on the ghungurus.

The suspense, built up with each successive variation, is released in an ecstatic catharsis with the perfect arrival at the final sum.

CHAPTER 15

THE RAS LILA OF BRAJ

The *Natya Shastra* describes 'ras' and 'rasak' as secondary forms of drama, but today the meaning is more specific and refers to the Ras which Krishna danced with the gopees of Vrindaban.

Krishna as a young man was so attractive that all the gopees were in love with him and longed for him constantly. Krishna, seeing that their love was sincere, promised each one that he would fulfil her desire by dancing with her by moonlight.

One night, when the moon was full, the silvery notes of Krishna's flute echoed through the forest. Each gopee left her home for the banks of the Yamuna, drawn by the irresistible call of the flute. Here Krishna awaited them. He projected himself in such a way that each gopee had a Krishna as a partner. They formed a big circle and the dance began. So enchanting was the dance, that even the gods and goddesses were envious and wished they too could join in. The dance lasted for six months, yet when the gopees returned home they found that their husbands and families did not even know they had been away.

There are five chapters in the *Bhagavad Purana* devoted to a description of the Ras.

The Ras Lila is found as a folk-drama in many parts of India, but the Ras Lila of Braj deserves special mention. It was here in the home of the Krishna legends that it was first enacted in its present form and has been danced in an unbroken tradition since the sixteenth century.

The stage techniques employed in Ras Lila are very simple. The stage, on the same level as the audience, is quite bare except for a small square platform on which there are two seats, for Radha and Krishna. The only curtain used is held up by two men when a special dramatic effect is required, such as before the *jhankis* or tableaux or sometimes before the introduction of a character. Jhankis punctuate the whole dance-drama and are an important feature of it. They have retained their authenticity and look like sixteenth-century miniatures brought to life.

The Ras Lila may be divided into three distinct parts, the prologue or *nitya ras*, the *sangeet* or didactic piece, and finally the *lila* or play proper.

The dance-drama has a traditional opening with Radha and Krishna seen seated. First the chorus sets the mood by singing devotional songs. The gopees then offer a puja and invite Radha and Krishna to join the dance in the *ras mandal* which is the actual dance area. They form a circle and the Ras begins.

The nitya ras introduces the chief characters but its main interest lies in its dance content. It is the only part of the dance-drama where stylized dance movements and interesting rhythmic pieces, called *parmuls*, are used. These have a strong affinity with the Kathak style of the story-tellers of the North Indian temples. There are special parmuls for the introduction of each character. This function of the parmuls can be compared with that of the Pravesar Nritya of Sattra Ras, which has similar dance pieces with distinctive boles for Radha, Krishna and the gopees. Parmuls are danced at speed and have fast pirouettes.

The nitya ras also contains short dance pieces rather like the gaths of Kathak, and even incorporate graceful chaals and eyebrow movements. The interesting choreography of the nitya ras makes a colourful and exciting opening to the Ras Lila.

The sangeet which comes next contains a sermon and devotional songs and poems sung by the chorus. Since, for Vaishnavites, the arts were a means of devotion and were used by them to teach people the traditions and practices of their religion, it was not unusual to find direct instruction such as sermons and expositions, sandwiched between acts in dance-dramas. The sangeet also served to remind people of the religious aspects of the Radha-Krishna legends.

The third and last part of the dance-drama is the lila or main play. For this, one story is chosen from the great wealth of Vaishnavite mythology. The selected story is then danced from beginning to end in one long sequence, without breaks or divisions into acts.

This part of the Ras Lila is entirely in the folk tradition. The gestures and abhinaya are a part of everyday language, used and known instinctively by the villagers. There is no single pattern of presentation. The characters may recite or sing their lines, and the chorus may repeat them. Sometimes the lines are explained in prose as they are being recited. The recitations are punctuated by short dances which include gaths, and by jhankis. Although the dancers appear to vary their styles a great deal they do, nevertheless, follow the chosen, carefully-planned pattern of presentation.

Much of the tradition of sixteenth-century Vaishnavism has been preserved in the Ras Lila. The numerous Radha-

Krishna miniatures show the same structure of presentation and the same costumes as are worn today, namely, ghaagra, choli and dupatta for women and dhoti for men. Even the language has a sixteenth-century flavour, and the similes used give an insight into the social conditions of those times.

There is much speculation as to whether the Ras Lila, which is a folk art, has borrowed from the classical style of North India. Certainly there are many points of similarity between the two, but these may have arisen because both deal with the same Vaishnavite themes, although Kathak is by no means restricted to these. Bhava in the mime of the Ras Lila, like that of Kathak, is natural although not as developed. Again this resemblance may exist simply because both grew in roughly the same geographical area. They share much Vaishnavite poetry which incorporates dance boles, and was intended to be expressed through singing as well as dancing. The kavita torah in Kathak and the kavita with dance boles in Ras Lila are examples of this. Now, while it is difficult to state categorically that the Ras Lila borrowed from Kathak, it is quite possible, since both dances were at their peak at the same time, that certain elements from Kathak, mainly the gaths, permeated into the Ras Lila through the influence of the professional Kathak dancers, so numerous and popular at that time.

Until comparatively recently, the Ras Lila was performed mostly in temple courtyards, and this sustained its religious character. The dance itself is far from the austere solemnity associated with religion in Western thinking. People enjoyed the Ras Lila. Through music, poetry and dance they brought the happiness of their own lives to their worship, but the religious experience was, nonetheless, profound. The dance is no longer confined to the temples, but has not in any way lost its religious significance.

During the festivals of Vasant, Holi and Janamashtami, the fairs of Vrindaban and Mathura resound to the rhythms of the mridang and the streets are crowded with pilgrims and visitors. The temples, decorated with buntings and marigolds, are filled with the heavy perfume of incense and the rhythmic chanting of Sanskrit hymns. The intermittent call of the conch shell penetrates the noise and bustle to remind the happy crowd that this is essentially a religious festival.

These festivals would not be complete without performances of Ras Lila in the *ras mandals,* dance enclosures, and the open spaces around the town. Meanwhile, the quiet glades and mango groves, so favoured for love trysts, pulsate with the fullness of life and the voice of the koel echoes to the throb of the distant drums.

CHAPTER 16

MANIPURI DANCE

*I*n the secluded north-eastern corner of India, where the majestic Himalayas loop southwards towards the sea, lies the picturesque valley of Manipur, the Jewelled City. This is the home of the Meities, a people of slight build with slanting eyes. The Meities are a deeply sensitive and artistic race that, by their very isolation from the rest of India, have evolved a unique pattern of life. Here, both the expression and the appreciation of art—and mainly of dance and music—seem to be the focal point in the everyday life of the people. The Meities love to dance. All their joys and sorrows, hopes and aspirations, are interpreted through the dance. Their graceful, rhythmic yet carefully-disciplined movements create their own vivid imagery, whether interpreting life or legend.

It was against this background that Manipuri dance, known as Jagoi in the Meitie language, first took shape. In order to fully comprehend it in its modern setting it is well to know the influences, religious, environmental and historical, that have fashioned the cultural ethos of Manipur; for any art that is so inextricably woven into the daily lives of a community, must surely be a reflection of them.

The Meities were originally followers of the Bratya religion, which was a Tantric cult with an admixture of primitive concepts of cosmology and a worship of Shiva and the Mother Goddess. The early history of the Meities and their religion is obscure, but as the Meities strongly adhere to tradition, many legends have been handed down through the generations and help to unravel some of the mystery surrounding them. Most of these legends relate to Shiva who, according to some authorities, was actually a pre-Vedic deity worshipped in many parts of India long before the advent of the Aryans. All these legends emphasize the Meities' inherent love for dancing, while some go as far as to attribute the very creation of Manipur to a dance. The story goes that once, while Shiva was seeking a beautiful but secluded spot for dancing the Ras with his consort Parvati, he came upon a lake surrounded by green hills. Seeing that the exquisite beauty of the scene provided an ideal setting for the dance, Shiva drained the lake. The enchanting valley that emerged was now the stage for a Ras that lasted seven days and nights. The hills echoed the strains of the celestial music played by the Gandharvas, heavenly musicians, while the whole valley was lit by the Serpent-god, Nagadeva, with the brilliant reflection from the Mani (Jewel) which he carried in the centre of his hood. The valley thus came to be known as Mani-Pur or the Jewelled City.

The people of Manipur also believe that they are descendants of the Gandharvas and refer to Manipur as 'Gandharvadesa' or the land of the Gandharvas (desa means country or homeland). They substantiate their claim by quoting various passages and episodes from the Hindu scriptures. For instance, Somara is a mountain peak on the eastern border of Manipur, lying directly on the Tropic of Cancer. Here, according to Manipuri tradition, is a gate set by the gods, and known as Mongpokhong. The people who guard the gate and live on this hill are the Tangkhus. Tangkhu is the Meitie name for Tandu, the disciple of Shiva who taught dancing to the sage Bharata. The Tangkhus, therefore, regard themselves as the descendants of Tandu. The *Ramayana* does in fact describe such a peak on the eastern border of India, where the sun starts its 'Dakshinayana' or its southward movement. There is also mention in the *Mahabharata* of a gate which stands on this peak.

Another passage in the *Ramayana* describes this same peak as the place where Usha, the goddess of the dawn, first made her appearance with the rising sun. It was Usha who taught the dance of Parvati to the women of India. The women of Manipur, therefore, regard themselves as disciples of Usha, and the black and red stripes which adorn their costume represent the dark night and the rays of the dawn. The Chingkheirol, one of the oldest of Manipuri dances, is a representation of Usha's dance.

These and similar legends are very much a part of Manipuri tradition and have guided and inspired the people through the centuries.

There are virtually no reliable records of the history of Manipur before 1714. Whatever little is known about the early period, therefore, has been pieced together from references to major events in contemporary literary works and archaeological discoveries. One of the earliest records is found on a copper plate inscription which gives King Khowai Tampak the credit for the introduction of the drum and cymbals into Manipuri dancing. It also describes him as a great patron of the arts. This is very much in accordance with an ancient tradition whereby the kings of Manipur were not only the patrons of the arts but were actually heads of the various art guilds. These guilds were called loisangs, and the guild for the dancers was the Palaloisang. Before gaining any recognized status as a dancer an artiste had to be accepted into his particular loisang. The kings, on the other hand, being the heads of all the loisangs, were the repositories of all art and were often accomplished artistes themselves. The loisangs continue to this day. All the leading present-day gurus are members of the Palaloisang, and it is one of their important duties to constructively criticize and approve all new dance compositions.

The next recorded event—one that found mention in several literary works of the eleventh and twelfth centuries—was the tender love story of Taibi and Khamba. The *Moirang Parba*, a Manipuri epic, is based on this semi-historical legend. Taibi and Khamba were both from a Moirang village just south of Imphal, but while Taibi was a wealthy princess from a high caste, Khamba was of humble birth. He won Taibi's heart by his many valiant deeds, once saving the Manipuris by killing a man-eating tiger single-handed with his spear. But the path of their love was never smooth. Taibi's family of course disapproved of Khamba and went to great lengths to dissuade her from marrying him. Finally, after overcoming several difficulties, the lovers were united, but their happiness was shortlived. One day Khamba, in a teasing mood, tried to frighten Taibi by driving his lance into her tent. Without thinking of the consequences, Taibi took the lance and hurled it back. It pierced Khamba through the heart and killed him instantly. Taibi was overcome with grief and decided to join her beloved. She took up the lance, drove it into her own body and fell dead beside her husband.

Khamba and Taibi are especially remembered for their dancing of the 'Lai Haroba', translated as the 'Merrymaking of the Gods', which is perhaps the best known of all Manipuri dances. They were such exquisite dancers that the Meities came to regard them as incarnations of Shiva and Parvati, known in Manipur as Nongpokningthou and Panthoibi.

The story of the two ill-fated lovers is related in detail in the *Moirang Parba* and has been incorporated into the main theme of the Lai Haroba of the Moirang School.

The history of Manipur between the twelfth and late seventeenth centuries is obscure, except for references at various stages to cultural exchanges between Manipur and its neighbouring kingdoms, Burma and China. It is said that dancers and musicians from the court of King Kyamba were sent in 1467 to the court of King Pong of Burma, who returned the gesture by sending some of his best musicians to Manipur.

The dawn of the eighteenth century was the beginning of an entirely new era. Vaishnavite missionaries from Bengal found their way into Manipur and propagated a form of Hinduism which regarded Vishnu, the Preserver, as supreme among the Hindu deities. They propagated the attainment of salvation through bhagti. The word bhagti is derived from the root 'bhaj' which means 'to adore'. Bhagti was thus adoration of, or devotion to God. This devotion demanded complete self-surrender, resulting in a union of the soul with the supreme spirit. Vishnu was worshipped chiefly as Krishna, the Blue God, whose love for the gopees of Vrindaban was symbolic of the love that united God with the soul.

The Vaishnavites recognized nine forms of bhagti. These included 'shravna', or listening to the praises of God, and 'keertana' or singing of hymns. Literature, music and art, thus received a great stimulus through Vaishnavism.

King Pamheiba, then ruler of Manipur, was greatly moved by the teachings of the poet-sages of this new faith and readily accepted Vaishnavism. He also tried to convert his subjects to the new religion, and even used force where necessary. Thus he ordered all earlier State records or any literature which referred to the Bratya religion to be burnt.

The earlier Meitie images were also destroyed and the use of the Meitie language, in song and worship, was forbidden. Several superstitions were evolved to force the people to give up their earlier beliefs. For instance, it was said that anyone who sang Meitie songs would be turned into an owl if he died at night and into a crow if he died during the day.

This sudden breaking away from earlier traditions proved to be very detrimental to the Meitie Jagoi (Manipuri dance) and Guru Amubi Singh and Guru Atombapu Sharma, in a paper on Manipuri dance in 1958, cited this as one of the main causes of the decline of Jagoi in the nineteenth century.

Nevertheless, Vaishnavism had taken root in Manipur and by 1764, when Pamheiba's grandson, Bhagyachandra, became the ruler, it had been firmly established as the religion of Manipur.

Bhagyachandra was himself an ardent devotee of Krishna. It is said that he once had a vision in which Krishna asked him to carve his image from the wood of a certain jack-fruit tree. The king gave orders for the image to be made and then built the famous temple of Govindji at Imphal.

In yet another vision the Ras dance of Krishna was revealed to Bhagyachandra. Inspired by the vision, Bhagyachandra composed the Ras Lila of Manipur, which was first performed at Imphal in the Govindji Temple. He is responsible for three of the six main varieties of Ras in Manipur, the Maha Ras, the Vasanta Ras and the Kunj Ras.

The Ras dances were performed mainly to help the people to understand clearly the divine nature of Krishna who, despite the fact that he lived and loved among the cowherds of Vrindaban, was really an incarnation of Vishnu. In the Maha Ras, Krishna dances with the gopees who, not realizing who he is, become very proud. Radha, when she gets tired, even asks him to carry her. In order to humble their pride Krishna vanishes. Radha and the gopees are extremely distressed. They search everywhere for him and are disconsolate. Krishna finally relents and returns to them; and when they dance again in the moonlight, Krishna appears beside each one. The love of Krishna in this story symbolizes God's love for man, and the search for him is the intense longing of the soul for union with God. The climax, with Krishna making each gopee feel that her fervent prayers have been answered and that she alone, above all others, has been favoured, depicts God's equal love for man, and His revelation to those who truly seek Him.

Dancing thus served an important purpose in Vaishnavite worship. It helped the common man to comprehend the true nature of God. Realizing this, Bhagyachandra erected ras mandals or halls as annexes to temples.

It is also said that Krishna revealed to Bhagyachandra the true nature of Manipuri dance. This resulted in the composition of the Achouba Bhangi Pareng, 'Bhangi' meaning dance poses and 'Pareng' a series. This is a dance which incorporates the fundamental body movements of Manipuri dance, and their variations.

The elaborate costume of the Manipuri Ras, known as Kumil, was also a result of Bhagyachandra's genius. The Kumil consists of a long skirt stiffened at the bottom, with a much shorter gathered overskirt of a very fine material. Both are beautifully embroidered with mirrors, silver sequins and silver and gold thread. A close-fitting blouse, usually of dark green velvet and decorated with fine embroidery at the neck and sleevebands, is also worn. At the waist a rectangular strip of material, which is also heavily embroidered in gold and silver, hangs above the shorter overskirt in front. A belt of similar material accentuates the narrow waistline.

Ornaments are profusely worn. There are a variety of necklaces, bracelets, armlets, rings, anklets and ear-rings. The head-dress is particularly beautiful, with a very fine veil covering the face and secured in position on the head by many silver ornaments.

Because it is stiffened at the bottom the long skirt or Kumin hides the movements of the legs, and gives the appearance of gliding when the dancer moves. According to an ancient custom in Manipur, it was improper for a female dancer to reveal the movements of the lower part of her body. The faces, which are half-hidden under the veils, also add to the elusiveness of the picture. This costume is ideally suited to the liquid grace of the Manipuri dance movements, for the overall effect it creates is one in which the dancers appear to float on to the stage, as if from another world.

The Kumil, which is today the main costume for the Ras, has never entirely replaced the earlier costume, Phanek, which is still widely used in some of the Meitie dances, especially the Lai Haroba. In the Phanek, the upper part of the body is covered by a tight fitting blouse. The skirt is a sarong-like garment which has black and red stripes with a border decorated in the traditional pattern of the lotus and the bee. The design of the lotus and the bee on the border of the Phanek is an ancient one, and even decorates some of the earthen pots excavated at Mohenjo Daro in the Indus valley.

Both the Kumil and the Phanek observe the rule of the Trikasta, or the tying of three knots at three places on the waist, as decreed by the shastras. There is one knot at the centre of the waist in front and one at the back, while the third knot is tied on the left side. The Trikasta was also observed by the Kshatriyas, the princely caste, during war.

Bhagyachandra's greatest contribution to the art, however, lies in his efforts to codify systematically all the rules and fundamental principles underlying the technique of Manipuri dance. Dance gurus, from all parts of Manipur, were summoned to his court to help in this work. The *Govindasangeet Lila Vilasa*, attributed to Bhagyachandra himself, is an important text detailing the fundamentals of the Ras and other dances.

Bhagyachandra died in 1789. His reign had seen some of the most significant changes in the history of Manipur. Vaishnavism had been established as the state religion, and with it music and dancing had received a great stimulus. In the field of classical dancing, Bhagyachandra, who was himself regarded as a guru, had composed several new dances, codified the classical dance movements and also fashioned an entirely new costume for the Ras. The kings who immediately succeeded Bhagyachandra carried on this tradition for a few generations and added considerably to the traditional repertoire.

Maharaja Gambhir Singh, who ruled from 1825–1834, was thus responsible for two parengs of the tandav variety, the Goshta Bhangi Pareng and the Goshta Vrindaban Pareng. In 1850 Chandra Kriti Singh ascended the throne of Manipur. He was a gifted drummer and he composed at least sixty-four Pung or drum dances. He also composed two more parengs, both of the lasya variety, namely, the Vrindaban Pareng and the Khrumba Pareng. The Nartana Ras is also attributed to him. The death of Chandra Kriti Singh in 1886 brought to an end the golden age of Manipuri dance which had begun with Bhagyachandra.

A period of decline and gloom now set in. In 1891, Manipur was annexed by the British. As in other parts of India, Indian traditions and customs came to be regarded as old-fashioned and a link with the ignorant past. Dancing, in particular, was frowned upon and regarded as immoral.

The true tradition of dance in Manipur was able to survive in only a few temples, such as the sacred temple of Govindji at Imphal. This state of affairs continued into the early part of the 20th century, when Rabindranath Tagore recognizing its potential, included it in his programme of study at his cultural centre, Santiniketan. The revival of Manipuri dance is almost entirely due to his untiring efforts.

Dancing was first tried out as part of the physical education course for the boys. Later, classes were started for the girls, mainly for the Ras. Naba Kumar, a celebrated teacher from Manipur, joined the staff of Santiniketan expressly for teaching the Ras Lila to the women students. Several dance-dramas by Tagore were choreographed by him and based on Manipuri techniques. The phenomenal success of this experiment resulted in a new interest in Manipuri dance among the educated classes of Bengal. Other leading gurus like Senarik Singh, Rajkumar and Nileswar Mukherji were also invited to teach at Santiniketan.

In general the dance style that evolved at Santiniketan was based on Manipuri and Kathakali, but its formulating force was the impelling creative genius of the poet himself. His songs and plays related to modern India and the dance style had to adapt ancient techniques to suit contemporary ideas. However, when Guru Atomba Singh came to Santiniketan as head of the Dance Department, Manipuri dance, naturally, underlined most of the new dance compositions.

It was due to Tagore's interest in it that this dance was first seen outside Manipur. This interest soon spread to other parts of the country. In 1928 Naba Kumar was invited to teach his art in Ahmedabad, and Bipin Singh of Assam popularized it in Mumbai and other cultural centres. Among Bipin Singh's most famous pupils are the Jhaveri sisters who are well known to Western audiences. The other successful dancers, who are not Manipuris by birth, Ritha Devi, Savita Mehta and her sister Nirmala, and Thambal Yaima, have had to spend considerable time in Manipur in order to imbibe some of the true spirit that characterizes this dance style.

This ancient art has received a great impetus in recent years. While much is being done in Manipur itself to recruit fresh talent, some interesting work is also being carried out in Delhi, Kolkata and Mumbai.

CHAPTER 17

LAI HAROBA, RAS LILA & OTHER DANCES

*M*anipur has a large variety of traditional dances. The best known of these are the Lai Haroba and the Ras Lila; both are dance-dramas that use the Manipuri technique of projecting bhava through body movements.

LAI HAROBA

This dance-drama dates back to the early Meitie culture and mirrors the synthesis of Tantric and early Hindu cultures. The word 'Lai' means God, and Lai Haroba is best described as 'The Festival of the Gods'. It is danced each year in the villages of Manipur, during the month of Chaitra. The performances last several days and nights. Although most of the villagers participate in the dances, the principal roles are danced by highly-trained professional male and female dancers, who are known as Amaibas and Amaibis in the Meitie language and also sometimes as Maibas and Maibis. The Amaibis are dancers who have dedicated their lives to the service of the temple and may be compared to the Devadasis of the South Indian temples. There are differences, however, for among the Meities these temple-dancers belong to both sexes. The institution is not generally a hereditary one and the Amaibis are allowed to get married and lead normal family lives.

The dancers have to undergo a long apprenticeship, after which their lives are spent in the service of God through the dance, which, as we have already seen, is an important mode of worship.

There is a striking similarity between the term 'amaiba' as used by the Meities and its equivalent 'ameebah' in the *Rig-Veda*, a fact strongly suggestive of the antiquity of the Meitie dance or Jagoi. Another interesting point about this dance is that the Amaibas, who are the male dancers, dress and regard themselves as the female attendants of Shiva and Parvati.

The dancers have a distinctive white costume, unadorned apart from the colourful striped border of the overskirt. The arms are completely covered by the long-sleeved blouses. The ornaments are less elaborate than those used with the kumil. Often a flower is worn behind one ear.

The Lai Haroba is a dance-drama based on the primitive Meitie concepts of cosmology, the belief being that the earth was brought down from heaven by nine gods and seven goddesses. The whole drama is danced in stages.

The first stage consists of seven dances in which the Amaibis summon the deities by placing flowers on the waters of a nearby stream. These flowers are then brought back to the village in procession and the Amaibis enact the *Laihunba* or the scattering of the flowers, symbolic of the infusing of life into the gods and goddesses. An Amaibi now prepares a seat by placing a cloth on a plantain leaf in the centre of the stage. She then worships Indra and moves anti-clockwise to the four corners of the stage, offering prayers to the deities that watch over the stage and the artistes. One can detect here the influence of the *Natya Shastra* which stipulates that every performance must commence with a puja in order to prevent any accidents that may be caused by the forces of evil. The Meitie word for dance, 'jagoi', means moving in a circle, and they claim that the tradition of moving anti-clockwise in the dance is taken from the *Rig-Veda*, which states that dancers must move in accordance with the movements of the planets.

The second part of the dance is the Lai Pou which begins with the chanting of the words 'Hoirou' and 'Hoya', seven times in seven different notes. The Lai Pou is concerned with the birth or incarnation of a god, the building of a temple to house him, and finally the making of fine garments for him. The miming is astonishingly detailed. Using the appropriate mudras, the dancer describes the development of the child inside the womb, and then its birth. In the building of the temple, we see the gathering of the sticks, the laying of the foundation and the thatching of the roof. After this the temple is blessed and dedicated to the god. The next part shows the growing of cotton from a seed to when it is ready for picking. The cotton is picked, and carefully woven into beautiful garments worthy of the deity.

We now come to the love duets which are performed by dancers enacting the parts of Nongpokningthou and Panthoibi, who are believed to be the incarnations of Shiva and Parvati. Meitie tradition has it that Panthoibi was not the wife of Nongpokningthou, just as Radha was not the wife of Krishna. The enchanting movements of these duets are restrained yet powerfully eloquent, and the imposing rhythms have an almost primitive appeal.

The last stage of the festival consists of several dances performed for the pleasure of the gods. In these the dancers depict various sports, fishing and hunting. After many days of dancing the Lai Haroba comes to an end, and the villagers bid farewell to the deities by placing them in boats and sending them downstream on their journey into the unknown.

Today there are three types of Lai Haroba. These are the Chakpa, the Konglei, and the Moirang, each slightly different and particular to its own region.

The Moirang Lai Haroba gives prominent place to the story of Khamba and Taibi, the legendary lovers and dancers. The Khamba-Taibi duet is a dance of fulfilment in which the lovers celebrate their marriage. It is set to an ancient and famous love song. This dance beautifully contrasts the forceful and virile movements of the warrior Khamba with the sweet and gentle ones of the princess Taibi. She wears a phanek with red, pink and black stripes and a flowered border at the bottom. Her emerald-green velvet blouse is embroidered in gold and silver. The hair is worn loose to the waist and the head circled with a red band with delicate gold fillets. Khamba wears a purple and gold dhoti and a green velvet jacket with gold trimmings. His head-dress consists of a handsome white turban decorated with red and gold embroidery and with a majestic peacock plume stemming from its white cloud-like centre. The white stands for truth and peace and the red for courage and sacrifice. The curve of the upper part of the turban represents the snake god Pak Hangba whom the Meities worshipped originally.

The Lai Haroba embodies the very essence of the Meitie cultural heritage. It has withstood the test of time; for even Bhagyachandra and his Vaishnavite descendants could not, for all their fanatic zeal, annihilate it. Its importance, however, did decline under the Vaishnavite rulers, who sought to replace it and fire the imagination of their subjects with a new type of dance, the Ras Lila.

THE RAS LILA

The love poetry of the Vaishnavite sages such as Chaitanya, Surdas, Jayadeva and others, was set to music and easily adapted for the dance. In Manipur, the Ras Lila of the Vaishnavites became very popular and soon acquired a significant place in the life and worship of the Meities. This may be attributed to the Meities' love for dancing and their natural interest in anything pertaining to God and religion.

The traditional Ras was of three varieties: the Tal Rasak, the Danda Rasak and the Mandal Rasak. In the Tal Rasak clapping was an important feature, while in the Danda Rasak the rhythmic effect was produced by sticks. Each dancer was provided with a pair of sticks and these were struck together as the dancers moved, weaving patterns as they danced. The Mandal Rasak consisted of a circle of female dancers representing the gopees and a male dancer, representing Krishna, in the centre. All three types of Rasak are found in Manipur.

Ras may be tandav or lasya. Of the seven generally accepted varieties five, Maha Ras, Vasanta Ras, Kunj Ras, Nitya Ras and Dija Ras—all of which relate to stories of Krishna and the gopees—are of the lasya type. Goshta Ras and Ulukhal Ras are of the tandav type and tell of the exploits of Krishna as leader of the youths of Vrindaban, of how he tended the cows, played games, rode horses and, even as a child, killed demons.

The Ras Lilas are performed at the appropriate times of the year in the Ras Mandals, or the specially erected halls adjacent to the temples. The performance usually continues from dusk to dawn and sometimes carries on for many days.

The predominant mood of the lasya variety of the Ras is shringar. Although each Ras Lila pertains to an incident in the Radha-Krishna theme, the action is not continuous. The drama is often interspersed with compositions like the Chalis and the Bhangi Parengs. The Chalis are short pure dance pieces which reveal the fundamental aspects of Manipuri dance technique and the Bhangi Parengs are dance compositions using a series of traditional dance poses. The Bhangi Parengs may be tandav or lasya and are used with the appropriate Ras Lilas. The Achouba, Vrindaban and Khrumba Bhangi Parengs, which are of the lasya variety, are used in the Maha Ras, the Vasanta Ras, the Kunj Ras, the Nitya Ras and the Dija Ras, while the Goshta Bhangi Pareng and the Goshta Vrindaban Pareng are used in the Goshta Ras and the Ulukhal Ras.

The sequence of each Ras Lila is strictly codified. Generally speaking the lasya types begin with short pieces such as the Krishna Abhisar (Krishna going to meet Radha), the Radha Abhisar (Radha on her way to meet Krishna secretly), the Krishna Nartan (dance of Krishna), the Radha Nartan (dance of Radha) and the dances of the chief gopees. These pieces are by way of introducing the main characters in the dance-dramas. The Chalis and Bhangi Parengs are also danced at this stage.

When the main theme of the dance-dramas is enacted the Bhangi Parengs serve as links between one scene and the next. The Ras Lila generally concludes with the Pushpanjali or the offering of flowers, and a prayer.

The story and significance of the Maha Ras, including the Antardhyan or the vanishing of Krishna, and his eventual reappearance to complete the dance with the gopees, has already been described in Chapter 16.

The Vasanta Ras describes the Spring festival of Holi. Vasanta means Spring and Holi is the festival of colours, when the young men and women of the village spray each other with coloured water or powder. The general air of festivity leads to many practical jokes. Many songs have been written about Holi and most of them tell of Krishna having the upper hand. Radha is described as being shy and hesitant and afraid that Krishna might overstep the limits of propriety in the presence of the village folk.

The story of the Vasanta Ras is one of Radha's jealousy and anger at Krishna's neglect of her. We see Krishna and the gopees dancing and enjoying themselves. Suddenly Radha notices that her lord is flirting with the other gopees. She tries to draw his attention, but Krishna is so enraptured by the other gopees that he does not notice her, or perhaps he pretends not to notice her. Radha's jealousy knows no bounds and she leaves the Ras Mandal. When at last Krishna realizes her absence, he is filled with remorse and goes out to look for her. One of Radha's sakhis (girl companions) leads Krishna to Radha, but Radha has been hurt too deeply and refuses to see him. Krishna uses all his charm to persuade her and in the end melts her anger with his winning words. The two are reconciled and dance together in happiness.

The Kunj Ras is a delightful dance describing how Radha and Krishna set out to meet each other (the Radha and Krishna Abhisars), and later of their tryst in the 'kunj' or bower. The Nitya Ras again describes the Abhisar, and the Millan or divine union of Radha and Krishna. This Ras ends on a devotional note, with Radha surrendering her soul to her lord.

In the Goshta Ras, Krishna and Balaram are taught how to tend cows. They play ball with the other cowherds and, when they are hungry, Balaram takes them to a palm grove. The palm grove, however, is guarded by the ass-demon, Dhenukasur, who challenges the boys. Balaram is angry and seizes Dhenukasur by the legs and hurls him into a tall tree. Dhenukasur falls off the tree and dies.

We see more of Krishna's pranks in the Ulukhal Ras. His foster mother in exasperation ties him to a mortar so as to keep him out of trouble. Krishna wants to join his companions and so escapes with the mortar. But in his hurry Krishna and the mortar, to which he is still attached, get wedged between two trees. He pulls, heaves and brings down the trees with a great crash, and in doing so he releases two youths who had been imprisoned in them.

The stories of the Ras Lilas strive to bring out the divine nature of Krishna; and even when describing the most passionate meetings with Radha they do not neglect to remind one of his real self.

The Lai Haroba and the Ras Lilas have many similarities. The Lai Pou of the Lai Haroba is very similar to the Bhangi Pareng of the Ras Lila, and the love duets that find such an important place in both dances are so alike that one may be led to believe that only the names of the principal characters have been changed.

The prominent role of the Maibas and Maibis in the Lai Haroba can be compared to that of the Sabaja Panthis in the Ras Lila. The men dancers among the Panthis also dress like women and play female roles.

Many authorities believe that with the coming of Vaishnavism, the Lai Haroba became the Ras Lila with a few minor changes in the dance technique. The costume and music, however, were changed considerably.

OTHER DANCES

Besides the Lai Haroba and the Ras Lila, three other dance-dramas have become important over the years. All three are associated with the Vaishnavite cult; but while the first two have mythological themes relating to the *Mahabharata*, in the one case, and the *Ramayana*, in the other, the third is based on the life of one of the celebrated Vaishnavite sages.

The Bharat Yuddha, or Battle of India, is a dance which recounts the story of the *Mahabharata* and is based on the war of succession between the Kauravs and the Pandavs. The Pandavs are generally regarded as the heroes of the dance-drama, as they were the eventual victors and the ones who were favoured by Krishna. Arjun, one of the Pandavs, had Krishna as his charioteer and counsellor during the decisive battle at Kurukshetra.

The Lanka Kand, the second dance-drama, is taken from the *Ramayana* and is the story of the saintly king Rama, whose wife was abducted by Ravana the king of Lanka. Rama eventually recovered his wife Sita after waging a fierce war against Ravana.

The Gouda Lila relates the story of Chaitanya the great missionary of Vaishnavism who came to be known as Maha Prabhu. It was he who instituted in Bengal the Goudiya form of Vaishnavism with its emphasis on Bhagti. Now Bhagti, or true adoration of God leading to ultimate union with Him, could be achieved in several different ways. Chaitanya believed that the most rewarding form of Bhagti was Sankeertan or community prayer, where the Lord's name was recited or sung in chorus. This form of worship, he maintained, would lead to 'the losing of one's self in rapture'. Chaitanya's disciples often reached a state of ecstatic delirium in which they would roll on the ground, embrace each other or burst into uncontrolled tears.

It was this highly emotional form of Vaishnavism that reached Manipur and took root there. Sankeertan, thus, became a part of community worship and today some of the most highly evolved Manipuri dances, such as the brilliant Pung Cholom and the Kartal Cholom are associated with the Sankeertan.

THE CHOLOMS

The Choloms are a tandav variety of dance belonging to the chalanam group. Both the Pung and Kartal Choloms are performed by large groups of well-trained dancers called Palas.

The Pung Cholom has rightly been called the king of the male repertoire. The dancers wear almost identical costumes consisting of white turbans, white dhotis and a folded shawl over the left shoulder. The pung or drum is secured in a horizontal position in front of the dancer by means of a strap which goes over the right shoulder and is then tied at the back. This leaves the dancer's hands free, either for playing the pung or for gesticulation.

The powerful rhythms of the pung match the dynamic grace of the dancers as they imitate several natural phenomena, such as thunder, rain, storms, or the beating of the human heart. The dancers produce the sounds with the pung and complement them with body movements. The dance includes some fiery drumming with high leaps and spins.

The Kartal Cholom is similar to the Pung Cholom, except that the rhythmic effects are achieved with cymbals or kartals. These are struck against each other to produce sounds which correspond with the syllables of the accompanying drum, the kartal marol. Although gestures are limited, for each performer has a pair of kartals, the dancers imitate the gaits of various animals and birds, at the same time exhibiting their mastery over the intricacies of rhythm.

The choreography of the Kartal Cholom is simple. The entire group of dancers and musicians forms one enormous circle and moves together in the same direction.

There is also a type of Kartal Cholom, the Mandilla Cholom, which is performed by women. This dance is used in a decorative way to accompany devotional songs about Krishna. Here, one cymbal represents Radha and the other, Krishna. Striking them, one against the other, denotes their playing together joyfully. Attached to these cymbals are long red tassels which make swirling patterns in the air.

There are two minor Cholom dances, both tandav in style. These are the Duff Cholom and the Dhol Cholom, the duff being a tambourine and the dhol a large drum used in folk music.

All the Cholom dances and the Sankeertans which form an integral part of them may be performed throughout the year, at births, deaths, or marriages and at the important religious festivals. They are also often danced as introductions to the Ras Lilas.

KUBAK ISHAI

The Kubak Ishai has sometimes been described as a variety of Tal Rasak. This dance stems from an ancient custom whereby a king's procession was accompanied by retainers who clapped rhythmically as they followed him. This tradition was absorbed into later Vaishnavite rites, so that the Kubak Ishai is now danced each year at the festival of Jagannath, when Vishnu is worshipped in all his splendour as the Sun God. Replicas of the god's chariot are taken out in procession to the singing of hymns and the chanting of sacred verses.

The Kubak Ishai is dominated by the mood of viyog or separation. It is said that once, when one of the sages was watching the chariots being drawn through the city, he fell suddenly into a trance and saw himself as Radha torn with grief, as she watched her lord mount his chariot to leave for Mathura. This incident is now enacted as part of the Kubak Ishai.

Kubak Ishai may be tandav or lasya, but in either case the predominant mood is still viyog.

Other traditional dances include the Ougrihangal, or Dance of Shiva in the tandav style, the Chingkheirol, or dance describing the rising of Usha or the dawn in lasya style, and the Ke Ke Ke or Thavalchongbi which is sometimes performed as part of the Lai Haroba.

Some tribal dances also form part of the Manipuri dance style. It is because of this, and the fact that in many of the dances (Ke Ke Ke for example) the audience participates in the performance, that all Manipuri dancing was sometimes classified as a folk-art. Manipuri, however, contains a very rich variety of codified interpretative movements and intricate rhythms and can, therefore, justly be regarded as one of the main classical dances of India.

Dancing in Manipur is often used in community worship so as to establish a close relationship between man and his Creator. The dancers are, as it were, at the High Altar, while the spectators by identifying themselves with the dancers, feel that they too are privileged to wait upon the Lord.

CHAPTER 18

SATTRA DANCES OF ASSAM

*T*he Sattra dances originated in the Brahmaputra Valley region of Assam at the close of the sixteenth century. They were the direct outcome of a new religious upsurge that was slowly spreading throughout India in the form of Vaishnavism. It has already been seen that all the arts received a great stimulus during this period and that most of the leaders of the Vaishnavite school of thought were themselves artistes of merit. Sankardeva, who brought Vaishnavism to this part of Assam, was no exception. He was a talented poet and musician who sought to teach his followers the fundamental truths in simple similes that could be easily understood. It was to achieve this end that most of his dance-dramas were written and performed.

The dance technique used in Sankardeva's dramas probably owed a great deal to the existing dance styles in the neighbouring regions. But whatever the origin, it soon became a distinctive style capable of holding its own alongside the other classical dance styles of India.

Most of the dance-dramas of the Sattra school were written by Sankardeva and his chief disciple, Madhavdeva, and portrayed incidents from the lives of Krishna and Rama. These plays are collectively known as *Ankiya Nat* or simply *Anka*.

Perhaps the most striking feature of the Ankiya Nat is the lack of prominence given to Radha. Krishna is worshipped here as the Prince rather than the cowherd, as the destroyer of evil and hate, rather than the universal lover rousing the passions of the simple gopees. This is because the Sattra dances are based on the *Bhagavad Purana* and the *Bhagavad Gita*, which are the earliest works relating to Vishnu's incarnation as Krishna. Krishna's life in Vrindaban, although mentioned in these works, is not given the same importance as his life after he left home, because it was then that he accomplished his first mission of destroying evil in the person of the cruel king Kansa. He never again returned to Vrindaban or to his childhood companions. Also, Rukmini is regarded as Krishna's wife and consort.

Radha, who is generally considered Krishna's favourite among the gopees, was not regarded as such in either the *Bhagavad Purana* or the *Bhagavad Gita*. The Radha-Krishna theme was emphasized by those who advocated the bhagti cult as a means of salvation for the soul. True bhagti demanded that the love for the Maker and Preserver be an all-consuming emotional experience, as is the love between a man and his beloved. A perfect example was found in Krishna. He was a god, and at the same time had been loved passionately by the gopees who had forsaken their homes and husbands for him. Radha was later singled out as the most favoured of the gopees. She symbolized the soul while Krishna was the god. In loving him above all else, she was showing that God must always come first in one's life.

Unlike most of the other dance styles of India, the Sattra dances adhere to the earlier image of Krishna and even dances like the Gopee Pravesar Naach and the Sattra Ras, which relate to the love of the gopees for Krishna, conspicuously refrain from any mention of Radha.

The Sattra dance-dramas start with a musical prelude known as Dhemali, where one or more musical pieces may be rendered. These include solos on percussion instruments like the *khol*, or even vocal items. The leader of the orchestra sometimes interprets the verses being sung by the use of simple abhinaya.

The Dhemali is followed by the entry of the Sutradhara who conducts the rest of the performance. The Sutradhara has the key role in the dance-dramas, for he announces the play and sets the scene for the action to follow.

In order to make the first appearance of the Sutradhara dramatic, a screen is held up to shield him from the view of the audience. The suspense is heightened by the chanting of verses and the beating of drums. Suddenly, the screen is pulled away and the Sutradhara appears kneeling at centre stage with his forehead touching the ground. He begins his dance in a very slow tempo, moving his limbs slowly as he rises. As the dance progresses, the tempo increases and the movements become much more vigorous.

A notable feature of the dance of the Sutradhara is the occasional recitation of slokas. The syllables of these slokas are reproduced by the orchestra and rendered in dance by the Sutradhara. This manner of rendering the syllables of the verses may be compared to that of the chhands in Kathak. Similar slokas are found in the Dances of Krishna and the Dances of the Gopees, that follow. While dancing a sloka the dancer also interprets it, using appropriate gestures.

The costume of the Sutradhara is the result of the blend of Hindu and Muslim cultures. He is dressed in a white long-sleeved coat or *jama* with a full, gathered skirt, rather like that of a figure from a Mughal miniature. He also wears a white turban and elaborate ornaments.

After completing his dance the Sutradhara introduces the characters in the play. These introductions consist of a succession of short dances, known collectively as Pravesar Nritya. The name comes from 'pravesh' meaning 'to present'. Each character appears on the stage in order of importance, the first to dance being the hero, either Krishna or Rama. This dance is called Gosai Pravesar Nritya, 'the Dance of the Lord'.

As the Sutradhara announces the hero, the orchestra begins to play a suitable hymn or song from the text of the play. A screen is held up and an arch of lighted torches is made. The audience bows low as, by the removal of the screen, Krishna or Rama is seen for the first time. The short dances of the Gosai Pravesar Nritya describe the hero's deeds of valour. Some slokas also are recited and rendered in dance.

The gopees are next introduced in the Gopee Pravesar Naach. The dancers are usually young boys, as women are not allowed to take part in these dance-dramas. The movements here are soft and delicate and the gaits of the dancers are very important because they reveal the characters of the persons being represented.

This procedure continues until every character has been introduced to the audience. Then the play itself commences.

The main dance-drama can take several hours and is enacted without a break. It is made up of dances such as the Jhumuras, the Yuddhar Naach, the Nritya Bhangi, the Natuwa Naach and the Sattra Ras.

The Jhumuras were introduced by Madhavdeva and are divided into two sections, the Ramdani and the Ga-naach. The Ramdani is danced before the songs of the women characters and the Ga-naach with the songs. The Jhumura costume combines both male and female dress, a turban, a jacket, and a gathered skirt. Krishna was for each gopee, as it were, a crown on her head, and in this dance they wear turbans to symbolize the fact that they still cherish him as such, even though he has left them.

The Yuddhar Naach depicts scenes of battle, mostly the deeds of Krishna and Rama, and so its movements are strong and in a very quick tempo. Because of its heroic nature this dance is a favourite with the village audiences.

Since Nritya Bhangi uses songs from the Jhumuras, the division of the dance into Ramdani and Ga-naach is also found here. Its choreography is particularly pleasing for the dance is performed by a group of six dancers, three gopees and three gopas. The songs are not interpreted through any elaborate or stylized facial expressions. Only a few simple gestures are employed from time to time.

The word 'natuwa' means an actor and was originally applied to all dancers who took part in the dance-dramas. In later years the term Natuwa Naach came to mean the particular type of dance which was based on the lyrics of the *Ankiya Nat*. The songs used for the Natuwa Naach were those sung by women characters.

The natuwas are generally young boys who wear women's costumes consisting of a ghaagra and a tight fitting blouse, with a veil draped over the head.

The Sattra school also has its own variety of Ras dances which are based on the description of the Ras in the *Bhagavad Purana*. These dances are performed by Krishna and the gopees, but again there is no mention of Radha.

The dancers of the Sattra school start to train when still very young. Special exercises for the body and limbs ensure the delicacy required in playing female roles. The dancers are also taught the art of make-up. Masks are used quite often, especially for characters like Hanuman and Dhenukasur the ass-demon.

Although the Sattra dance style does not use any codified or systematic method in movement or abhinaya, the influence of the *Natya Shastra* is unmistakably present. The hastas used bear a resemblance to those prescribed in the shastra, and it also stresses the fundamental rule that the eyes must follow the hand if true representation is to be achieved. The Dhemalis too have their counterpart in the Purvaranga of the *Natya Shastra*.

CHAPTER 19

ODISSI

$\mathcal{T}$he Odissi dance of Orissa is considered one of the oldest in India. It was rediscovered comparatively recently and even then was thought to be an offshoot of Dasi Attam and Kuchipudi. However, research has shown that there are many differences, not the least of which is the music, which in Dasi Attam and Kuchipudi is Karnatic and in Odissi Hindustani.

Orissa has been called the land of temples. The greatest of these are at Bhubaneshwar and Puri, and it was these temples which were the centres of art and culture as well as of religion, and where dance took shape and grew. It follows, therefore, that the development of dance was closely associated with that of religion. Shaivite, Buddhist, Jain and Vaishnavite temples, some dating from as early as the second century B.C., show sculptures and friezes of dance poses. Dancing girls have been dedicated for service in the temples from very early times, but there is evidence of an unbroken tradition of this in Orissa from the ninth century A.D. These girls, known as Maharis, together with their male counterparts, the Gotipuas, have preserved the art. The Maharis led chaste lives and had a high position in society. There is at least one instance of a princess who became a Mahari. The Gotipuas dressed and danced like the Maharis but had to leave the temple at the age of eighteen. They then usually became dance teachers. Because they had left the temple their style of dancing was open to outside influences and has, therefore, not come down in the same pure form as that of the Maharis.

One of the most celebrated temples of Orissa is the temple of Jagannath at Puri. Jagannath is another epithet of the god Vishnu and means 'Lord of the Universe'. The temple was built during the reign of Chodaganga Deva (1077–1147) when Vaishnavism was in the process of being established in Orissa.

There are many versions of the story about how the three most sacred of the statues came to this temple. In one, Krishna is said to have been accidentally killed by the bird-hunter Jara. Arjun, Krishna's companion, tried to cremate the body but, unable to do so, floated it out to sea where it changed into a log. Now, King Indradyumna was forewarned in a dream about the true nature of the log which would be washed onto the shores of his kingdom. He therefore arranged for it to be retrieved and carved into the image of Vishnu. However, none was able to touch it until one Vishvakarma, an old carpenter, undertook the task on condition that he would not be disturbed until it was finished. One day the eager king, unable to contain his curiosity any longer, entered the room where the carpenter had closeted himself. He found to his surprise not one but three images, all half finished. Of the carpenter himself there was no trace. He then had these images of Vishnu, his brother Balaram and their sister Subhadra taken to the great temple.

Puri thus became a place of pilgrimage and during the great festival of Jagannath the statues were placed in gigantic chariots, called raths, which were drawn through the streets by pilgrims and devotees. In former times, the more ardent of the pilgrims used to throw themselves under the wheels of the chariots, in the belief that by this sacrifice they gained salvation. The English word 'juggernaut' derives from the name of the god. In all such processions the Maharis attended upon the gods with hymns and dances.

The temple was later extended by King Kapilendra Deva, who built the Nata Mandir especially for the devotional dancing of the Maharis. He also defined their duties which have since always retained the form laid down by him. They danced twice every day. At the time of the god's mid-day meal or Bhog, the Bahir-Jani Maharis danced in the Nata Mandir. The specially selected Bheetar-Jani Maharis danced before the deity in the inner shrine at the Barah-Shringar ceremony when the deity was adorned and made ready for the night. In addition, the dancers accompanied the gods on their periodic exoduses such as the Chandan Jatra when they were taken out in boats, and the Jhoolan Jatra when they were amused and entertained on swings.

One of the duties of the Maharis was to perform bhava to songs. From the fifteenth century these songs had been taken from the *Gita Govinda* and other books, but with the firm hold of Vaishnavism in the sixteenth century they were instructed to use songs from this work only to the exclusion of all others.

Odissi did not escape a decline any more than the other dances of India, but now the old gurus are helping towards its re-establishment. The Orissa State government and the Sangeet Natak Akademi are financing research and the translation of ancient texts. There are four institutes which now offer courses in Odissi, the Kalavikas Kendra, the Utkal College of Music and Dance, the Bhubaneshwar Kala Kendra and the Orissa Sangeet Parishad.

The leading gurus of this dance style are Kelucharan Mahapatra who was once a gotipua and now teaches at the Kalavikas Kendra, and Pankaj Charan who is from a Mahari family and teaches at Puri. Perhaps the most widely-known teacher is Deba Prasad Das who was the guru of Indrani Rehman.

Indrani Rehman was the first contemporary professional dancer to have studied Odissi seriously and to have performed it in other parts of India. However, the credit for bringing Odissi out of Orissa must go to Priyambada Mohanty. I saw her present an Odissi item in Delhi in 1954 and from then on critics and scholars sat up and took notice of this dance form. Since then many dancers have devoted themselves to Odissi and among them the late Sanjukta Panigrahi must be mentioned.

TECHNIQUE

Odissi draws upon several ancient texts in Sanskrit and Oriya, most important of which are the *Natya Shastra*, the *Abhinaya Darpanam* and the *Abhinaya Chandrika*. Some of the works have illustrations and these, together with the temple sculptures, have been of great help in recreating certain postures and movements of the dance.

The training begins with eight *belis* or basic body positions and movements, each of which has many varieties.

The *uthas* are the positions used in rising and jumping. The various sitting positions are called *baithas*. The *sthankas* are the standing positions, and detail the varying distances between the feet and the positions of each knee, whether bent or straight. The gaits and walks are the *chaalis*. The quick movements, *burhas*, suggest joy and excitement. The alternate bending of the body from left to right is called *bhasa*. *Bhaunris* are spins executed on one spot, either clockwise or anti-clockwise and the *palis* are the stylized retreats on the stage which end short dance sequences.

Bhumi means the earth, but in this context it refers to the movement of the dancer on the stage and the patterns thus created. Usually the dancer moves round the outside of an imaginary circle or square and sometimes spins in one place. Also included here are movements in which the dancer comes forward, inscribing a small arc with each step.

Apart from the belis and the bhumis there are six foot positions called *pada bhedas*. Two of these are not found in other dances, the movement on the heels, and the *stambha pada*, which comes at the beginning of the dance. For this the feet are kept close together and the big toe of the right foot rests on that of the left one.

There are sixty-three hastas used in Odissi today. Some are identical with those in the ancient texts and have the same names, others are identical with those in the texts but have different names, yet others are unique to Odissi. A likely reason for the large number of hastas is that they were necessary in order to do justice to the ornate poetry of Upendra Bhanj, Surya Baladev Rath, Banamali Das and others whose works were especially favoured by Odissi dancers.

Some of the karanas used in Odissi are found in the *Natya Shastra*, but the majority are taken from the *Abhinaya Chandrika*. There are others which are recorded only on the temples of Orissa.

COSTUME

The *Abhinaya Chandrika* also lays down the details of costumes and ornaments to be worn by Odissi dancers. The women wear the patta sari, a brightly coloured silk sari which is nine yards long and a black or red blouse called the kanchula, which is embroidered with various stones and gold and silver thread. An apron-like piece of silk known as the nibi bandha is tied from the waist. The waistband itself, called the jhobha, is a length of cord with tasselled ends.

The kanchula of the Gotipuas is somewhat different as is the method in which their patta sari is draped.

The tendency of dancers, nowadays, is to wear fewer ornaments than those prescribed in the *Abhinaya Chandrika*. Three ornaments are worn on the head, one along the hair-line of the forehead, one down the centre parting and one in the hair. There are two types of necklace, a choker and a longer one with a pendant. The ears are adorned with ornaments known as kapa. Decorative wristbands and armbands are also used.

There are three permissible hair styles: the pushpa-chanda with the hair coiled into the shape of a flower, the ardh-bathaka or semi-circular bun and the kati-beni which is a single plait down the back.

An elaborate design is made on the forehead with a vermilion mark in the centre. The eyes are made up with kohl and there is a small mark on the chin.

Some dancers do not use the authentic costume and ornaments and this has caused misgivings in Orissa.

AN ODISSI PERFORMANCE

Although Odissi recitals are nowadays given on the stage, they are nevertheless essentially a form of worship in which the dancer performs an act of adoration. She uses a balanced combination of nritta and nritya and although the style is lasya there are in it some elements of tandav. There are no breaks between the different items which make up the whole dance but they do come in a set order.

The accompanying instruments have now been reduced to the mardal, a drum, the gini (cymbals), and a flute. A violin or veena may also sometimes be used. It was customary in former times for the dancer herself to sing but now a singer is usually included among the musicians.

The performance opens with the *bhumi pranam* which is a salutation to the earth or stage. With feet in *stambha pada* the dancer stands erect in the *sthai bhangi*. Tribhanga poses then follow and the *vandana* commences. She touches the ground in an act of obeisance. This short invocatory piece was originally performed behind a curtain held up by two people.

The *bighnaraj puja* now begins and she performs bhava to a recital of slokas.

For the next item, Batu Nritya, there is neither song nor recitation and the mardal becomes the chief accompaniment. This is a very elaborate and difficult passage of dance dedicated to Shiva. It should show sixteen modes of prayer-offering but is now shortened to include only the last five. These are the offerings of flowers, incense, light, in the form of tiny earthenware oil lamps, food, and last of all pranam, or salutation.

To rhythmic syllables called *ukuttas* the dancer begins slowly with poses representing the playing of instruments to welcome the Lord. Between each mode of offering is an interlude of pure dance, where there is a fine interplay of complex rhythm patterns between dancer and drummer. Sometimes tals other than the basic ones are introduced so that the dancer is able to display her skill. Each consecutive nritta passage increases in tempo and complexity of footwork.

The dedication of Shiva is followed by the *ishtadeva vandana*, which is a devotion honouring the guardian deity of the dancer. Here the dancer interprets slokas through bhava.

Next comes the *swara pallabi nritta*, the structure of which is the same as that of the rendering of a raga and indeed, as the name implies, the stress is on the musical aspect. During the singing of the alap the dancer too sets the mood by using decorative poses and eye movements as in the thaat of Kathak. After this the dancer interprets the musical notation of the raga in movements. Occasionally ukuttas are danced in place of this, in which case the name *badya* is substituted for swara.

The same raga is used to provide the melody of the song or poem interpreted in the next item, which is the *sabhinaya*. Another name for this is *gita-abhinaya*. Each couplet or verse of the poem is punctuated with nritta, which becomes progressively more intricate, so that at the end it blends into the pure nritta of the finale. This is the *tarijham*, a dance of sheer joy. The excitement mounts as dancer and drummer play with different rhythms and the dance ends in a very fast tempo with long and intricate ukuttas.

In the past this was not the final item. Instead, the dancer bowed to the gods, the stage and the earth, and the audience. This triple leave-taking was called the *trikhandi majura*.

CHAPTER 20

SANTINIKETAN

$\mathcal{R}$abindranath Tagore represented in his life and work the cultural renaissance of modern India. His rich liberalism drew its inspiration from India's ancient philosophy and, being a true traditionalist, he was always ready to accept the age and its challenges. Poet, novelist, playwright, philosopher, actor, painter and educationist, he also left his imperishable mark on the history of India's dance. Indeed, he was, with Vallathol, the pioneer of the revivalist movement that uplifted and restored the art to its proper place in the cultural life of the people. The task was by no means easy, for dancing had come to be regarded as synonymous with prostitution and loose living.

In 1901 Gurudev, the Preceptor, as he was known to his countrymen founded Santiniketan, the Home of Peace, where he experimented with his new educational methods. This school which later became a university was set in quiet surroundings away from the bustle and turmoil of Calcutta. The students led very simple lives and were encouraged to live in close communion with nature. The atmosphere was relaxed and there were no 'rules', as the poet insisted that the only discipline worth striving towards was the inner discipline which emanated from the soul. Santiniketan attracted some of the foremost thinkers and humanists from East and West and it was Tagore's inspiration which made it a great meeting place of the best minds. Although the curriculum included general academic subjects such as science and mathematics, great stress was laid on the arts. Painting, sculpture and music were taught, while Tagore himself wrote the plays which were regularly produced at Santiniketan and in some of the larger cities.

Tagore's plays were novel in that the dialogue was in blank verse and often set to music. Tagore had studied the classical ragas from a very early age and in composing the music for his plays he laid particular stress on raga-bhava, that is, he set the words to ragas that would best relate to the mood of the dialogue. A system of mixed ragas thus resulted. The actors were also the singers and remembering that his actors did not all have the same background in classical music as himself, he used only simple ragas together with popular Bengali folk melodies. Expressionistic movements and gestures were employed and dancing as such was not introduced till much later.

While on a lecture tour of Assam in 1919, Tagore saw the Goshta Lila or dance of the shepherd boys performed by a group in Sylhet. So impressed was he, that he invited the dance guru Budhimantra Sinha to come to his school and teach there. But even Tagore had to tread carefully and he could only introduce dancing as part of the physical education programme for the boys. In 1926, Tagore ventured further. With the help of the Maharaja of Manipur he brought Guru Naba Kumar to Santiniketan. This was a major breakthrough for now the girls too started their dance training. By this time the climate of opinion had begun to change and moreover, with Tagore's backing the girls had little fear of social stigma.

In the May of that same year he presented his first dance-drama in Calcutta with a cast composed wholly of girls. This drama, *Natir Puja*, is the story of a nati or dancing girl who becomes a Buddhist nun. The king, however, forbids the worship of Buddha and commands the nati to dance again. Much against her will the girl dresses herself in her most beautiful costume and dances at court. But as she dances she thinks only of Buddha. As the dance progresses she sheds her jewels one by one and finally throws off the costume as well. We see her, not naked, but in the humble habit of a nun. As she kneels in silence to worship Buddha, the king's soldiers close in and slay her for defying his orders. The princess, who has been watching, is so moved by the nati's devotion and sacrifice that she too becomes a follower of Buddha's teachings.

Natir Puja was a great success and Tagore had at last brought home his message that dancing was a medium of expression like any other art. It could uplift the soul and was not necessarily a corrupting influence. Calcutta had been converted and many Bengali girls from the best families began to learn dancing.

Tagore composed other dance-dramas; *Chitrangada, Shyama* and *Chandalika* are the best known. They were all based on ancient mythological tales and legends and he continued to use raga-bhava as the basic principle for the music. He took care to give the songs a well-defined rhythm which would lend itself to dancing. The tals generally used were the simple ones such as dadra, kaharwa, ektal and teental. The tempo was increased or decreased according to the mood, a slower tempo for the sad pieces and a faster one for joy or excitement. Sometimes, in order to heighten the dramatic effect, as in tragic scenes, the songs were sung without any rhythmic accompaniment. In *Shyama,* for instance, the last few songs of the heroine are without tabla or dholak. She tells her lover how she had saved his life by sacrificing the life of her admirer Uttiya. She begs his forgiveness for any wrong that she may have done him and then finally tries to appease her guilt-stricken conscience by prayer and meditation.

Tagore, though not a dancer himself, devised the choreography for most of the dance-dramas. He was fortunate in getting the services of three more gurus, Senarik Singh, Nileswar Mukherji and Atomba Singh who came to Santiniketan to teach and assist with the ballets. He found, however, that Manipuri techniques alone could not do justice to his plays. Accordingly, he brought gurus from South India to teach his students the elementary movements and mudras of Kathakali. A new dance style was evolved which used simplified Manipuri and Kathakali techniques along with some folk dance movements. Now this style had obvious drawbacks arising from the dancers' limited foundation in any one classical dance. Moreover, the dancers were not required to interpret the text exactly so long as they were able to convey the general mood. This naturally led to a great deal of improvisation. Nevertheless, these compositions were colourful and light and brought new blood to rejuvenate the theatre of the time.

In recent years, when the classical dances of India are receiving increasing attention, the Santiniketan style has been criticized for its lack of a precise technical basis. Although this is largely true, it cannot eclipse the significance of Santiniketan's main contribution. Its greatest service lay in helping to change the attitude of the public towards dancing, and while it paved the way for modern ballet groups it also helped to rehabilitate the classical dance styles, especially Manipuri, which till then had never been seen outside

Manipur. As Tagore toured India with his ballets giving his message through dancing, people began to set aside their prejudices and accept the art as part of their heritage.

CHAPTER 21

UDAY SHANKAR

*U*day Shankar, the pioneer of modern ballet in India, put Indian dance on the world map. He rose to fame at a time when, because of dancers like Pavlova and Ruth St Denis, oriental dancing had already excited considerable interest in the West. Shankar, by his very presence on the stage, crystallized the popular image. His face and figure and the line of his hand and body movements seemed to be, in Western eyes, the quintessence of the mysterious dance of India. Even today there are many to whom Indian dancing is synonymous with his name.

His impact was somewhat different in India, where he was successful in the first instance because of his novel ideas, brilliant stagecraft and a kind of professionalism then almost unknown to the Indian theatre. At the same time he was misunderstood and even condemned by some critics because of the style of dance he had created. His dancing, though basically Indian, was nevertheless his own personal creation, although it was influenced by European expressionist schools as well as the dances of the Far East. It was a combination of the many influences, both Eastern and Western, which were synthesized in, and had moulded, his own life.

Uday Shankar was only eighteen when he went to England as an art student under Sir William Rothenstein. Here he danced in a few charity performances organized by his father and was noticed by Anna Pavlova. Impressed by his dancing and magnetic stage presence, she asked him to help her to choreograph two oriental ballets, *The Hindu Wedding* and *Radha and Krishna*.

Shankar stayed with the Pavlova company for a year and a half and danced Krishna to her Radha. He then launched out on his own in Paris. This was the next formative stage in his career, for here he took advantage of the museums and art galleries to make a careful study of the art and culture of many countries, particularly the Far East. He also missed no opportunity of seeing the performances given by visiting international companies. All this influenced his dancing to some extent, but the style he developed was in no way imitative and matched his own personality.

For many years Shankar was based in England, where he rehearsed his company in the picturesque setting of Dartington Hall. He was assisted by his dance partner Simkie, a French girl who had been his pupil in Paris.

During his stay abroad, he had visited India several times and collected new material for his ballets. He made sketches of the dance sculptures in temples, filmed many Indian folk dances and learned the technique of the classical dances of India. Nevertheless, his dancing was not based on these classical styles any more than on foreign styles, although he incorporated movements, footwork and mudras with imagination wherever they served to enrich his own style of dancing.

Shankar also evolved a successful system of training. It was entirely his own and not in any way based on traditional Indian methods. The effect of this training was, that his corps de ballet earned a reputation for perfect harmony and co-ordination. All the exercises were classified as A, B, C, D and so on, and then numbered A1, A2, A3, etc. For example, the exercises for the hands and wrists belonged to the 'A' group. There were many of these, such as those where both hands moved together, palms facing up and then down, or where the hands moved in opposite ways, right palm facing up while the left faced down. As the 'A' exercises became more complicated the wrists naturally played an increasingly active part in them.

Walking to rhythm was given great importance. A characteristic of Shankar's style was the way in which the dancers moved down and up between steps. This was referred to as the *dip* in the exercise count which went, 'one dip, two dip, three dip, and four dip'. As the tempo increased the shorter time lapse between counts meant that the body would have to move much faster. The second stage in these exercises used the double dip where, as the name implies, the dancers had to dip twice between beats.

In 1938 Shankar returned to India and opened his India Culture Centre at Almora. To this centre he invited gurus of the classical dance styles so that his pupils were able to learn the fundamentals of these, although the primary aim was always that they should learn the Shankar style of dancing. Kandappa Pillai was responsible for Bharata Natyam, Amubi Singh for Manipuri and Sankaran Nambudri for Kathakali. In addition, the great Ustad Alauddin Khan taught classical music.

Uday Shankar was very interested in the folk dances of India and adapted their simple rhythms and movements for the stage with great success.

His choreography was such that the existing classical ragas and tals would not have fitted it in their normal form.

A certain amount of experiment was therefore necessary. He wanted music which was Indian, of a high quality without being too complex, and which would also allow for orchestration. The challenge was accepted by Tamir Baran, whom he commissioned to do this work. Baran used an orchestra of fourteen, which included various kinds of stringed as well as percussion instruments. The musicians were seated on the stage in full view of the audience. In terms of European music, fourteen instruments could hardly be said to comprise an orchestra, but for Indian classical music this is a very large number indeed, since this music is not based on harmony and so does not need a multiplicity of instruments which might easily endanger its particular unity. Since some of the ballets needed special sound effects as well, such as thunder, ploughing and harvesting, these too had to be devised. The experiment was successful and the audiences liked it, for the music skilfully complemented the choreography. Another successful composer and music director who worked with Shankar was Vishnudass Shirali.

When Uday Shankar first established himself in India his ballets were extremely popular. The themes were new for India, and based on contemporary situations. *Labour and Machinery* depicted the struggle of mill workers against the owner. *The Rhythm of Life* emphasized the need for a spirit of unity among Indians. It was at about this time that the classical dances were beginning to be revived and gaining popularity, so people were able to compare them with Shankar's ballets. The new-found love for the older styles showed itself in criticism of Shankar. He was accused of not restricting himself to one style and indeed, of not being classical, and of putting in movements from his own imagination. All these charges were, of course, quite justified, but these were the very things Shankar was trying to do. He wanted to forge a dance which would be relevant to modern conditions, in which contemporary problems could be expressed, and which would have meaning for his audiences. To do this he employed all the resources at his disposal irrespective of their origins, and still created an art which could not be mistaken for anything but Indian.

Quite apart from the quality of his work, Shankar is a turning-point in the history of Indian dance for many reasons. He was the first dancer to produce modern Indian ballets. His successful experiments in orchestration paved the way for those who were to use it later. Above all Shankar will be remembered for the finish and the professionalism of his productions. His programmes were carefully planned. The sets, lighting, costumes and make-up were given detailed attention at a time when all these had tended to be overlooked in the Indian theatre.

Shankar produced some brilliant dancers and directors among whom were Shanti Bardhan, Sachin Shankar, Kameshwar and Zohra Segal, Narendra Sharma, Debindra Shankar and his own wife Amala. Many of his pupils later formed their own troupes and carried on the tradition. The late Shanti Bardhan was particularly successful with his production of the *Ramayana*, and stories from the *Panchatantra*. *The Cranes* of Narendra Sharma is among the best of his many ballets. He also choreographed *Ramlila* for the Bharatiya Kala Kendra. The late Kameshwar Segal composed a ballet for human puppets and choreographed the beautiful *Lotus Dance*. Among Sachin Shankar's many ballets are *The Fisherman and the Mermaid, Utsav, Sanjh Savera* and *Jay Parajaya*.

In addition to dancers and directors Uday Shankar trained many much needed technicians and stage managers.

Uday Shankar was full of creative ideas till the end of his life in 1977. Concluding his London *Times* obituary I commented: "More recently, however, he was criticised by the orthodox purists for having the audacity to innovate and fashion was in their favour. He died largely disillusioned but a lord of dance nonetheless."

His youngest brother Ravi Shankar, still active as a master musician in his eighties, started his career as a boy dancer in his brother's company. He writes: "It is a rare thing for a person with no formal training to become a great dancer and a pioneer in the art as well...He appeared, really, like a god, filled with an immense power and overwhelming beauty. To me, he was a superman."

CHAPTER 22

CHHAU

$\mathcal{T}$he Chhau dances constitute a peculiar blend of the tribal, or pre-Hindu, with the Hindu. They are performed in Seraikella (Bihar), Mayurbhanj (Orissa) and Purulia (West Bengal) during the Chaitra-parva festival which is usually held during the middle of April. It is a time for rejoicing and for remembering, with gratitude, the bounties of Mother Nature.

The worship of Mother Nature has been amalgamated with reverence for Shiva, the male principle, and Shakti, the female principle, so that today the dancing celebrates Ardhanarishvara which is a composite male-female figure. With greater Hinduization deities such as Krishna have also become part of the dance ritual. The best known Chhau exists in Seraikella where the rulers themselves were both patrons and dancers. Even today, the members of the erstwhile ruling family carry on the dance tradition.

The five-day festival begins with a few women of the lowest caste carrying earthen pots, filled with water from the Kharkai river, to a sacred spot near the palace where they dance with great frenzy and go into a trance. Cockerels are then sacrificed. After this thirteen men—representing all the castes from the lowest to the highest—are chosen to dance and conduct the ceremonies that include the slaughter of goats and lambs. Each devotee is presented with a cane that he carries as a symbol of high rank. The chosen thirteen undergo austerities and fast from morning till night. In order to prove their devotion, as it were, they throw themselves on thorns before the fast is broken. There is then rejoicing and dancing late into the night. An interesting observance is worth mentioning, for while the pot of holy water is kept in the Shiva shrine near the god's *lingam* or phallus, the *jarjara* or decorated banner is taken to the temple of Raghunath (Rama) who is the god that the ruling family venerates.

On the second day the chief persona is Hanuman the monkey god while the third day is devoted to Krishna. The fourth day is reserved for Kali—a form of Shakti—who calls for blood sacrifices. The dancer is attired in black and many animals are slaughtered to propitiate the fearsome goddess. The Kali dance is the only performance that no member of the ruling family is allowed to witness. This is possibly a device meant to shield royalty from the evil eye.

The last day which symbolizes death and rebirth is called Pat Sankranthi. The chief devotee is made to lie on a makeshift funeral pyre and he acts as if he is dead. The body is covered with a cloth, ready for cremation. But then the ruler arrives in procession and by the simple act of touching the dancer's body brings him back to life. The ruler is thus invested with the god-like gift of restoring life to the dead. The next morning the water from the pot that was kept in the Shiva temple is poured over the god's *lingam* to the accompaniment of chants and prayers. Another pot of holy water is buried near the *lingam* and the pot that was buried after the previous year's ceremonies is taken out of the earth. There is an air of expectancy for if last year's pot is still full and the water still drinkable then the year to come will be full of good luck and fortune. If, however, the water has seeped away or gone brackish then the year will be blighted with famine and drought.

The dance, therefore, is much more than mere entertainment for the people of Seraikella.

As well as taking material from the Indian epics, the Chhau performers also use local myths. One of the best known dances tells the story of Chandrabhaga the moon maiden. Kama Dev, the god of love, mischievously makes the Sun god fall in love with her but, at the same time, he most irresponsibly fires an arrow of hatred for the god into the heart of Chandrabhaga. Thus for reasons, which even she does not understand, the moon maiden cannot bear the thought—let alone the touch—of the Sun god. She flees from his advances but he persists in following her and will not be rebuffed. Eventually, in sheer desperation the moon maiden throws herself into the sea, staining the waters with her blood.

And that is why every night before he sleeps the grieving Sun god lingers by the edge of the carmine waters where his beloved perished.

This touching tale is an example of the rich repertoire of Chhau.

The masks of the Seraikella dancers are made of *papier mâché* by skilled craftsmen and are normally of a pale pink colour. Since the mask precludes facial expression the Chhau artists have to excel in the use of body language. Indeed, to see them perform is a lesson in the eloquence of limbs.

The Mayurbhanj dancers do not wear masks and so their style is somewhat different from that of their Seraikella colleagues. The Mayurbhanj rituals are also different. There is, for example, a marked tendency towards extreme types of penance and protestations of faith. Devotees walk over red hot charcoal, swing from poles with iron hooks in their backs and are suspended upside down over flames. All this, it seems, only serves to heighten their frenzy during the Chaitra-parva festival.

Apart from Purulia the Chhau also exists in Nilgiri, Karswan and Keonjhar. Minor offshoots of the style can be detected in a few even more remote areas of the region.

CHAPTER 23

FOLK DANCES

$\mathcal{T}$here can be no doubt that Indian classical dance—perhaps a better term would be 'art dance'—has evolved from and been nourished by the vast variety of the country's traditional folk dance. India is big not only in terms of geographical area but, more so, on account of its great diversity. The variety of India's ethnic types, religious beliefs, languages, dress, social customs, climate and food habits very often bewilders Indians themselves. Indeed, one of the chief tasks of Indian education ought to be the dissemination of knowledge about India within India itself.

There is much lip service paid to 'national integration': in fact, very little is being done. What might be attempted first is inter-state understanding which would foster the appreciation of the finer points of each State and its constituent parts. An effort in this direction was made by Jawaharlal Nehru and his daughter Indira Gandhi when they encouraged folk dance participation during the annual festivities in Delhi to mark India's Republic Day. In January— one of the best times of the year to be in North India—dance troupes from the remotest parts of the country come to the capital to present dances particular to each region. It is a rare pageant and gives a glimpse of the glories of India.

The dances of the tribal peoples and those from the so-called 'backward areas' are perhaps the most striking. These can, for example, be identified as sacrificial, instructional, martial, talismanic, celebratory, seasonal, or devotional. There are also several forms of dance-drama which use both religious and secular themes.

The Himalayas serve as the northern borders of India and have a rich store of folk dance tradition. Kapila Vatsyayan has astutely observed, 'All the dances of the mountains have something in common, whether they come from Kashmir, Himachal Pradesh or Uttar Pradesh or Darjeeling. The bend of the knees, the long swaying movements, the intertwined arms recreate the undulating ranges of the Himalayas. The agitated movements and abrupt changes of posture in the otherwise flowing lyrical movements of the eastern region, particularly Assam and Manipur, speak of sudden storm and uprooting of trees. The tense and watchful and carefully choreographed attitudes in the dancing of the Nagas of NEFA (North East Frontier Agency), Meghalaya, Manipur and Assam denote the unknown perils of the jungle.'

In Kashmir the men of the Wattal tribe perform a type of maypole dance known as Dumhal and this phenomenon itself is worthy of anthropological study. Also interesting is the swaying Rouf so popular with Kashmiri women during Spring. This dance has several features in common with East European folk forms. Another Spring dance is the Hikat which is the preserve of girls and boys.

Kashmir is a Muslim majority area and the tombs of *pirs*, saints, become the venue of much music and dance during anniversary celebrations known as Urs. The Jashan Pather is danced by professional performers during the festivals of various *pirs*. Also popular are the Bacha Nagma, when a boy takes the part of a young woman, and the Hafiza Kalam danced by Muslim counterparts of the Hindu devadasis.

The peasant dances of the Hindu majority Jammu area include Phumaniyan and Kud. Both have circular formations and celebrate harvesting.

Himachal Pradesh has several well-known folk dances. Losar Shona Chuksum is the dance of the New Year while Namagen usually closes the year before the onset of the snows. Tushimig dances have the girls leading the boys and give an indication of the equality of the sexes, whereas some of the dances of the Gaddis actually have the girls wooing the boys. The Pangi valley's many Jatra dances are performed near temples and form part of the religious rituals.

In Sirmur goats and sheep are sacrificed during the Lohri and Baisakhi festivities and the Gee is performed by men and women, both young and old. However, only those girls born in the village—married or unmarried—are permitted to join in the dance. Girls from other areas who have married into the village have to go back to their parents' homes should they wish to dance during these festivals. Another dance is the Rasa which is a series of chain formations with men and women dancing with interlocked arms. Their songs tell of love and sacrifice.

Northern Himachal retains a strong Buddhist tradition and the slow Dakyang relates how the lamas carried the Buddha's teachings far and wide. Polyandry is still practised in some parts and hence Draupadi, the wife of the five Pandav brothers, is raised to the status of a goddess. The Khayang, danced mainly by women, takes its themes from the *Mahabharata*.

Kulu is known as the Valley of the Gods and legend has it that in ancient times the Gandharvas or heavenly musicians lived here. This claim, incidentally, is also made by the inhabitants of Manipur in eastern India. However, during Dussehra the village deities are taken out in colourful procession and there is much singing, dancing and merrymaking. Dussehra in Kulu is always a memorable occasion and the best known dances are the martial Kharait and the mixed Bashari and Dhili Pheti.

The Dhuring of the Bhotiyas, an Indo-Mongoloid tribe of north Uttar Pradesh, is a typical death-ritual dance. The Bhotiyas believe that a dead person's soul inhabits the body of a particular animal and the only way by which the human soul can be released is to slaughter the animal, usually a goat. Before this is done a sword dance is performed in a circle with the goat in the centre. The animal is then hacked to death. The meat, regarded as unclean, is never eaten but is thrown to the jackals.

Trance dances, known as Jagar, are fairly common in the Garhwal and Kumaon Hills. These are supposed to cure serious illnesses, both physical and mental. On a happier note there is the Chhapeli of the Kumaonis which is a duet danced to the accompaniment of love songs.

The Nagas of North-east India have a dance appropriate to every activity in their lives, but the most dramatic is their head-hunting dance. Not very long ago head-hunting was an integral part of Naga war ritual. Now, however, though the practice has gone the dance survives. Another interesting survival is the trance dance of the Bodos. A *deodhani*, woman dedicated to God, dances with a sword and a scarf. After dancing late into the night she goes into a deep trance and then questions are put to her by the presiding priest. Like an oracle, the deodhani tells her audience about the weather, the harvest and forthcoming joys and sorrows.

Manipur, as we have discussed in a previous chapter, is the birthplace of the well-known Manipuri classical style, but there are several other types of folk dance still much in evidence. Indeed, it can be said that dance for the Manipuris is as important as air, food and water.

Throughout Punjab, the Land of the Five Rivers which lies on either side of the Indo-Pakistan border, the virile male Bhangra is danced on all festive occasions and particularly after the *kanak*, wheat, is sown. The lively and often lusty songs tell of the pleasures of life and the heroic deeds of lovers. The Gidda is like the Bhangra but danced only by women. At the tail-end of this dance the girls form up into pairs; and then holding tightly on to each other's hands, with arms outstretched, they spin at great speed to the accompaniment of loud and fast song. This is the Kikli which is known to every Punjabi peasant girl. A much slower dance is the Karthi in which both men and women participate.

The *duf* is a tambourine type of instrument and duf dances, during which the performers sing and play on the duf, are very popular in Haryana. Here the women's dances are the Holi and the Lahoor; the former marks the coming of Spring and the latter the sowing of the Winter crop.

In Uttar Pradesh the folk theatre, Ram Lila and Ras Lila, has elements of dance and each occupational caste has its own special dance form. The *dhobis*, washermen, *ahirs*, cattle breeders, *chamars*, leather workers, and *gujars*, milkmen, for example, have their own dances for each occasion. These and the castes of professional musicians and dancers such as the *harjalas, mirasis, bhagatas, dufalis, bairagis* and *bhands* constitute some of the 'Backward Classes' of presentday India. What a terrible tragedy that in village India traditional musicians and dancers have been relegated to the lowest rungs of the social order. In earlier times, however, there can be no question as to their infinitely higher status. The *Ahirs*, for instance, claim affinity with Krishna himself who, apart from being a god, was a cowherd. Thus in India while some groups, like the Patels of Gujarat, have moved up the caste and social ladder in recent years others— such as the *Ahirs*—have moved down.

Bengal, Bihar and Madhya Pradesh have several types of tribal dance. The best known are the dances of the Oraons, Santhals, Hos, Gonds, Murias, Marias, Bhils and Juangs. Rajasthan's community Jhumar, martial Raika and acrobatic Bhavai are justly famous. Gujarat's Garba and Dandiya Ras are often seen abroad since Gujaratis take their dance with them wherever they go. Maharashtra's Kolis, fisherfolk, have several dances depicting their life by the sea as do the Muslim Moplahs of Kerala who occupy the coastal strip.

In Andhra Pradesh the Banjaras, the Lambadis, the Mathuris and the Siddhis—who are of African origin having been brought over by the Nizams as bodyguards—each retain their own dance traditions. This also applies to the Todas, the Irulas and the Kumrumbas of Tamil Nadu as well as to the Mavilans, the Maratis and the Meras of Karnataka.

Stick and ribbon dances known as Koll-attams and dummy horse dances, Puravi-attams, are common to all the southern States. Also common throughout the South are various types of trance dances and dances of exorcism.

INDIA'S DANCERS

Abhimanyu Lal
(Photo Courtesy: Ashwani Chopra)

A Kathak dancer of the younger generation, Abhimanyu was trained by his mother Geetanjali Lal. In 1999 his polished dancing was noticed by the critics when he appeared in a programme organised by the Kathak Kendra. Since then he has been busy in India and abroad. Most recently he has been interested in Kathak-Flamenco collaborations with the participation and interaction of Rajasthani and Spanish musicians.

Aditi Mangaldas

(Photo Courtesy: John Panikar)

A brilliant student of Kumudini Lakhia's Kadamb Centre for Dance and Music in Ahmedabad, Aditi Mangaldas later spent many years in Delhi under the tutelage of Birju Maharaj. Her training in the Lucknow school of Kathak was therefore thorough. After having performed in several dance dramas choreographed by Kumudini Lakhia and Birju Maharaj she became a solo dancer of distinction and was invited to major festivals in India and abroad.

Currently she is artistic director and principal dancer of the Drishtikon Dance Foundation but often works closely with New Delhi's Natya Ballet Centre.

Although many of Aditi's dances, solos and ensembles, have been within the repertoire and traditional form of Kathak, she has also explored contemporary themes and new avenues of expression. In *Movement and Space* she used Kathak, Chhau and yoga to unfurl the body's full potential. However, with *When Eternity Ends: journeys in love* there were new departures. Much use was made of Pablo Neruda's poetry and there was a love poem by Jalal-ud-din Rumi. The concept and motivation are best described by the dancer-choreographer herself: "At some stage in life one feels the need to sky dive. In *Footprints on*

Water I had held on to the parachute of 'tradition'. But suddenly, I felt the need to free fall, to feel the air rushing by me at a pace all of its own, to land where I will. If this endeavour was to find a place within the traditional Kathak repertoire, that was all right by me; but even if it didn't, I felt the need to explore my limits. In *When Eternity Ends...* I have attempted to capture the spirit of a top spinning freely. I have let myself go, let my body mould itself to the winds of time, and the journey of love to traverse its own course."

In her far ranging and perceptive book *Indian Dance: The Ultimate Metaphor* Shanta Serbjeet Singh states that artists such as Aditi Mangaldas are holding up the mirror to A.K. Ramanujan's observation: "In a culture like the Indian, the past does not pass. It keeps on providing paradigms and ironies for the present."

Aditi Mangaldas is aware that the traditional and contemporary can co-exist and even stimulate each other. There is, however, continuous flux with the passage of time and changing circumstance. She quotes a Sufi who said, "Just as the traveller after walking in the scorching sun reaches the shade of a tree, the sun moves on."

Her travels as an artist, nonetheless, go on.

Asavari Pawar

(Photo Courtesy: Avinash Pasricha)

Asavari Pawar, Pratap Pawar's daughter, learnt to dance from an early age when she was a member of her father's dance troupe in London. This initial Kathak training was followed by three years under the tutorship of Vijai Shankar in India. She has also learnt classical singing from Girija Devi.

A busy dancer and teacher in India and Britain, Asavari's earliest production was a ballet titled *The Coat* which won the first John Major award in the United Kingdom. Among her many honours in India are the Shringar Mani and Aadharshila awards. She has appeared on various television channels in India and abroad. Her future as a Kathak artist is bright. In *The Dancing Times* (September 2003) I commented on her artistic intelligence.

Bharati Shivaji
(Photo Courtesy: Avinash Pasricha)

Mohini Attam, the enchanting dance of Kerala, has found an outstanding exponent in Bharati Shivaji. She has made it her life's mission to reinstate this dance form to its former glory and for over two decades has delved into its origins and history. As a professional dancer she has reconstructed its concert format and expanded the range of its idiom and technique.

Bharati Shivaji's sponsor and inspirational patron was Kamaladevi Chattopadhyay and her academic guru was Kavalam Narayana Panicker. Her book *The Art of Mohini Attam* is an authoritative document on the subject and her researches into Kerala's *Gita Govinda* tradition have been widely appreciated.

An innovator, she has presented group productions using Mohini Attam movements. Her dance centre in Delhi is devoted to the training of Mohini Attam artists. She appeared at the Edinburgh Festival in 2002.

Birju Maharaj

(Photo Courtesy: Marcus Massey)

It is impossible to give any accurate account of this master's achievements in what has to be a short summary. He is the jewel in the crown of Delhi's dance world. The only son of Achhan Maharaj, he is now the head of the Lucknow gharana and though no longer a young man continues with his dancing and dance experimentation. As a choreographer he is unique.

His father died when Birju Majaraj was very young and so his *taleem*, training, was taken over by his two uncles Lachhu Maharaj and Shambu Maharaj but principally the latter. He followed Shambu Maharaj as the head of the Kathak department at the Bharatiya Kala Kendra and has over the years trained scores of dancers who

Jai Krishan Maharaj

(Photo Courtesy: Avinash Pasricha)

are now well known names in their own right.

There is not a single aspect or element of Kathak that Birju Maharaj has not expanded or illuminated. He has created several *boles* and *bandishes*, fixed compositions, and his ballets have become landmarks of the Kathak dance. He is also a very accomplished percussionist and singer and not many know that he is an avid sketcher and miniaturist.

Birju Maharaj is universally loved and respected. Perhaps it is only he who could have brought together no less than seven leading hereditary gurus representing the seven major dance styles of India. In 1994 he choreographed a presentation titled *Saptrang* at Calcutta's Victoria Memorial which included Kalyan Sundaram Pillai (Bharata Natyam), Kelucharan Mahapatra (Odissi), Kalamandalam Khemavati (Mohini Attam), Birju Maharaj (Kathak), Satyanarayana

Deepak Maharaj

Sarma (Kuchipudi), Govindan Kutty (Kathakali), and Bipin Singh (Manipuri). Also taking part were the following leading dancers: Leela Samson (Bharata Natyam), Madhavi Mudgal (Odissi), Bharati Shivaji (Mohini Attam), Saswati Sen (Kathak), Jaya Rama Rao (Kuchipudi), Sadanam Balakrishnan (Kathakali) and Priti Patel (Manipuri). The welding together of so much tradition and talent was, in terms of dance, an historic event.

Showered with several honours including the Padma Vibhushan, Birju Maharaj is innately modest and, in a child-like way, very unworldly. His sons Jai Krishan Maharaj and Deepak Maharaj, both of whom he trained, are following in his footsteps. He has started Kalashram, a Kathak institution of excellence.

Deepti Omchery Bhalla

(Photo Courtesy: Invis Multimedia)

A brilliant scholar-dancer, Deepti Omchery Bhalla is Professor of Karnatak Music at Delhi University. Her mother Dr Leela Omchery and Guru T.S. Raghavan initiated her into the classical music of south India while her teachers of the north Indian genre were Ustad Yunus Khan of the Agra gharana and the Dagar brothers, the dhrupad masters. Her Kathakali gurus were Gopinath, S.K. Nair, P.M. Panikkar and Sadanam P.V. Balakrishnan. Mohini Attam she learnt from the legendary Kalyani Kutti Amma. Her doctoral studies investigated the Sopana music of Kerala, the indigenous classical music of the region. Her researches into the origin and development of Mohini Attam have been praised by dance academics.

Deepti Omchery Bhalla has danced at many festivals in India and abroad and amongst her many awards mention must be made of the Natya Ratna.

She supervises doctoral students and a number of Mohini Attam artists of the future (such as Sapna Menon, Aruna Nair and Tanushree Bhalla) are her pupils. Hisayo Adachi, the first Japanese dancer to learn Mohini Attam, is her disciple.

Devayani
(Photo Courtesy: Rakesh Shreshta)

Born in Paris and dance conscious from early childhood, Devayani first absorbed ballet, jazz, flamenco and Middle Eastern traditions. It was, however, to India that she eventually turned and, it must be said, India accepted her warmly and wholly. Bharata Natyam became the essence of her life. She went to Chennai and studied under Ellapa Mudaliar and Muthuswamy Pillai. Later she came under the influence of Vempati Chinna Satyam (Kuchipudi), Kalanidhi Narayanan (Abhinaya), Balamurali Krishna (Karnatic vocal), Malavika Sarukkai and Yamini Krishnamurti (Bharata Natyam). Yamini Krishnamurti has choreographed some compositions specially for Devayani.

Having danced in various cities in India, Devayani then performed in a number of European capitals. She became the Arts Council of Great Britain's first artist-in-residence to promote Indian dance in the United Kingdom. Her creation *Devadasi* fused the classical styles of east and west.

Devayani's dancing and acting was widely appreciated when she performed Kuchipudi in the Telugu film *America Ammayi* ('A Girl from America'). Later, at the XXIV Algarve International Music Festival she got star billing with Luciano Pavarotti and Olga Borodina.

The world vision of Devayani's art is praiseworthy.

Divya and Diksha Upreti

(Photo Courtesy: Avinash Pasricha)

Known as 'The Dancing Twins', Divya and Diksha have spent many years learning Kathak and are beginning to gain well earned recognition. At the Sriram Bharatiya Kala Kendra they studied under Bhaswati Misra and later, at the Kathak Kendra, they learnt from Bharati Gupta and Munna Shukla. From such firm foundations one can only expect a fine edifice.

Geetanjali Lal

(Photo Courtesy: Ashwani Chopra)

A senior dancer and teacher, Geetanjali Lal heads the repertory unit of New Delhi's Kathak Kendra. Her teachers were Roshan Kumari, Gopi Krishna, Mohan Rao Kalyanpurkar and her husband the late Devi Lal. Music she learnt from her father Professor Rajnikant Desai of Mumbai, a well known musicologist.

She has performed in many dance dramas, the most notable being her lead role in *Habba Khatoon* which was directed by Birju Maharaj. Herself a choreographer and director, her *Meghdoot* which she produced in Mauritius attracted favourable attention. She had at the time been sent by the Indian Council for Cultural Relations to perform and teach at the Indira Gandhi Centre in Mauritius. Later she also taught at the Dartington College of Arts in Devon, England. She has toured abroad several times and is a respected member of her profession.

Geeta Mahalik

A fine Odissi artist whose *nayanabhinaya* is remarkable, Geeta Mahalik's teachers were Mayadhar Raut and Deba Prasad Das. She has appeared at various festivals in India and abroad and has choreographed dances from the works of Jayadeva, the Pancha Sakha poets and Upendra Bhanj.

Geeta Chandran

(Photo Courtesy: Avinash Pasricha)

Founder of Natya Vriksha, a dance school in Delhi, Geeta Chandran is a leading Bharata Natyam dancer. In 1999 she was the youngest choreographer to present her work at the first National Festival of New Choreographies. Her piece, *Sivam*, was critically acclaimed.

Geeta Chandran is a significant bridge between the Thanjavur school and the contemporary dance idiom and aesthetic. Trained by many gurus (her first teacher was Natya Kalanidhi Srimati Swarna Saraswathy who hailed from the devadasi tradition) she has imparted her imprint on a combined legacy.

Conscious of dance as an instrument of social change, her work has often tackled contemporary issues. In 1998, *Sihanvlokan* raised her concerns about violence against women. *Her Voice*, produced in 2000, was a collaborative effort of dance and puppetry and gave womanhood's perspective on war. Draupadi, the victim in the Mahabharata, became a powerful metaphor not only of agony but also of sanity.

Geeta Chandran has toured widely and has won the All India Critics Award.

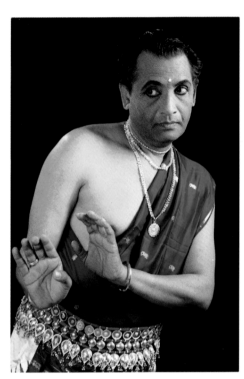

Hare Krishna Behera

(Photo Courtesy: Avinash Pasricha)

After he had completed his training at the Kala Vikas Kendra in Cuttack, Hare Krishna Behera started Nritya Niketan in 1964. It was the first Odissi school in Delhi. He invited his gurus Kelucharan Mahapatra and Mayadhar Raut to teach at Nritya Niketan as well as his former pupil Surendra Nath Jena. Several of the institution's students later became well known dancers.

Hare Krishna Behera's experience has been wide and varied. As a youngster he joined a Jatra touring troupe; Ramhari Behera and Ramchandra Dey trained him to become a *gotipua*; under Birju Maharaj's direction he learnt Kathak; at Delhi's Natya Ballet Theatre he studied choreography; he learnt vocal music from Siddheshwari Devi; he also mastered the *tabla* and the *pakhawaj*.

He has taught at the Bharatiya Natya Sangh and the Gandharva Mahavidyalaya. The Odissi Kendra in Delhi, of which he is founder president, trains both dancers and musicians. He has choreographed over fifteen dance dramas based on Sanskrit, Hindi and Oriya classics and many of his original dance creations which embody both the *gotipua* and the *mahari* traditions have been widely appreciated and emulated.

A respected guru, Hare Krishna Behera has danced and held workshops in several countries. His eldest daughter Kavita Dwibedi is now a leading Odissi artist; the other two daughters, Kaveri and Kalyani, are also beginning to make a mark.

Jaya Rama Rao and Vanashree Rao

(Photo Courtesy: Avinash Pasricha)

This husband and wife team, who have partnered each other since 1978, direct the Kuchipudi Dance Academy in Delhi which has a high reputation. Jaya Rama Rao, who was born into a Bhagvatulu family of dancers and singers, trained first at the Siddhendra Kala Kshetram in Kuchipudi village. He learnt from Chinta Krishnamurthi, Pasumarti Venugopal Krishna Sarma and Vempati Chinna Satyam. Later, in 1969, he moved to Delhi where he worked with Raja and Radha Reddy, Swapna Sundari and Meenakshi Seshadri.

His wife Vanashree was initiated into dance by him and then studied under Vempati Chinna Satyam and Nataraja Rama Krishna.

The Raos have represented India in many dance festivals from Moscow to Mauritius, from Edinburgh to Adelaide.

Their honours include the Sangeet Natak Akademi Award.

Kavita Dwibedi

(Photo Courtesy: Avinash Pasricha)

The eldest daughter of Hare Krishna Behera is an exciting new talent. She has appeared at various dance venues in India and has performed abroad several times. Her experiments with exponents of other styles and forms (Kathak, Bharata Natyam, Manipuri, French theatre and Indian puppetry) have been lively and interesting.

In 2001 she was invited by the All Pakistan Music Conference and danced Odissi to the accompaniment of *thumris* rendered by the celebrated Farida Khannam. This cultural connection with Pakistan was not insignificant. In 2002, the Jayadeva Utsav which she organised in Delhi was well received.

Kavita Thakur

(Photo Courtesy: Avinash Pasricha)

A dancer of the younger generation, Kavita Thakur has had a firm academic foundation in music and dance. Her training began in Shimla, Himachal Pradesh, where she was born; she then went on to the Bhatkhande Vidyapeeth, Lucknow and later to the Indira Sangeet Vishwavidyalaya, Khairgarh. Finally, in 1994, she came to Delhi and studied under Munna Shukla at the Kathak Kendra. She assists him in many of his productions and lecture-demonstrations.

Kavita has danced in several festivals in India in both solo and group items. Abroad, she has danced in China and Germany. Her dedication will one day reap rich rewards.

Kiran Segal
(Photo Courtesy: Avinash Pasricha)

Daughter of Kameshwar and Zohra Segal who were well known dancers and choreographers, Kiran Segal imbibed dance and choreography from a very early age. Zohra Segal, the first Indian to study in Germany under Mary Wigman, is even today a respected actress of stage, television and film. She and her husband worked in Uday Shankar's dance company (she and Madame Simkie were Shankar's leading ladies) and, later, she became one of the leading ladies of Prithvi Theatres which was owned and run by none other than Prithviraj Kapoor, the founding father of the Kapoor acting dynasty. It would be true to say, therefore, that Kiran Segal was born into the fraternity of dance and drama.

Kiran was trained in Bharata Natyam by Govindarajan Pillai and in

Odissi by Mayadhar Raut, an important figure in the development of the style. Her adherence to the true spirit and form of Odissi has been noteworthy and her *Panchaakshara Stotram* was widely hailed as the finest prayer to Shiva in the Odissi style. *Taalaangiya*, a form of worship through mind, body and rhythm, is her most recent piece of choreography.

As a teenager Kiran lived in London and appeared at the Commonwealth Institute in a dance drama titled *Nurjehan*. It was choreographed by Sunita Golvala, a student of Shirin Vajifdar, and produced by Ramesh Patel's Nava Kala company. Reviewing the programme in *The Times* (March 24, 1969) I noted that "...Kiran Segal as the bereaved *dhoban*, washerwoman, evoked much pathos in the final scene." She showed promise even then but has since moved on to greater things.

Her reputation as a misssionary for Odissi is well deserved as she has taken the dance to about 40 countries all over the globe. She has represented India at various international dance festivals in France, Germany, Morocco and Russia. She broadcasts on the subject of dance extensively and America's Lincoln University has recorded her work for its archives. Her dance school in New Delhi is known as the Pallavi Odissi Nritya Sangeet Vidyalaya.

Among the honours she has won are the Kala Shreshta Samman, the Nritya Saraswati, the Parishad Samman, and the Padma Shree.

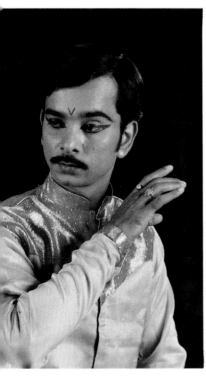

Krishan Mohan Maharaj
(Photo Courtesy: Avinash Pasricha)

Bhaswati Misra
(Photo Courtesy: Avinash Pasricha)

This husband and wife team are established Kathak artists and often dance together. Krishan Mohan Maharaj, son of the late Shambu Maharaj, was first taught by his father and then by his cousin Birju Maharaj. He is a member of the Kathak Kendra production unit and has performed in many dance dramas.

Bhaswati Misra, younger sister of Saswati Sen, was first taught by Reba Vidyarthi and later by Birju Maharaj. She teaches at the Shri Ram Bharatiya Kala Kendra.

Leela Samson

(Photo Courtesy: Avinash Pasricha)

Having mastered the grammar and technique of Bharata Natyam at Kalakshetra, Leela Samson's dance art has grown in several directions. According to her "adherence to any school is a point of reference only". She is today one of the leading Bharata Natyam exponents of her generation.

A teacher of distinction, she is also an important choreographer and writer on dance. Her book *Rhythm in Joy* deals with the major Indian styles. Arun Khopkar's *Sanchari* and Ein Lall's *The Flowering Tree* are two documentary films that explain and explore her achievement and experimentation.

In 1995 Leela Samson started Spanda, a group that works creatively within the Bharata Natyam tradition. She has performed in many foreign countries and has been showered with honours and titles. In 1990 she received the Padma Shree and ten years later the Sangeet Natak Akademi award.

Madhavi Mudgal

(Photo Courtesy: Avinash Pasricha)

In 1995, Jay Visva Deva's Sama Performing Arts Network presented an Indian dance festival at London's Queen Elizabeth Hall. The Odissi component was comprised principally of Kelucharan Mahapatra and his pupil Madhavi Mudgal. Reproduced here is a relevant passage from a longish review that I wrote in *The Dancing Times*: "Madhavi Mudgal is a worthy disciple of her great master. Her *pallavi*, a flowering, as it were, of musical motifs in movement, was excellent and her portrayal of the woman waiting for her lover—who never came—was touching. The last dance, *Sohamasmi* (*I am That*), was on the subject of all-pervading reality and the essential unity that binds the cosmos. It was cleverly choreographed by Madhavi Mudgal and danced beautifully by her, Bindu Juneja and Rekha Tandon. The vocalist Madhup Mudgal was excellent throughout."

Madhavi Mudgal's family background is artistic. Her first Odissi teacher was Hare Krishna Behera; it was later that she became the disciple of Kelucharan Mahapatra. However, she has also been trained in Bharata Natyam and Kathak; her Kathak teachers were Durgalal and Birju Maharaj. Her performances therefore are influenced by the best elements of three distinctive styles.

She has appeared at some of the world's leading festivals such as the Vienna Dance Festival, the Budapest spring Festival and the Festival d'Avignon. In 2002 she danced at the Edinburgh Festival and made a great impression. Madhavi teaches at the Gandharva Mahavidyalaya, an institution of high reputation. She has been honoured with the Padma Shree, the Sanskriti Award and the Orissa State Sangeet Natak Akademi Award.

Madhumita Raut

Mayadhar Raut taught his daughter Madhumita from a very early age. She is now an accomplished Odissi dancer who has performed at the major Indian festivals as well as important venues in twenty-two countries.

She manages her father's school in Delhi and also teaches at its affiliated institutions abroad.

A dedicated artist, she also choreographs and is currently writing a book on Odissi.

Malti Shyam

(Photo Courtesy: Avinash Pasricha)

After having been trained by Reba Vidyarthi for four years, Malti Shyam continued her training under Birju Maharaj for seven years. Currently a member of the production unit of the Kathak Kendra, she has danced at a number of festivals in India and abroad.

A polished and dedicated dancer, she is also a devoted teacher.

Mayadhar Raut

(Photo Courtesy: Avinash Pasricha)

Like his late elder brother Harihar Raut, Mayadhar Raut started as a boy dancer-actor in a theatre group in Orissa. He studied under a galaxy of teachers which included Kali Charan Patnaik, Durlav Singh, Mohan Mahapatra, Yudhishtar Mahapatra, Mohan Sunder Dev Goswami, Pankaj Charan Das and Dayal Sharma. Kathak he learnt from the Jaipur master Ram Gopal Misra. In 1955 he won a scholarship to Kalakshetra where he studied Bharata Natyam under Rukmini Devi and Kathakali under T.K. Chandu Panikar.

As a teacher his experience is vast; he has taught at the Kala Vikas Kendra, the Natya Ballet Centre, the Nritya Niketan and the Sri Ram Bharatiya Kala Kendra. His own institute in Delhi, the Mayadhar Raut School of Odissi Dance, has offshoots in Germany, Holland and the USA. He has tutored and guided many of India's leading dancers and the list of his foreign students is impressive. They are as far afield as Japan, the USA, Holland, Switzerland, Germany, Vietnam, Pakistan and the West Indies. His tours abroad began in 1972 and since then he has been on several cultural missions.

Shri Subbudu, the critic of *The Statesman* of Delhi, observed that not only did Mayadhar Raut bring a scientific approach to the teaching of dance but he had also enriched the *abhinaya* vocabulary of Odissi. He is the first guru to introduce *sanchari bhava* in Odissi items.

He has choreographed a number of well known dance dramas of which *Tapasvini*, *Meghadoot*, *Singhala*, *Krishna Charitam* and *Geetagovindam* must be mentioned. Three successful Oriya films have dance sequences directed by him. In collaboration with D.N. Patnaik he has researched and documented many of Orissa's folk dances.

In 1985 he received the Sangeet Natak Akademi award.

Munna Shukla
(Photo Courtesy: Ashwani Chopra)

This well known Kathak dancer and teacher is the son of Vidyavati, a sister of Birju Maharaj. Achhan Maharaj was, therefore, his *Nana-ji*, maternal grandfather. After initial training from his father Sunder Lal Shukla, he migrated to Delhi from Lucknow on a Ministry of Culture scholarship and studied at the Bharatiya Kala Kendra. His guru was now Birju Maharaj, his *Mama-ji*, maternal uncle.

After completing his training Munna Shukla taught at Prabha Marathe's Kala Chhaya institute in Pune. He choreographed many duets and group items as well as some full-length dance-dramas. He returned to Delhi in 1976 and since then has been a guru at the Kathak Kendra where he has trained a large number of dancers.

Munna Shukla is a creative choreographer of high repute. His credits include *Shan-e-Mughal, Tratak, Kathak Prasang, Kaliyadaman, Makhanleela, Shyam Bansuriya, Inder-Sabha, Ameer Khusro, Azeezunisa, Shahi-Mehfil, Kathak ki Kahani* and *Talmala*. His foreign tours have taken him to Japan, the USSR, and many countries in Europe and Africa.

He is the recipient of the Sarangdeo Award and the Uttar Pradesh Sangeet Natak Akademi Award.

Pasumarti Vithal and Bharati

(Photo Courtesy: Avinash Pasricha)

This husband and wife team have established the well regarded Kuchipudi Kala Kendra in Delhi. Pasumarti Vithal hails from Kuchipudi village where from an early age he was coached by his father Pasumarti Venugopal Krishna Sarma. Bharati, trained by Vedantam Prahlad Sarma, partners her husband on the stage.

Both are first class teachers and their workshops, duets and dance dramas have been widely praised.

Pratap Pawar

(Photo Courtesy: Avinash Pasricha)

Pratap Pawar was Birju Maharaj's first *shishya*, student or disciple, in Delhi and has carried his master's style of dance to distant parts of the globe. He has taught in the West Indies, Canada and Britain and has toured several countries. In the summer he lives in Britain for long periods but in the winter is always in Delhi. His India-wide dance tours from his base in Delhi are a regular feature.

His talented daughter Asavari, whom he has trained, lives permanently in Delhi.

Formerly the Kathak teacher at London's Bharatiya Vidya Bhavan, he now runs with the assistance of his son Prashant a dance company and a school. The school has many foreign students. I once remarked: "Not many male Indian dancers have the stamina and strength of Pratap Pawar and he is therefore a rare commodity." The last time I saw him perform was in February 2002 during Birju Maharaj's Kalashram Kathak Festival in Delhi and have no reason to revise my opinion.

Reviewing a Pawar production in 2001, I wrote in *The Dancing Times*: "London's Queen Elizabeth Hall was the venue of a unique event on July 10 when the Kathak maestro Birju Maharaj starred in a programme titled *Legacy of Tradition*. So far as Indian dance in Britain is concerned the evening marked a point of maturity and Pratap Pawar's Triveni Dance Company is to be congratulated for celebrating it so fittingly... Never before had an audience in this country seen what amounted to three generations of Indian dancers appear together. Even in India such an event would be rare... Saswati Sen, Pratap Pawar and Birju Maharaj swept on to the stage and in a matter of minutes mesmerised the packed hall with fantastic footwork, pirouettes and flashing arms... After Pratap Pawar had presented a powerful invocation to the god Shiva within the framework of the 14-beat time cycle he was joined by Saswati Sen. Together they danced a charming duet which symbolised the eternal and divine bond that existed between Shiva and Parvati; he the masculine principle, the *tandav*, and she the feminine, the *lasya*."

Currently he has regular teaching assignments in various Indian, British and Canadian cities. Many of his students, such as the British Asian Akram Khan, have already made a name for themselves.

Prerana Shrimali
(Photo Courtesy: Avinash Pasricha)

A fine representative of the Jaipur school of Kathak, Prerana Shrimali studied under Kundanlal Gangani at the Kathak Kendra. Endowed with imagination and intelligence she has choreographed several dances based on the works of leading poets. *Reaching for Each Other*, which she presented at the Avignon Festival in 1995, was a multi-media production which pooled vast resources: the poetry of Ashok Vajpeyi, the painting of Sayed Haider Raza, the music of Satyasheel Deshpande, the scenography of B.V. Karanth, the costumes of Purnendu Shekhar and the photography of Avinash Pasricha. It was widely praised.

She has danced in all the main Indian cities. Her foreign tours have taken in Kabul, Calgary, London, New York, and Moscow. She teaches at New Delhi's Gandharva Mahavidyalaya.

Raja and Radha Reddy

(Photo Courtesy: Avinash Pasricha)

It can be claimed with some justification that this duo has brought Kuchipudi to the attention of dance lovers the world over. Through the sheer force of their personalities and their amazing dancing skills they have set standards for Kuchipudi dancers of the future.

In 1977, I wrote the following in *The Dancing Times* under the title *Kuchipudi Classics*: "That wonderful pair Raja and Radha Reddy did a whirlwind tour of Britain during October, taking almost literally in their stride places as far apart as Dartington Hall and the Nottingham Playhouse...

The Reddys come from Andhra and both have had a long and arduous period of training under Guru Prahlad Sarma and Guru Krishna Sarma. The Reddys are today the leading performers of Kuchipudi... Each performance was varied, well thought out and carefully presented, and due importance was given to lighting and acoustics—a refreshing change from what one usually gets in Indian dance programmes. Moreover, the Reddys are in peak form: in item after item they demonstrated virtuosity, expression, and a talent for choreographically editing the dance dramas to manageable length. An outstanding example of this was *Usha Parinayam* which in its original setting often spans three nights. It is the story of Usha, a princess, who sees a lotus-eyed prince in a dream and falls in love with him... *Usha Prinayam*, in the Reddys' version, had charm, feeling and touches of humour."

They have a vast repertoire of dance dramas, duets and solo items.

Raja has always been a powerful, masculine dancer and personifies the *tandav* aspect of Shiva. Radha, on the other hand, was always quintessentially *lasya*, utterly feminine. Hence their dancing duets in the roles of Shiva-Parvati, Rama-Sita, and Krishna-Radha have touched and thrilled audiences wherever they have appeared. In 2002 they caused a sensation at the Edinburgh Festival.

Radha's younger sister Kaushalya is now a leading dancer as are some of their other students. Yamini and Bhavana, their daughters, are also showing great promise.

The Reddys have been honoured by many cultural organisations. They have received the Sangeet Natak Akademi Award and, unusually, both the Padma Shree and the Padma Bhushan.

Andhra's classical dance art will always bear the Reddy imprint.

Kaushalya Reddy

(Photo Courtesy: Avinash Pasricha)

Now a Kuchipudi star in her own right, Kaushalya Reddy's apprenticeship in dance has been long and arduous. She was initially trained by Rattiah Sarma and then by Raja and Radha Reddy. When I first saw her dance I compared her to an *apsara*, heavenly nymph. After having seen her perform at Sadler's Wells in London (September 2002) I made the following comment in *The Dancing Times*: "She has grown from strength to strength and can now be called the definitive *apsara*." She has also matured to become an accomplished choreographer and *nattuvanar*, conductor and dance mistress.

Sunil Kothari has praised her thus: "Once again she has started giving solo performances...bringing to her recitals a freshness, competence and quicksilver quality in her *nritta*. She succeeds in giving dramatic touches to the depiction of various *sanchari bhavas* in solo exposition."

Kaushalya is a dedicated teacher at Natya Tarangini, the dance institution of the Reddy family in New Delhi, and is inspiring and training many Indian and foreign students. She has also travelled widely and danced in Japan, South America, South East Asia, Mauritius, Nepal, Britain, France, the Caribbean countries, Poland, Hungary and Bosnia.

Raja Reddy, with the moral strength of the true artist, has declared: "It is true that behind every successful man there is a woman. I am twice lucky and the credit goes to the two women in my life, my two wives, Radha and Kaushalya." He added that with the birth of his two daughters, Yamini and Bhavana, his success was quadrupled. "Then our family became the Kuchipudi family like the *panchendriyaas*, the *panch-tatvaas* (the five elements) the earth is made up of."

Kaushalya's future in the dance world is assured.

Yamini and Bhavana Reddy

(Photo Courtesy: Avinash Pasricha)

Raja Reddy's daughters (Yamini from Radha and Bhavana from Kaushalya) are now well set to continue the family tradition. Both are being trained by their parents and their performances are already getting favourable notices. Their tours, within India and abroad, have been successful and the future for both these talented young dancers is bright.

Rajkumar Singhajit Singh
and Charu Mathur

(Photo Courtesy: Avinash Pasricha)

Born into a family of dancers and musicians of Manipur, Rajkumar Singhajit Singh was initiated into dance at an early age. Trained by eminent gurus, he has mastered the Manipuri style and is an outstanding performer, scholar and choreographer. He and his wife Charu Mathur have toured abroad many times and in 2002 they appeared at the Edinburgh Festival. He has received the Padma Shree and the Sangeet Natak Akademi award.

A dedicated Manipuri artist, Charu Mathur was born and brought up in Delhi. She is equally adept in solo and balletic works. She is also a respected teacher. Her lead roles in her husband's several ballets have won wide recognition. She has been honoured with the Sangeet Natak Akademi award.

Ramani Ranjan Jena

(Photo Courtesy: Avinash Pasricha)

Rashmi Ranjan & Itisri Jena

(Photo Courtesy: Avinash Pasricha)

A widely travelled dance guru, Ramani Ranjan Jena has the distinction of teaching Odissi not only in Cuttack, in his home state of Orissa, but also in Chennai and Delhi. In Chennai his students were established Bharata Natyam dancers such as Malavika Sarukkai who has recently been awarded the Padma Shree. For three years he was also the Odissi guru at Kalakshetra.

His own teachers were Kelucharan Mahapatra, Raghunath Datta and Mayadhar Raut. He teaches at Delhi's Triveni Kala Sangam. His son Rashmi Ranjan Jena and daughter-in-law Itisri Jena are making their reputations as fine Odissi artists.

Ram Mohan Maharaj

(Photo Courtesy: Ashwani Chopra)

After he was initiated at the age of six by his late father Shambu Maharaj, Ram Mohan Maharaj, like his elder brother Krishan Mohan Maharaj, was trained by his cousin Birju Maharaj. Over the years he has made a name for himself as a soloist, choreographer and teacher. His *abhinaya* is outstanding and reminds critics of the sensitivity of Shambu Maharaj. Though he is based at the Kathak Kendra in New Delhi, Ram Mohan Maharaj's tours and workshops all over India have attracted much attention.

He has danced in several countries and in 1992 was invited to teach and perform in Surinam where he stayed for over three years.

Ranjana Gauhar

(Photo Courtesy: Avinash Pasricha)

Apart from being a well known Odissi dancer, Ranjana Gauhar is a painter and theatre artist. She was for a time based in Britain where she gave lecture demonstrations and stage performances.

Her gurus were Srinath Raut, Mayadhar Raut and Kelucharan Mahapatra. Now based in Delhi she is busy performing and teaching.

An independent film producer, she holds a Ministry of Culture senior fellowship. She is currently working on two films: the first is on the Jagannath temple and the second deals with India's cultural connections with Vietnam and Cambodia.

In 2003 she was awarded the Padma Shree.

Rashmi Singh
(Photo Courtesy: Kiron Pasricha)

An outstanding pupil of Kalyani Shekar, Rashmi Singh is making a reputation as a Bharata Natyam dancer. She has a strong interest in Karnatic vocal music and has won many competitions thanks to the teaching of Vijayalakshmi Krishnan.

Rashmi has also learnt Chhau and folk dance and often participates in dance dramas and national festivals. When she was sixteen she represented India in the Asian Youth Festival at Seoul. Her school, Kalyani Kala Mandir, imparts training in music and dance.

Reba Vidyarthi

A dedicated and respected teacher, Reba Vidyarthi has taught many of today's leading dancers. Birju Maharaj's children started their Kathak training under her watchful eye as did Saswati Sen and her sister Bhaswati Misra. For many years Reba Vidyarthi taught at New Delhi's Bahawalpur House as a senior staff member of the Bharatiya Kala Kendra and, later, the Kathak Kendra.

She was a pioneer of dance therapy in India and worked with the deaf and dumb and children stricken with polio. She has received awards from the Sahitya Parishad and the Sangeet Natak Akademi. Her gurus were Achhan Maharaj and Shambu Maharaj.

Sadanam P.V. Balakrishnan

(Photo Courtesy: Avinash Pasricha)

This guru heads the justly famous International Centre for Kathakali in New Delhi which has been propagating Kerala's dance-drama since 1961. The centre's performing group has several outstanding artists.

Sadanam Balakrishnan was trained by K.N. Nair, T.R. Nair and K.K. Nair. After teaching in leading institutes in Kerala, he joined the I.C.K. in 1974. Under him the institute has expanded its repertoire to include material from other theatrical traditions, from classical Greek to Shakespeare. *Othello*, choreographed in Kathakali style and idiom, has been widely appreciated.

Guru Balakrishnan and his company have danced in festivals all over the world. Kathakali has enriched the culture of India's capital.

Saswati Sen
(Photo Courtesy: Marcus Massey)

Since her father was a doctor, Saswati Sen wanted to follow her father and so started on a pre-medical course. She later turned to anthropology. In the meantime she took Kathak lessons from Reba Vidyarthi and finally decided to become a professional dancer. In 1968 she became Birju Maharaj's disciple and has since then served him as dance partner and manager.

I first saw Saswati Sen dance in 1974 and made the following observation in *The Dancing Times*:

"Miss Sen has, quite clearly, a good future ahead of her." I was wrong. I should have said that Miss Sen had a great future ahead of her. However, in 1981 I had the sense to write the following in *The Guardian*: "The celebrated Roopmati-Baaz Bahadur love affair of 16th century India has been the subject of much poetry and painting and certainly offered Birju Maharaj's choreography and dramatic sense the widest scope. With only a few dancers he orchestrated movement and pace and filled the stage admirably. The naturalistic grace of Kathak was well used throughout. Saswati Sen as the tragic Hindu heroine Roopmati evoked tremendous feeling and often reminded one of the sad-eyed ladies so beloved of Rajput art." Then in 1994, after a lapse of thirteen years, I noted:

"Later, we were regaled with subtle nuances of meaning extracted from dance syllables that on the surface seemed meaningless. Saswati Sen possesses energy and emotion, fire and finesse and is blessed with a Rajput type of beauty. Hence her interpretations of the classical Kathak repertoire are invested with the stamp of authenticity."

Appearing with Birju Maharaj at the 2002 Edinburgh Festival, she made an enduring impression in the tragic role of Ahilya, wife of the sage Gautam, who was violated by the lustful god Indra.

Seeing her dance over a period of almost thirty years one can only marvel at her stamina for technical and intellectual improvement.

Sharmistha Mukherjee

An accomplished Kathak dancer and experimentalist, Sharmistha Mukherjee was trained by Durga Lal, Uma Sharma and Rajendra Gangani. She has toured abroad many times and has created choreographies based on the work of Tagore (Bengali), Ghalib (Urdu) and Maithili Sharan Gupta (Hindi). At Jordan's National Conservatory of Music she interpreted 12th century Arabic poetry through the rich idiom of Kathak.

Sharon Lowen

(Photo Courtesy: Avinash Pasricha)

Delhi can justly lay claim to Sharon Lowen though she was born and brought up in the USA. In the early seventies after taking a master's degree in modern dance she won a Fulbright scholarship to study Indian dance. Since then she has lived in India for long periods.

She first studied Manipuri while a student in America and continued at New Delhi's Triveni Kala Sangam. Her teacher was Singhajit Singh. Later, under Kelucharan Mahapatra, she became an accomplished Odissi exponent and toured the United States with her *guru*. A dedicated missionary of Odissi, she has given lecture-demonstrations all over America. In India she performs regularly and is recognised for her devotion and immense talent.

After having learnt Chhau from Krishna Chandra Naik she made a comparative study of the different forms of Chhau. Her television documentaries on Indian dance have been well received and her performance in *Golden Lotus*, voted the best Telugu film of 1988, was noteworthy.

Though looking remarkably Indian with the eyes and body language of an Odissi danseuse, she has yet another important advantage. Her approach to the aesthetics of Indian dance is refreshingly intelligent. By dint of her devotion Sharon Lowen has shown that Indian dance can certainly be mastered by dedicated artists foreign to the soil and culture of India.

Dance speaks an international language independent of politics, religion, persuasion and bias. Sharon Lowen is the proof.

Shovana Narayan

(Photo Courtesy: Ashwani Chopra)

Born into a family that has played an important role in the struggle for Indian independence, Shovana Narayan is ever conscious of the responsibility carried by the artist in today's India. Her themes therefore often concern social, mental, human rights, health and women's issues. At the same time she has not neglected the traditional repertoire of Kathak which is wedded to the Radha-Krishna story. Shovana has often been compared to a Mughal miniature because of her grace and sensitivity but that is only one aspect of her. She is endowed with great intelligence and introspection. Leela Venkataraman has commented that Shovana's dance "evokes a message of power and emotive depth".

Not only has she used other Indian dance styles in her choreography but she has gone further. From the west she has worked with ballet dancers, a flamenco artist and even an American tap dancer. In *Moonlight Impressions* she used the music of Beethoven, Mozart, Debussy and Ravel. In late 2001, in instant response to the ghastly destruction in New York, she presented *Sound of Emptiness and Harmony* accompanied to the chanting of Buddhist monks. She has used ancient and modern poetry from several countries and cultures to enrich and irrigate her thematic range.

The well known dancer-actress Sadhana Bose initiated her into Kathak at the age of four and she then went on to learn from Kundan Lal. Shovana was finally trained by Birju Maharaj and became one of his best known disciples. Her Kathak can best be described as a fine combination of the elegance of the Lucknow school and the rhythmic precision of the Jaipur school. Thanks to Shovana's teaching many of her students are already making a name for themselves.

Her two books *Kathak: Rhythmic Echoes and Reflections* and *Dance Legacy of Patliputra* have been well received and she has written several papers on a variety of subjects from Kathak to urbanisation, women's empowerment and the environment. She is Visiting Lecturer at the Theatre Wissenschaft, University of Vienna.

Shovana Narayan has boundless energy; apart from being a dancer and teacher she is a high ranking bureaucrat and a mother. She also has diplomatic duties as the wife of an Austrian ambassador.

Her many honours include the Sahitya Kala Parishad Samman Award of Delhi, the Japanese Oisca Award, the Sangeet Natak Akademi Award and the Padma Shree.

Sonal Mansingh

(Photo Courtesy: Avinash Pasricha)

An acclaimed Odissi dancer of the highest order, Sonal Mansingh has a rich and varied background of art and culture. She is blessed with natural grace, expressive eyes and a strong personality; qualities that mark her out amongst her contemporaries. Her Odissi *guru* is the legendary Kelucharan Mahapatra but she also learnt from Shri Jiwan Pani, Hare Krishna Behera, Mayadhar Raut and Srinath Raut. She had, however, a considerable reputation as a Bharata Natyam exponent well before she began her Odissi career. Her principal Bharata Natyam teachers were the Bangalore based U.S. Krishna

Rao and his wife Chandrabhaga Devi. She also went to Gauri Amma to take lessons in the art of *abhinaya*. Kuchipudi she learnt from Vempati Chinna Satyam. She has also been trained in vocal music; her Hindustani teacher being Professor Ginde and her Karnatic teacher Sri Venkataraman.

"After mastering the technique from the *gurus*," observes Sunil Kothari, "Sonal has charted her own path; her approach to dance has been both artistic and cerebral."

Apart from being a practising artist, she is a scholar and linguist. Her study of Sanskrit and Oriya literature, painting, sculpture and poetry have influenced her life and work. It is no wonder, therefore, that her dancing has always been possessed of a fine poetic quality which is, at the same time, stamped with authority. Her dance items based on the *Gita Govinda* are still recalled with great affection and respect.

Sonal Mansingh has also concerned herself with the relationship between art dance and folk dance and to that end studied the Chhau dance of Mayurbhanj from Anant Charan Sai.

Widely travelled in about seventy-five countries, she has danced in many world capitals and represented India in several international festivals. She has received rave reviews wherever she appeared. Her workshops and lecture-demonstrations are always well prepared and brilliantly presented. The Centre for Indian Classical Dances which she founded trains students in both Odissi and Bharata Natyam.

Among her many honours are the Sangeet Natak Akademi Award and, in 2003, the Padma Vibhushan.

Surendra Nath Jena

(Photo Courtesy: Sangeet Natak Akademi)

A respected figure in both Odissi and Jatra folk theatre, Surendra Nath Jena was trained at the Kala Vikas Kendra, Cuttack. Among his teachers were Mayadhar Raut and Kelucharan Mahapatra. In 1967 he came to Delhi and joined the Triveni Kala Sangam where he still teaches. Among the hundreds of dancers that he has coached can be numbered luminaries such as Yamini Krishnamurti, Dr. Kapila Vatsyayan, Ranjana Gauhar and Melissa Ruth Sprout.

As a teenager he joined a travelling folk theatre troupe and his choreography has always displayed a distinctly earthy element. His Odissi creations therefore are a unique blend of classicism and folk culture.

Surendra Nath Jena's teaching and workshops have been greatly appreciated in the USA. His three daughters Pratibha, Rekha and Rama and son Nirmal are also dancer-teachers.

Swapna Sundari

(Photo Courtesy: Kiron Pasricha)

A noted performer and scholar, Swapna Sundari was first taught classical singing by her mother V. Sarala Rao and grandmother C. Sundar Amma. This she has put to purposeful use in that she has brought back to Kuchipudi the former practice of dancers themselves singing the traditional texts. She has had an array of dance teachers. For Bharata Natyam she went to G. Kalyana Sundaram and Adyar K. Lakshman; for special tuition in *abhinaya* to Kalanidhi Narayanan; and for Kuchipudi to Vempati Chinna Satyam, P. Sitaramayya, J. Rama Rao and Y.S. Sarma. She has also interested herself in the dance art of the devadasis of Andhra which is now called Vilasini Natyam. Under the guidance of M. Lakshminarayana she has made an effort to revive many neglected and lesser known dances.

Swapna Sundari's corpus of choreography is large. *Om Shakti,*

Amrapali, Prahlada Natakam, Quli Qutb Shah, and *Radhika Shantvanam* are only some of her well known works. Her busy teaching schedule takes in lecture-demonstrations and dance workshops which highlight the finer and subtler aspects of the Kuchipudi form.

For over twenty years her Kuchipudi Dance Centre has been doing excellent work in teaching, research and creating new dance dramas. Many trained at the centre have embarked on rewarding dance careers.

After I had first seen her dance in 1973, I made the following observation in *The Dancing Times*: "Swapna Sundari's short Kuchipudi dance gave an inkling of what she might achieve..." Since then she has clearly achieved much and any critic rejoices when a passing observation proves to be true.

"Endowed with a large pair of eyes and a mobile visage, Swapna registers *bhavas* with all the relevant and artistic nuances," writes Sunil Kothari. He goes on to say, "She is the first exponent to have released audio cassettes and CDs of Kuchipudi dance music. She has received several awards and honours among which noteworthy are *Svara Vilas* of the Sur Sagar Samsad, Bombay and the Sahitya Kala Parishad of Delhi." In 2003 she received the Padma Bhushan.

Tirath Ajmani

Tirath Ajmani was awarded a government scholarship which enabled him to train in Kathak under Birju Maharaj. Prior to that he was a student of Shanti Bardhan, the well known dance director of the Little Ballet Group, who was one of Uday Shankar's most outstanding protégés.

Tirath Ajmani has himself choreographed some interesting dance items and has toured abroad several times. I first saw him on stage at London's Queen Elizabeth Hall in 1972 and noted, "Tirath Ajmani, a pupil

of Guru Birju Maharaj, proved himself a most able partner in a number of duets." Six years later he partnered Shovana Narayan at the same venue and I was moved to write that their Mughal court dance "set the stage afire".

For many years he taught at the India Cultural Centre in Paramaribo, Surinam and in Delhi he was a member of the Kathak Kendra's production unit. His wife Reba is a talented Odissi artist and folk dance exponent.

Tirath Ram Azad

Not only is Tirath Ram Azad a well known Kathak dancer, he has also been trained in drama and Hindustani classical music. From a very early age he started learning Kathak from Giri Raj and Narayan Prasad. Later he studied with Chiranji Lal and Krishna Kumar. Apart from teaching at the Gandharva Mahavidyalaya for many years he also started his own dance school in Delhi.

His three books (*Kathak Praveshika, Kathak Shringar* and *Kathak Darpan*) show his understanding and commitment to the art of dance. As a scholar, he has made a detailed study of the fixed dance compositions of the great gurus. Among his several dance dramas special mention must be made of *Madhushala, Shakuntala, Mahabharat*, and two with Christian themes, *Prakash-ki-Ore* and *Vijayata*.

For two years (1967–1969) he taught and performed in England, Germany, Denmark and Holland.

Uma Sharma

(Photo Courtesy: Avinash Pasricha)

An outstanding and versatile Kathak star, Uma Sharma is an established figure on Delhi's cultural scene. She was trained by Shambu Maharaj, Sunder Prasad and Birju Maharaj. Later, her interest in the Ras Lila of Braj took her to learn from Ladli Sharan Sharma and Devaki Nandanji. I first saw her dance at the Scala Theatre, London, in 1967 and was impressed by her vivacity and wide range of expression. The accuracy of her incredibly fast pirouettes and footwork showed her mastery of *tal*.

Her competitive duets, *jugal-bandhi*, with Devilal generated excitement and were danced with panache and style.

In *The Guardian* (July 2, 1981) I wrote: "The Sanskritik Festival of Indian Music and Dance opens with an invocatory piece using artists from both north and south India... The north-south dialogue was sustained commendably right up to the final fireworks from Uma Sharma, the doyenne of Kathak... Earlier, in an expressive solo, she interpreted a Surdas poem which told of the first love meeting of Radha with the god Krishna. Here Uma Sharma, with the help of Bashir Ahmed's singing, recreated the passionate atmosphere of bygone nights on the banks of the Yamuna."

Later that year I wrote the following in *The Dancing Times*: "The dancer was Uma Sharma whose career I have followed over a number of years. Her repertoire has steadily expanded and she has branched out into the realms of creative choreography.

Progress of Kathak was an example of the latter in which she danced the exciting history and development of her particular style... Uma Sharma's range is quite amazing for, in the same dance, she was able to transform from a devout vestal virgin to a *femme fatale*, a *dame sans merci*. And it was done convincingly with a surprising suspension of disbelief. I did not know that she could sing so well, but this is what makes artists of her class so interesting. One is always discovering new aspects of their art and personality. The excerpts from the *Ramayana*, which told of the adventures of the man-god Rama and his wife Sita in the forests, was a *tour de force*."

One of Uma's latest productions is *Stree* which tackles women's issues. Her teaching, meanwhile, continues apace at the Uma Sharma School of Dance which is part of her Bhartiya Sangeet Sadan.

She is the recipient of several honours and awards including the Padma Shree.

Yamini Krishnamurti

Yamini Krishnamurti has the distinction of having become a living legend. Her powerful personality and vitality have made a lasting impression on all those, the world over, who have had the pleasure and privilege of seeing her perform. For the record let me quote my 1982 review in *The Dancing Times*: "Yamini Krishnamurti, the Bharata Natyam and Kuchipudi dancer, had a full night's programme on July 8 at the Queen Elizabeth Hall and on July 30 she was presented by Nadabrahman in the Great Hall of Imperial College. On the evidence of both nights—but particularly of the second—I have no hesitation in stating that she is still India's leading Bharata Natyam dancer. The strong Kalakshetra line, the immense stamina and the charisma are all there to behold and to marvel at. Her *varnam* to Lord Someswara is a masterpiece. At one moment there was tenderness, at another pride, at yet another lasciviousness. Her arms flashed like the sword of a Samurai and her eyes wrought destruction. Here was direct communication. Barriers of culture and language were trampled into the dust by the sheer strength of her artistry. This was not 'pointless' dancing as the critic of *The Times* would have us believe. It is rather dancing that is at once earth-bound, abstract, significant to the human condition but well suited to imaginative flight. And it is precisely on account of these qualities that Pavlova and many other dancers after her went to India for inspiration."

After being trained at Kalakshetra, Yamini started her career in 1957. Later, Pasumarti Venugopal Krishna Sarma taught her Kuchipudi. Her portrayals of the many characters that she danced—such as Satyabhama and Mohini—received rapturous acclaim all over India and abroad. She was fortunate in that she had Professor Krishnamurti and her sister Jyotishmati, a talented singer, always by her side. They inspired and assisted her to attain vast success and an international reputation.

Her academy in Delhi which bears her name is a hub of activity and is by no means confined to children and students from well-to-do families. She has received several honours and awards including the Braid of Bhama, the Padma Shree and the Padma Bhushan.

Listed below are some of the other dancers, choreographers and teachers living in Delhi. Their pictures have not been included only because the photographs and transparencies were unavailable when this book went to press.

Aloka Panikar, Anusha Lall, Apunni Karta, Arjun Mishra, Bharat Sharma, Bharati Gupta, Bipul Das, Brojen Mukherjee, Darshina and Shobha Desai, Govindrajan Pillai, Jayalakshmi Eshwar, Jayashankar and Radha Marar, Jeetandra Maharaj, K.N. Dakshinamurti, Kalpana and Suparna Bhushan, Kalyani Chakravarty, Kanchan Maradon, Manisha Sathe, Manjushree Chatterjee, Margi Vijayan, N.V. Venkataraman, Nandkishore Kapote, Narinder Sharma, Navtej Singh Johar, Neera Batra, Nupur Banerjee, Paromita Moitra, Parvati Dutta, Prachi Anand, R.L.V. Radhamohanan, Raghav Raj Bhatt, Raj Kumar, Rama Vaidyanathan, Rasika Khanna, Sadanan Harikumar, Saroja Vaidyanathan, Shri and Smt. Nana Kasar, Shri and Smt. Srinivasan, Sonar Chand, Sushila Duraiswami, Swati Mahalaxmi, Tara Ramaswamy, Trinath Maharana, Urmila Nagar, Usha Narayan and Valmiki Banerjee.

GLOSSARY

abhinaya	expression
adavu	dance unit (Bharata Natyam)
adbhuta (ras)	wonder
aharya abhinaya	costume, make-up and jewellery expressing the dramatic element, sentiment, or mood
alap	introductory passage in music which establishes the atmosphere
amad	entry
angik abhinaya	gestures of the body expressing the dramatic element, sentiment, or mood
apsara	divine nymph
arangeetram	debut of a dancer (South India)
ashtapadi	hymn
asura	demon
bhagti	devotion of one who is dedicated to the truth (North India)
bhagta	devotee
bhagvata	devotee of Vishnu (Bhagvata Mela Nataka)
bhagvatulu	devotee of Vishnu (Kuchipudi)
bhajan	hymn

bhangi pareng	dance embodying the traditional Manipuri poses
bhava	mood
bhayanaka (ras)	terror
veebhatsa (ras)	disgust
boles	rhythmic dance syllables (Kathak)
chaal	a Kathak walk or gait, also called *gati*
chakkar	a turn or pirouette in Kathak
chakkiyar	reciter of sacred texts in the temples of Kerala
chali	a pure dance piece (Ras Lila of Manipur)
chari	foot movement (Manipuri)
charnam	final part of a verse or poem
chela	disciple, follower
chenda	upright cylindrical drum (Kathakali)
chhand	form of ancient religious poem
cholom	a masculine variety of dance (Manipuri)
chutti	rice paste used for beard (Kathakali)
daru	introductory dance for important characters (Kuchipudi)
desi (dance)	for the pleasure of humans
devadasi	woman servant of the gods, temple dancer (Dasi Attam)
dhoti	loin-cloth
dupatta	veil, also called *orhni*

gath	dance in which a story is told (Kathak)
gati	a Kathak walk or gait, also called *chaal*
ghaagra	long gathered skirt
gharana	school or style
ghazal	Urdu poem set to music (Kathak)
ghungurus	ankle bells
gopee	milkmaid, young woman
hasta	hand gesture (Kathak)
hasya (ras)	humour
jati	complex rhythm pattern in footwork of Bharata Natyam
jhanki	tableau
kalari	Kathakali training school
kalasam	short piece of pure dance (Kathakali)
karana	a unit of dance including poses and hand and foot movements
kartal	small cymbals used in Manipuri
karuna (ras)	pathos
keertan	devotional song
khandas	four-line stanzas which make up the text of the Kathakali dance-drama
kriti	dance-song
kumil	costume used in Manipuri
kumin	long skirt stiffened at the bottom (Manipuri)

lasya	feminine aspect of the dance
laya	tempo
layakari	the dancer's mastery of the variations of rhythm within the time measure (Kathak)
lehra	single phrase of music played repeatedly (Kathak)
maddalam	mridangam-like drum (Kathakali)
mahari	female temple dancer (Odissi)
margi (dance)	sacred to the gods
mridangam	South Indian drum with two striking surfaces, one bigger than the other
mudra	hand gesture
mukhabhinaya	facial expression
nattuvanar	musician, dance master (South India)
natya	the dramatic element
nayaka	young man, hero
nayika	young woman, heroine
nayanabhinaya	expression through the eyes
nritta	pure dance
nritya	the expression of sentiment and mood in dance
orhni	veil, also called *dupatta*
pada	love lyric

padam	that part of a Bharata Natyam performance where the padas are interpreted through abhinaya
pakhawaj	North Indian drum with two striking surfaces, one bigger than the other
palta	a pure dance figure involving a turn (Kathak)
phanek	sarong-like costume (Manipuri)
puja	service of devotion
pujaree	person taking part in a service of devotion, also temple priest
pung	drum (Manipuri)
raga	musical mode, melody archetype
rajasik	character with particular flaws or vices (Kathakali)
rakshasa	demon
ras	sentiment, emotional state
rudra (ras)	anger
sahitya	literature, literary content
sakhi	confidante
sambhoga	union in love
sankeertan	communal prayer
sarangi	fretless stringed instrument played with a bow
sargam	sol-fa syllable
satvik	heroic, virtuous character (Kathakali)

satvik abhinaya	physical manifestation of mental or emotional states (Natya Shastra)
shanta (ras)	serenity
shishya	student, disciple
shringar (ras)	love
sloka	short religious verse in Sanskrit
sollukuttus	rhythmic dance syllables (Bharata Natyam)
sum	the first and key beat of the time measure
swara	musical sound, note
tablas	drums popular in north India
tal	time measure in dance or music
tamasik	evil character (Kathakali)
tandav	masculine aspect of dance
tatkar	footwork (Kathak)
therissila	the curtain held up by two people (Kathakali)
tirmana	a short brilliant succession of adavus (Bharata Natyam)
torah	short dance piece, similar to a *tukra* (Kathak)
vipralambha	separation in love
vir (ras)	heroism
viyog	separation from the loved one (Manipuri)

BIBLIOGRAPHY

Abhinaya Darpanam, Nandikesvara, trans. Manomohan Ghosh, Metropolitan Printing & Publishing House, Calcutta. 1934.

All India, Reginald Massey (Editor), The Apple Press, London. 1986.

Anatomy of Ballet, Fernau Hall, Melrose, London. 1953.

Art of Indian Dancing, Projesh Banerjee, Sterling Publishers, New Delhi. 1985.

Asian Dance in Britain, Reginald Massey, The National Resource Centre for Dance, University of Surrey, Guildford, UK. 1996.

Classical and Folk Dances of India, Mulk Raj Anand (Editor), Marg Publications, Bombay. 1965.

Classical Dances and Costumes of India, Kay Ambrose, Adam & Charles Black, London. 1952.

Classical Indian Dance in Literature and the Arts, Kapila Vatsyayan, Sangeet Natak Akademi, New Delhi. 1968.

Dance Dialects of India, Ragini Devi, Vikas, Delhi. 1972.

Dance Dramas of India and the East, K. Bharatha Iyer, Taraporevala, Bombay. 1980.

Dance in Thumri, Projesh Banerjee, Abhinav Publications, New Delhi. 1986.

Dances of India, Ragini Devi, Susil Gupta, Calcutta. 1962.

Dances of the Golden Hall, Ashoke Chatterjee with photographs by Sunil Janah, Indian Council for Cultural Relations, New Delhi. 1979.

Discovery of India, Jawaharlal Nehru, O.U.P., New Delhi. 1983.

Festivals of India, B.N. Sharma, Abhinav Publications, New Delhi. 1978.

419 Illustrations of Indian Music and Dance in Western Style, Vidya Sarabhai Nawab, S.M. Nawab, Ahmedabad. 1964.

India's Kathak Dance: Past, Present, Future, Reginald Massey, Abhinav Publications, New Delhi. 1999.

India's Heritage, Humayun Kabir, Meridian Books, London. 1947.

Kathak: Indian Classical Dance Art, Sunil Kothari, Abhinav Publications, New Delhi. 1988.

Kathakali, K. Bharata Iyer, Luzac, London. 1955.

Krishna Theatre in India, M.L. Varadpande, Abhinav Publications, New Delhi. 1982.

Kuchipudi: Indian Classical Dance Art, Sunil Kothari & Avinash Pasricha, Abhinav Publications, New Delhi. 2001.

Lesser Known Forms of Performing Arts of India, Durgadas Mukhopadhyay (Editor), Sterling Publishers, New Delhi. 1978.

Life and Works of Amir Khusro, M.W. Mirza, Panjab University, Lahore. 1935.

Living Dolls: Story of Indian Puppets, Jiwan Pani, Publications Division, Government of India, New Delhi. 1986.

Marg—Special issue on Chhau Dances of India, Sunil Kothari (Editor), Marg Publications, Bombay. 1968.

Marg—Special issue on Sattriya Dances of Assam, Sunil Kothari (Editor), Marg Publications, Bombay. 1971.

Music and Dance in Indian Art, Edinburgh Festival Society, 1963.

My Music, My Life, Ravi Shankar, Simon & Schuster, New York. 1968.

Natya Shastra, Bharata, trans. Manomohan Ghosh, Royal Asiatic Society of Bengal, Calcutta. 1950.

Odissi: Indian Classical Dance Art, Sunil Kothari & Avinash Pasricha, Marg Publications, Bombay. 1990.

Religion and Theatre, M. L. Varadpande, Abhinav Publications, New Delhi. 1983.

Rhythm in the Heavens, Ram Gopal, Secker and Warburg, London. 1957.

Sangeet Natak Akademi, Dance Seminar Papers (New Delhi, 1958):

Dance Traditions in Assam, Maheshwar Neog.

Kathakali, Gopinath.

Manipuri Dancing, Atombapu Sharma and Amubi Singh.

Manipuri Dancing, Nayana Jhaveri.

Music in the Dance-Dramas of Tagore, Santidev Ghose.

Ritual Dances of South India, Mohan Khokar.

Shaivism and Vaishnavism in Indian Dance, Mohan Khokar.

Tagore, Poet and Dramatist, Edward Thomson, O.U.P., 1962.

The Ajanta Caves, Benjamin Rowland, Collins & U.N.E.S.C.O., 1963.

The Art of Kathakali, A.C. Pandeya, Kitabistan, Allahabad. 1961.

The Dance in India, Faubion Bowers, Columbia University Press, New York. 1953.

The Dance of Shiva, Ananda Coomaraswamy, Asia Publishing House, Bombay. 1956.

The Dances of India, Reginald & Jamila Massey, Abhinav Publications, New Delhi. 1995.

The Encyclopedia of Dance and Ballet, Mary Clarke & David Vaughan (Editors), Putnam, New York. 1977.

The Indian Experience, Ken Barrett & Suresh Sharma (Editors), Media Transasia-Thomson Press-Air India, Bangkok. 1982.

The Indian Theatre, Mulk Raj Anand, Dennis Dobson, London. 1950.

The Indian Civilization, Ernest Mackay, Lovat Dickson & Thompson, London. 1935.

The Kathakali Complex — Actor, Performance & Structure, Phillip Zarrilli, Abhinav Publications, New Delhi. 1984.

The Music of India, Reginald & Jamila Massey, Kahn & Averill, London/Pro-Am, New York. 1987 / Abhinav Publications, New Delhi. 1996.

The Rāga-s of Northern Indian Music, Alain Daniélou, Barrie & Rockliff, London. 1968.

The Rāgs of North Indian Music, N.A. Jairazbhoy, Faber & Faber, London. 1971.

The Splendours of Indian Dance, Mohan Khokar with photographs by Gurmeet Thukral, Himalayan Books, New Delhi. 1985.

Theatre in India, Balwant Gargi, Theatre Art Books, New York. 1962.

The Wonder That Was India, A.L. Basham, Sidgwick & Jackson, London. 1954.

Traditional Indian Theatre: Multiple Streams, Kapila Vatsyayan, National Book Trust of India, New Delhi. 1980.

Traditions of Indian Classical Dance, Mohan Khokar, Books From India, London/Clarion Books, New Delhi. 1979.

Traditions of Indian Folk Dance, Kapila Vatsyayan, Indian Book Company, New Delhi. 1976.

Uday Shankar, Sunil Kothari & Mohan Khokar (Editors), RIMPA, New Delhi. 1983.

Yakshagana, Martha Bush Ashton & Bruce Christie, Abhinav Publications, New Delhi. 1977.

INDEX